# THE
# LIBRARY OF
# DISTINCTIVE
# SERMONS

❧

## VOLUME ONE

GARY W. KLINGSPORN
*General Editor*

QUESTAR PUBLISHERS • SISTERS, OREGON

*General Editor*
Gary W. Klingsporn, Ph. D.

*Associate Editor*
Pat Wienandt, M.A.

*Contributing Editors*
Gary W. Downing, D. Min.
Ron Durham, Ph. D.
Gary Furr, Ph. D.
Perry J. Hunter, M.A.
Peter Smith, M. Div.

THE LIBRARY OF DISTINCTIVE SERMONS, VOLUME 1
published by Questar Publishing Direct
*a part of the Questar publishing family*

© 1996 by Questar Publishers

*International Standard Book Number: 0-88070-979-0*
Design by David Uttley

Printed in the United States of America

Scripture quotations are from:
*The Holy Bible, New International Version* (NIV) © 1973, 1984 by International Bible
Society, used by permission of Zondervan Publishing House.

*The New King James Version* (NKJV) © 1984 by Thomas Nelson, Inc.

*The New Revised Standard Version Bible* (NRSV) © 1989 by the Division of Christian
Education of the National Council of Churches of Christ in the United States of America.

*The Revised Standard Version of the Bible* © 1946, 1952, 1971, 1973, Division of Christian
Education, National Council of the Churches in the USA.

Acknowledgment is made for "Psalm 23" excerpted from *Psalms Now,* by Leslie Brandt.
Copyright © 1973 Concordia Publishing House.
Reprinted by permission of Concordia Publishing House. All rights reserved.

97  98  99  00  01  02  03 — 10  9  8  7  6  5  4  3  2

# TABLE OF CONTENTS

*For all who preach*

How beautiful upon the mountains
are the feet of the messenger
who announces peace,
who brings good news,
who announces salvation,
who says to Zion, "Your God reigns."

ISAIAH 52:7

# PREFACE

The idea of *The Library of Distinctive Sermons* originated in painful practical circumstances rather than in an academic context. A pastor friend of mine went through a prolonged ordeal of tension and conflict with a congregation before he was terminated primarily "because his sermons were dry and hard to follow." As a new, young pastor, he was doing the best he could without the benefit of much experience in ministry. By and large, however, he was not connecting with the congregation in his preaching. The congregation became impatient and was less than compassionate in handling the situation. This led to a bitter parting of the ways.

As a lay person sitting in the pew and aware of the tension, I felt the pain on both sides of the issue. I began to ask myself what more might be done to assist ministers in learning and sharing the insights which contribute to effective preaching. *The Library of Distinctive Sermons* originated from that experience. It is a resource designed to promote vital and effective preaching through the sharing of sermons and insights on preaching by working pastors.

*The Library of Distinctive Sermons* brings together a collection of powerful contemporary sermons of diverse style and content, along with careful reflection as to what makes each sermon effective, and how each sermon relates to biblical, theological, and practical ministry issues facing pastors today.

It is important to note that we have chosen not to engage in an academic critique of each sermon. No sermon is flawless. We have chosen good sermons and have asked some simple questions: What makes each of these sermons good? What can we learn from the creative elements of style and content in each sermon to assist us in the art of preaching?

Discussion of these questions in the Comment section following each sermon makes *The Library of Distinctive Sermons* unique among sermon publications. We have enlisted only working pastors for the task of commenting on each sermon. While there are many excellent books on homiletics, we discovered that few are written by pastors for pastors. The Comment sections are a means of sharing practical ideas and insights from pastor to pastor in a way that is helpful to pastors of all backgrounds and levels of experience. Our desire is that *The Library of Distinctive Sermons* will enhance your own process of developing new sermons and contribute to the continual renewal of your preaching ministry.

Many people gave of their talents to this series. First, we are deeply grateful to all of the preachers whose sermons appear in this volume. Their commitment to the proclamation of the gospel and their willingness to share their sermons "out of context" with a wider audience beyond their local congregations, have made this series possible. Special thanks go also to those pastors who shared their wisdom, perspectives, and insights in the Comment sections. Appreciation goes as well to the General Editor, Dr. Gary W. Klingsporn, whose special gifts and talents in communication and publishing are reflected throughout the series. Special thanks to Pat Wienandt, who, as Associate Editor, kept us all in line with her wonderful editorial expertise in the written word.

In a rapidly changing consumer culture which is increasingly visually oriented, the sermon "competes" as never before with a multiplicity of media and voices vying for our attention. In a culture where the entertainment world sets the pace and celebrities are often the measure of "success," preaching today is subjected to intense scrutiny and is regarded by many as outmoded, especially if it does not "entertain." And yet, since the beginning of Christianity, followers of Jesus Christ in every age have found preaching the most powerful and effective form of communicating the gospel. Indeed, there is something about the gospel that seems to demand this particular expression, this form of communication, and none other. Through preaching, lives continue to be saved and transformed, liberated, healed and reconciled. We pray that *The Library of Distinctive Sermons* will encourage you and help you create new and effective ways of proclaiming the gospel of Jesus Christ in today's world.

*Stephen E. Gibson*
Executive Editor

INTRODUCTION

Much has been written on the subject of preaching. Seldom, however, do we find good sermons brought together with commentary on why those sermons constitute effective proclamation of the gospel. Among the literature available today, we can read sermons. Or, we can read about preaching. But seldom do we have the opportunity to do both at the same time: to read good sermons, and to reflect on the art of preaching as it is embodied in those sermons.

*The Library of Distinctive Sermons* is designed to promote the enrichment of preaching through the sharing of good sermons and careful analysis of their style and content. The purpose is to read a sermon and ask, "What makes this sermon effective as the proclamation of God's Word?" The philosophy underlying this series is that, whether we are novices or seasoned preachers, we can always learn from others who preach. One of the best ways to do that is to "listen" to others, to observe how they preach, and pick up on some of the best of what they do in a way that is natural and appropriate in our own preaching.

Each of the sermons in this volume is accompanied by a Comment section. Here working pastors reflect on what makes each sermon distinctive and effective. To some extent, of course, this is a very subjective undertaking. What makes a sermon "good" or "effective" to one person is not always the same in the opinion of others. Given the subjectivity involved, it would be easy to avoid ever undertaking the task of serious reflection about our preaching. However, in the Comment sections in this volume, the writers have taken the risk of opening the dialogue about what constitutes effective preaching. There is much to be gained in this process: new ideas and techniques, new perspectives on texts, creative forms and structures, new stories and illustrations for preaching.

It is one thing to hear or read a good sermon and to have some sense of why we like it. But how often do we give serious analytical reflection, asking what we can learn from a sermon? *The Library of Distinctive Sermons*

8

provides an opportunity for the enrichment of preaching through thoughtful consideration of why each sermon has been done in the way it is done.

In the Comment sections in this series the writers reflect on the style and content of each sermon. They look at such things as the genre and structure of the sermon, its use of biblical texts, illustrations, literary or rhetorical techniques, tone, and language. They also comment on how the content of each sermon proclaims biblical faith; remains true to the biblical text; reflects sound theology; deals with faith questions; addresses ethical and social issues; and shows the relevance of the gospel in today's world.

The Comments are presented in a fairly nontechnical way. The focus of this series is not on an academic analysis or critique of sermons, nor is the focus on theoretical aspects of communication and homiletics. The purpose of this series is to offer practical reflection aimed at stimulating our thoughts and improving our preaching in very practical ways. The Bibliography at the end of this volume lists excellent resources for additional reading, including many recommended academic and theoretical discussions of preaching.

The format of this volume is simple. Each sermon is presented as closely as possible to the original form in which it was preached. Obviously, in moving from the original oral medium of preaching to the written form represented here, some editing has been necessary to facilitate literary style, clarity, and comprehension.

The Comment following each sermon assumes that every effective sermon includes at least three basic elements. First, every sermon addresses questions relating to the problems and needs of the human condition. Second, every good sermon has a thesis and makes an assertion. It proclaims truth from the Scriptures using one or more biblical texts. Third, every good sermon invites people to respond or motivates them to think, act, or believe. These preaching elements can be described in many different ways using varieties of language. In their Comments the writers commonly use the terms Text, Problem, Proclamation, and Response (or Invitation) to refer to these elements of sermonic structure and content.

In the Comments, then, you will notice frequent discussion of the following items which are intended as helpful tools of reflection and analysis:

**1) Text.** How does the preacher interpret and apply the biblical text(s) in the sermon? What techniques are used? What insights into the text(s) are found in the sermon?

**2) Problem.** What human problem, need, question, or life situation does each sermon address? How is the problem of the human condition understood and presented in the sermon?

**3) Proclamation.** How does the sermon proclaim the good news of the Christian gospel? What is the truth or "kerygma" drawn from the Scriptures and applied to the human situation?

**4) Response.** How does the sermon invite us to respond? What does the preacher invite, urge, or encourage us to believe or to do? What motivation is there to act or to change, and how does this flow out of the interpretation of the biblical text(s), the human problem, and the proclamation of the gospel?

**5) Suggestions.** Each Comment section concludes with some practical suggestions for thought or discussion, for further reading, or for incorporating some of the insights from the sermon into one's own preaching.

*The Library of Distinctive Sermons* features a wide variety of sermon styles and subjects. This is important in a series designed for the enrichment of preaching. You will undoubtedly like some of the sermons more than others. You will react differently to different sermons. You may agree or disagree with some of the Comments. But all of these reactions can be learning experiences. So as you read, ask yourself: "What do I think about this sermon? Why do I feel as I do?" Interact with the material! Reflect on your own preaching and ministry as you enjoy this volume. Then the sermons and Comments will become a valuable resource for your own ministry.

It is important to remember that each of the sermons in this volume was preached in an original context, most of them in congregations on Sunday mornings. Each was spoken with the presence and guidance of the Holy Spirit to a particular people in a particular time and place. Each sermon had a life of its own as the Word of God in that specific moment.

While the sermons that appear here are removed from those original contexts, there is much we can learn from them. Whenever possible, the attempt has been made to acknowledge significant aspects of the original context. But now these sermons appear in a new context. God can use them in this context to speak home to our hearts and to create new understanding and possibilities for ministry.

The apostle Paul wrote, "So then faith comes from what is heard, and what is heard comes through the word of Christ" (Rom. 10:17). It is in and through the preached word of Christ that God directs us to faith in Christ and imparts to us the gift of faith. In preaching, the wonderful work and mystery of God take place: the living Christ becomes present through the preached word. Bonhoeffer said, "The word of Scripture is certain, clear, and plain. The preacher should be assured that Christ enters the congregation through those words which he [or she] proclaims from the Scripture...."[1] Preaching is a holy calling filled with the mystery and promise of God. We do well to give all the careful time and attention we can to this holy task, while always giving ourselves to God. As Augustine said of preaching, "Lord, give me the gifts to make this gift to you."

*Gary W. Klingsporn*
General Editor

Note

1. Dietrich Bonhoeffer, *Worldly Preaching*, ed. Clyde E. Fant (Nashville and New York: Thomas Nelson, Inc., 1975), p. 130.

# BETWEEN TWO WORLDS: FROM EASTER TO ETERNITY

LUKE 24:13–35

REV. DR. DAVID L. WILLIAMSON
FIRST PRESBYTERIAN CHURCH OF HOLLYWOOD
HOLLYWOOD, CALIFORNIA

REV. DR. DAVID L. WILLIAMSON

# BETWEEN TWO WORLDS: FROM EASTER TO ETERNITY

LUKE 24:13–35

The Final Four is over. The NCAA banner is hanging proudly in Pauley Pavilion. But, the band has stopped playing, the crowds are gone and it's back to school, into the office, life as usual. The Academy Awards have been presented, the post-award parties are over and Chasens' is closed! Hardly anyone remembers the awards from a year ago or last year's World Series or January's Super Bowl. (A little clue, there was no World Series last year.) The promotion or a wedding, a birth, a prom or a graduation has come and gone, and life is back to routine. Great spiritual experiences, discoveries, ecstatic moments, even miracles, have happened, but that was yesterday or last week or last year or many years ago.

And, we muddle through ups and downs of everyday life, here and now, trying to live a life of faith. We bade farewell to our Senior Pastor and we have entered into an interim, wondering what God has in store for us. We had an inspiring Palm Sunday, Good Friday, and Easter Sunday that have come and gone. No brass fanfares in the balcony, no enormous floral spreads across the choir loft and across the front, no combined choirs. All of the excitement is gone; even last Sunday's crowds are gone. And, we wonder, now what?

Two disciples are heading down from Jerusalem to Emmaus to their home late Easter afternoon. Easter has happened. They have heard the report that their friend and spiritual leader who was brutally executed on Friday was alive! That was astounding, perplexing, and exciting news that left them uncertain, cautious, confused. Remarkable news, but it wasn't what they had expected. It had not transformed all of the world: Jerusalem was still in the hands of Rome and the Risen Jesus was nowhere to be found. So, back on the road, back home, back to the mundane and to business as usual, with dashed hopes, unfulfilled dreams, squelched enthusiasm, a disappointing and questionable future. An ending with no beginning in sight.

Do you ever feel that way?

Easter has happened, you have heard God's voice, you have celebrated the Resurrection, and you believed. You felt transformed, born anew. You were here last Sunday and went away feeling good: God had met you here. "Christ is risen," we said. "He has risen indeed." But, Monday came, or, at least by Friday afternoon, life was much the same. Heaven had not arrived, the Kingdom had not come in its fullness and power. On top of that, Wednesday's tragedy in Oklahoma City shattered our sense of security. Life as we have known it is gone forever, and we wonder, "Where is God?" We have tried to be faithful, and we go on trying to live by faith, but yet in the ordinary struggles of life, it is somehow difficult. We feel caught between two worlds, caught between the way life is and the way it ought to be, caught between the bookends of Easter and eternity.

We are in transition from one experience of life to another, constantly moving from where we have been to where we are going. We are on a journey, leaving the past behind, making a transition to the future, and we find ourselves somewhere in between.

What spiritual valley are you in today? What spiritual mountaintop experience have you left behind? What transition are you in? Perhaps it is a predictable transition — going through the stages of life: retirement, aging, the death of a loved one. And there are unpredictable changes that come along — changes in our employment; our financial ups and downs and sideways; a divorce, a move, the loss of a dream, or the ending of a project. How we manage our transitions, how we deal with the spiritual valleys makes a huge difference in our lives.

Psychologist William Bridges says that there are three stages of transition. There are endings and beginnings and a neutral zone in between. All transitions involve losses. Loss and separation is hard, and we tend to avoid it, but we can't hang on, we can't live in the future hanging onto the past. Bridges writes, "New growth cannot take root on grounds still covered by the old. Every transition is an ending that prepares for new growth and new activities."[1] Jesus says, "Unless a grain of wheat fall into the ground and die, it cannot produce fruit."

You see, before leaving from endings to beginnings, we pass through the wilderness of our neutral zones. This is often a time of confusion and considerable uncertainty. We have left our comfort zones — the familiar — looking for a new understanding that is not yet there. We are up in the air, out in the dark, the honeymoon is over, and we feel betwixt and between. And, sometimes in the uncomfortableness of this neutral zone — the wandering through the wilderness — we want to go back. We want to go back to Egypt, to the Mount of Transfiguration, or to some place of security, comfort, or calm. But we can't, nor should we, for God is doing a new thing and we need to journey on by faith through the neutral zone. We need to embrace the present with all the questions and all the struggles and find our way through.

So, what transition are you in this morning? At work, at home, with God — what valley are you traveling through with the tantalizing taste of Easter behind you, and eternity and the Kingdom of God and your spiritual fulfillment seemingly a long way off? In what way do you identify with the two disciples on the Emmaus Road who said, "Our own hope had been that he was the one to redeem Israel and set us free!" Where is he?

On the road, coming off a high, on the journey through the neutral zone, a stranger joins us. And, that encounter with that stranger makes all the difference in the world. Cleopas ("Cleo") and another disciple have just entered their neutral zone. The ending has happened, the ecstasy of Easter is over, and the new beginning that they had placed all of their hopes in has not yet come. So, walking away quietly from Jerusalem, they are joined unobtrusively, gently, imperceptibly by a third who walks with them and listens. He has a word with them and joins them for dinner.

Dear friends, the risen Christ comes to join us on the journey through the mundane, the ordinary, the perplexing places of our lives. He meets us sometimes obviously, powerfully, wonderfully, but perhaps most often subtly, gently, as a stranger or friend. Jesus comes to us in the in-between, bringing his loving, caring, encouraging presence. Perhaps he comes through the life of another Christian brother or sister like a Stephen minister, or a member of Rod & Staff or an elder or deacon praying with us at the steps. Perhaps he comes at a hospital bedside or over a cup of coffee in the lunchroom. In a restaurant, a living room, with a small group of spiritual buddies, a mentor, a therapist, or at a Bible study group in a downtown restaurant in the middle of the week — and in that encounter Jesus fulfills his promise to us, "Lo, I am with you always, I will not leave you alone, I will send you another."

The stranger who joins Cleopas and the other disciple, and who joins us on our journey, comes as the one who listens to their story and to our story. We have a persistent need to have someone who will listen, listen, listen — who will understand us from our frame of reference and from God's frame of reference. The resurrected Jesus comes to the disciples on the road, and he comes to us, to listen. Listening is the highest act of love that we can give to another, short of laying down our lives for that one. The Lord never tunes us out; he never walks away. He pays attention to us. And, whenever someone comes alongside you to listen to you, you have evidence of the continuing reality of the resurrection.

Then the stranger opens up the Scripture. In the midst of their confusion and their uncertainty, the Word of God is offered to shed new light, to bring insight and understanding of the awareness of God and God's understanding of life. Meaning begins to take form; clarity comes to these confused and uncertain disciples. Later, they remember that their hearts burned as they heard the Scripture revealed and explained. I am amazed at how often in my transitions, in my in-betweens, in my valleys, God will give me a word of Scripture that day for that particular situation. And, notice that the word of God comes to the disciples not in private; rather Jesus forms a small community to discuss and explore the Scripture together.

So the fourth thing that Jesus does for the disciples on the Emmaus Road and that he does for us on our Emmaus roads, is to create for us a community. In the breaking of the bread, their eyes were opened. The breaking of the bread has a reference not only to the experience of communion, but also to the experience of the fellowship. We say to each other when we want to have intimacy or friendship, "Let's break bread." Community is formed. Yes, Jesus does meet us in private, and in our own personal spiritual retreats. But more often he meets us in the context of the people in the community of the faithful. Christ meets us here in the sanctuary of our church. He also meets us in our adult Sunday School classes, in small groups, and in Bible studies. He meets a group of high school kids as they journey out to the mountains at Forest Home, or on a mission trip to Mexico.

Then, he vanishes. Do you experience Jesus vanishing from you right after that moment of glory? Jesus says to us and to all the disciples, "It is good for you that I go away, for faith is the assurance of things hoped for, the evidence of things not seen." Ecstasy needs to be transformed into trust, knowing that in our neutral zones God has provided for us a people, a book and a Person: the listening, loving, and empowering continuous Presence. Easter, dear friends, has happened, and it continues to happen all the way through to eternity.

What then is our response? As we come down off our highs and as we live down in our valleys, as we walk the road to Emmaus and the streets of Los Angeles, the Risen Christ is here. We need to accept the reality of those difficult journeys to mourn our losses (as a church we have had several in a relatively short period of time — Lloyd, Ralph, Jack, Dorothy, and Bob). There is no shame in our grieving and having to live the in-between! We live one day at a time — life in interim!

We need to recognize that God is not interested in lifting us out of here until we finally take our place in his presence in eternity. Yet, he does promise, always, to be with us in the midst, giving us the Scriptures, giving us a community of people to share the journey with us, giving us himself — and then he sends us on a mission. When the disciples recognized that Jesus was there, present with them on the road to Emmaus, away from the mountaintop in Jerusalem, down into the valley, their instinctive response was to go and tell the disciples and eventually, to tell the world.

Dear friends, on this week after Easter, it is my invitation to you and to me, to welcome transition, to let the Risen Christ come, and to let our hearts burn within as we welcome his presence. And then be the stranger who brings the Risen Savior to your companions and to the world. It is an incomparable and remarkable journey, full of new life in every way. "Therefore," Paul says, "if anyone is in Christ he is a new creation; all things have passed away, and behold, everything with him becomes new." Happy Easter, every day!

Notes

1. William Bridges, *Transitions: Making Sense of Life's Changes* (Reading: Addison-Wesley, 1980), p. 91.

# COMMENT

"Timing is everything" goes the saying in politics, sports, and business. Timing is also crucial in preaching. There are teachable moments and appropriate occasions when just the right word can bring great change or healing in the life of an individual or a community.

Knowing what is appropriate to do and when to do it is part of the art of preaching. Such timing requires that we learn to listen carefully and perceptively to our own lives, to our people, and to God. Time is important to God. God acts "in the fullness of time" (Gal. 4:4) not only in the Incarnation but in the pulpit and in the shared life of Word and Sacrament in the church. Good preaching requires good listening and God's own timing, when the Word proclaimed can speak to human need and to the seasons of human life.

David Williamson's sermon "Between Two Worlds: From Easter to Eternity" is a fine example of appropriate timeliness in preaching. The sermon was originally preached on the Sunday after Easter, a fitting occasion for considering the post-Easter experience of the two disciples on the road to Emmaus in Luke 24. The sermon addresses the common human experience of transition in people's lives. It speaks of the spiritual high and low moments as well as the in-between times on the journey of faith. The sermon was also preached to a congregation experiencing transition in its pastoral leadership. A beloved long-term senior minister had just departed. The church was beginning a prolonged interim period without the familiar pastoral leadership it had known for many years.

This is an eminently pastoral sermon. It is a wonderful example of pastoral care from the pulpit! The preacher is aware not only of the seasons of the church year, but of the seasons of people's lives. He has reflected on the changes and transitions which inevitably come to us all. He has listened attentively and perceptively to where people in the congregation are. In the sermon he draws us in alongside the two disciples on the road to Emmaus at a time of profound confusion and transition in their lives. Easter has happened. But has it? We become fellow travelers with those disciples, and we meet the Stranger who falls in alongside us unrecognized along the way.

In this sermon the preacher allows the text to interpret us. The story of the Emmaus disciples becomes our story. God comes through the text and speaks to us who find ourselves living between two worlds. Here, through the preacher, the Word of God meets us where we are and we encounter the living Christ. Timing is crucial to that experience. The right word at the right moment has the power to change us, nurture us, and give us new hope.

### PROBLEM

The human need or life situation Williamson addresses in this sermon is described as the experience of "living between two worlds." By this he means two things: (1) the distance or contrast between Easter faith and the reality of life as we daily experience it; and (2) the practical transitions we face as we move through the various stages of life.

1. *Faith and reality.* In the opening paragraphs of the sermon Williamson points to the contrast we experience in life between the high moments of joy or celebration and the return to the mundane ups and downs of everyday life. He gains our attention by alluding to popular sporting events and special moments in every person's life. Great moments come and go so quickly — the NCAA Final Four, the Academy Awards, a wedding, a birth, or a promotion. They are here and gone. Life is suddenly back to the routine, and we "muddle through" the day-to-day activity.

In the same way, Williamson says, Easter has come and gone again in the life of the church. After an uplifting and inspiring Easter celebration, there are no longer any brass fanfares in the balcony, no enormous floral spreads, no combined choirs. "All of the excitement is gone; even last Sunday's crowds are gone. And, we wonder, now what?" (para. 2). "Easter has happened,…you have celebrated the Resurrection… You…went away feeling good…. But, Monday came…[and] life was much the same. Heaven had not arrived, the Kingdom had not come in its fullness and power. On top of that, Wednesday's tragedy in Oklahoma City shattered our sense of security. Life as we have known it is gone forever, and we wonder, 'Where is God?'"

In these words the preacher is pointing to the gap or distance we often feel between the high moments of our faith and the stark reality of life in a routine and violent world. Placing the Easter celebration of the Resurrection alongside the reality of the Oklahoma City bombing painfully makes the point: "We feel…caught between the way life is and the way it ought to be, caught between the bookends of Easter and eternity."

What does it mean then to live by faith in a world where we are always on the journey between "the *is* and the *ought,*" between faith and reality? What difference does Easter make? What difference does faith make? These are critical questions in the life of faith similar to those asked by the Emmaus disciples in Luke 24.

2. *Life's transitions.* Williamson also points to the natural life transitions we encounter as part of living between Easter and eternity. There are predictable transitions (aging, retirement, death of loved ones) and unpredictable transitions (divorce, a move, changes in employment). All transitions involve loss. Life's transitions can be "wilderness experiences" filled with struggles that test our faith.

In presenting the problem that the biblical text will address, notice how Williamson uses key questions throughout to invite the listener to identify with the human need or life situation. He says: "We wonder, now what?" (para. 2). "Do you ever feel that way?" (para. 4). "We wonder, 'Where is God?'" (para. 5). "What spiritual valley are you in today?" (para. 7). "So what transition are you in this morning?" "In what way do you identify with the two disciples on the Emmaus Road?" (para. 10).

By asking these questions the preacher draws the listener into the story and into identification with the problems the sermon addresses. Too many questions can overwhelm the listener. But here, minimal questions are placed appropriately throughout the opening paragraphs to draw the reader into the problem and into the text.

TEXT

In the first six paragraphs of this sermon Williamson beautifully inter-
weaves the biblical text with his description of the human problem it
addresses. Immediately after his description of the high celebration of
Easter with its fanfares, flowers, crowds and choirs, he turns immediately
to the scene of the two downcast disciples heading toward Emmaus late on
Easter afternoon. There had been reports of Jesus' resurrection, but were
they true? No one had seen Jesus alive.

Jesus' life had ended with no new beginning in sight. At this point the
preacher asks us to think about our own experience: "Do you ever feel that
way?" "Yes," we may want to cry out, "life is filled with endings in search of
new beginnings. I know just how those two disciples felt!" We are now
drawn into the text.

Williamson goes on to describe more fully the human experience of
high moments of faith followed by shattered security, disillusionment, or
the confusion of transition. Then he returns to the text asking specifically
how we may identify with the two disciples' question "Where is God?"
Having now related the text to the human condition, namely, the challenge
of faith in a bewildering world, Williamson is ready to let the text proclaim
the good news of the gospel which addresses our human need. He introduces the Proclamation portion of the sermon by recreating the scene
of the Stranger coming in alongside the disciples. This Stranger journeys
with them, asks questions, listens, speaks some words, and joins them for
dinner.

PROCLAMATION

In the remainder of the sermon Williamson walks through the Emmaus
story telling how the living Christ engaged the two disciples and how the
living Christ meets us today. He begins the proclamation portion of the sermon by saying: "Dear friends, the risen Christ comes to join us on the journey through the mundane, the ordinary, the perplexing places of our lives.
He meets us sometimes obviously, powerfully, wonderfully, but perhaps

most often subtly, gently, as a stranger or friend." Notice how this statement beautifully joins the proclamation of the text with our human need and struggle. This is the very heart of the sermon. It is good news for all of us living between two worlds.

The sermon proclaims four truths from the story:

1. The Risen Christ comes to us in many ways, through friends and strangers alike. Jesus is present with us in the darkest moments of our lives, in the violence and insecurity of our world, and in the uncertainty of our transitions.

2. The Living Lord comes as One who listens to our story, as he listened to the disciples on the road to Emmaus. God loves us by listening and understanding our need.

3. In Word and Sacrament today the Living Christ proclaims to us the truth and wisdom of God.

4. Jesus creates for us a community.

"Then, he vanishes!" (Luke 24:31). The high moment of spiritual recognition does not last. We walk by faith, not by sight, the text proclaims. "Ecstasy needs to be transformed into trust" — trust in the listening, loving, empowering Presence of Christ. The preacher concludes, "Easter, dear friends, has happened, and it continues to happen all the way through to eternity." That is the good news of the gospel this sermon proclaims.

## RESPONSE

The invitation to respond is placed in the closing three paragraphs of the sermon and is signaled by the question "What then is our response?" The pastoral counsel is to accept the reality of life in-between, to welcome transition, and to recognize that the Risen Christ is always present with us here between Easter and eternity. Finally, as the response of the Emmaus disciples was to go and tell the other disciples (Luke 24:33-35), we are encouraged also to bring the good news of the Risen and Present Savior to our friends and to the world.

This sermon allows the biblical text to speak effectively to the human condition. It moves from the recognition of the human struggle to live by faith to the proclamation of the assurance of the presence of God. In the midst of all the darkness, the loss, and the confusion of life, we are invited to believe ever more boldly that Easter is real, that Christ is present, and that the journey of Easter faith is an incomparable journey full of new life in every way.

One of the powerful mysteries in preaching is how God often leads the preacher to just the right word at the right moment. In that moment, through the power of the Holy Spirit, the Scripture becomes the Word of the living Christ bringing salvation, hope and healing. This doesn't happen in the same way or to the same degree every Sunday. But when it does happen in an unusual and powerful way, you know it. The "success" of the sermon is obvious in the responsive chord it strikes in the hearts and lives of the people. The preacher is often surprised, not expecting the result nor perhaps even thinking beforehand that the sermon was "that good." One walks away that day knowing that the power of the sermon was not primarily in its language or content nor in the eloquence or accomplishment of the preacher. Rather, the power was that of the Spirit of God leading the preacher from the text to the human condition of need in a way that proclaims the good news and brings response according to God's own timing.

As this sermon reflects, timing is crucial in preaching. One who proclaims the gospel must continually listen for the voice of God speaking through the Scripture and the various experiences of one's life and one's congregation. If we are faithfully attentive to those voices and to the contours of human life and experience, God will speak through us in powerful ways and Easter will continue to happen all the way through to eternity.

## SUGGESTIONS

- Take some time in the next few weeks in your prayer, quiet time, and study to focus on the question of timeliness in your preaching. What needs, issues or texts do you feel led to address? Why?
- Talk to friends or lay leaders in your church and ask their feelings about the needs in your congregation. How might you do some good

pastoral care from the pulpit as David Williamson has done in this sermon?

- Special holidays and seasons of the church year (Advent, Christmas, Epiphany, Lent, Holy Week, Easter, Pentecost, etc.) offer important opportunities for timeliness in preaching. Do a special study of the meaning and significance of these seasons in the history of the Christian church. Offer a teaching or preaching series about them in your congregation. How can you use the timing of these seasons to proclaim the gospel more creatively and effectively?
- Consider preaching some sermons on the two key issues addressed in David Williamson's sermon: the contrast between faith and reality as we often experience it; and the experience of transitions in our lives. Make a list of biblical texts that speak to each of these issues.
- On timeliness in preaching, locate a copy of John Claypool's *The Preaching Event: The Lyman Beecher Lectures* (Word, 1980/Harper, 1989) and read chapter 5, "The Preacher as Nurturer." On transitions in the stages of human life, see Gail Sheehy's book *New Passages: Mapping Your Life Across Time* (Random House, 1995).

*Gary W. Klingsporn*

# Good Luck,
# Bad Luck—
# Who is to Say?

PHILEMON 1–25

REV. DR. JOHN R. CLAYPOOL
ST. LUKE'S EPISCOPAL CHURCH
BIRMINGHAM, ALABAMA

# GOOD LUCK, BAD LUCK— WHO IS TO SAY?

PHILEMON 1–25

I once heard a professional humorist claim that there are only ten basic joke patterns in all the world, and that all the funny stories going around are simply adaptations or variations of these primal themes. I do not know whether his number is correct, but think of the same punch lines you have heard across the years, although the details vary widely.

Anthony de Mello makes a similar claim for certain basic story forms. During his lifetime, this Indian Jesuit made an extensive study of literature of many cultures, and what he discovered was that certain story patterns turn up everywhere. The details are very different, but the basic structure or point of the stories is the same. Carl Jung uses the term *archetypal* to describe such stories, and both men suggest that we need to look very carefully at those places where stories from all over the world coincide. We can be confident that what is being expressed here is important and universal truth.[1]

One such archetypal story comes out of the Chinese culture. It seems that a poor old farmer had a single horse on which he depended for everything. He pulled the plough, drew the wagon, and was the old farmer's sole means of transportation. One day a bee stung the horse and in fright he ran off into the mountains. The old farmer went in search of him, but was not able to find him. He came home and his neighbors in the village came by and said, "We are really sorry about your bad luck in losing your horse." But the old farmer shrugged and said, "Bad luck, good luck — who is to say?"

A week later his horse came back, accompanied by twelve wild horses whom he had obviously encountered, and the old farmer was able to corral all these fine animals, which turned out to be an unexpected windfall. Again news spread throughout the village, and his neighbors came and said, "Congratulations on your good luck, this bonanza out of the sky." To which the old farmer once again shrugged and said, "Good luck, bad luck — who is to say?"

The only son of the farmer decided to make the most of this good fortune, so he started to break the wild horses so they could be sold and be put to work in the fields. But, as he attempted to do this, he got thrown off one of the horses and his leg was broken in three places. When word of this accident spread through the village, again the neighbors came, saying, "We are sure sorry about the bad luck of your son getting hurt." The old man shrugged and said, "Bad luck, good luck — who is to say?"

Two weeks later a war broke out between the provinces in China. The army came through conscripting every able-bodied male under fifty. Because the son was injured, he did not have to go, and it turned out to save his life, for everyone in the village who was drafted was killed in the battle.

De Mello draws two basic conclusions from this archetypal story. First, we humans are in no position to make final judgments on the things that happen to us. A certain event may have every appearance of evil at the time it occurs, like a valued horse running away, or a leg getting broken. And yet, in the mysterious unfolding of life, what seemed so bad at the time turns out to be the means to unexpected good. Had the horse not run off, the twelve new horses would not have come. Had the leg not been broken, the son's life might have been lost. Therefore, the old farmer's reaction each time was profoundly wise. He accepted the shape of his creatureliness and refused to hand down ultimate verdicts on things until they had run their course.

He knew what the book of Genesis tries to teach us; namely, that the fruit of the Tree of Knowledge of good and evil is deadly poison for human beings. We did not create this universe and therefore do not have the capacity to determine the ultimate nature of these realities. What is finally good and evil is literally beyond our finite abilities, and stories like this in every culture underline the importance of humility and openness to mystery on the part of humankind. I spoke a few weeks ago about St. Paul's image that we humans "know in part and prophesy in part, that our seeing is always as through a glass darkly," and this is precisely the witness of this archetypal story.

De Mello's other conclusion, however, is a very bright and hopeful one; namely, God is at work for good. The One who created the universe and knows fully the essence of good and evil is, in fact, an ingenious Alchemist, capable of taking what looks for all the world like lead and bringing forth from it astonishing gold. This One is rarely obvious or predictable in how he works, but again and again in history, he takes the worst of times and does the best of things with them like he did with the runaway horse and the broken leg.[2]

Years ago, Herb Gardner wrote a wonderful play called "A Thousand Clowns." The title comes from a metaphor the chief character uses in trying to help his young nephew understand the wonder of being alive. He said, "Every day is like going to the circus. You remember how a little car always drives into the middle of the ring, and it looks so tiny, and then all of a sudden, all of the sides open up and out pop a thousand clowns? You never dreamed that all those people could be in such a tiny vehicle, but somehow they were.

"This is the shape of life, my boy. There is always so much more to any event than we humans can see on the surface. Do not ever assume you know everything about anything. Every day is a little car filled with a thousand clowns — learn to be humble and a friend of mystery and who knows how you will be surprised?"[3]

Here is a beautiful image of that "knowing and not knowing" that is the essence of faith. We can have confidence in this One who in all things is at work for good at the same time that we do not understand completely how it is all going to work out. "Do not jump to premature conclusions about either good or evil" seems to be the import of this story, and right in the center of our Scripture lessons this morning is a story that proves de Mello's point.

If you look at it carefully, it has the same structure as the Chinese story, although the particulars are different. I am referring to the Epistle lesson — the reading from Philemon. This is the only personal letter of St. Paul's to be included in the New Testament. All his other epistles were addressed to churches, but this one is different, and the story behind it is intriguing indeed.

Years before, Paul had gone to a city named Colossae, and there he had been instrumental in the conversion of one of its leading citizens, a man named Philemon. Through Paul, the Risen Christ had done for another what he had done for Paul on the Damascus Road. Like so many people of that era, Philemon was a slave owner. It is estimated that at the time Paul lived there were sixty million slaves in the Roman Empire. The whole ancient world rested on this social arrangement, and one of Philemon's possessions was a young slave named Onesimus. It seems that one day he did a very dangerous and risky thing — he stole some money from his master and fled into the night. As a runaway slave, he headed for Rome and proceeded to lose himself among the throngs who made up that ancient megalopolis.

We have no details as to how Onesimus happened to cross paths with his owner's old friend, the Apostle Paul. By this time, the great missionary was under arrest and being held in prison in Rome on the hope he might gain an audience with the Emperor and be exonerated. It could be that Onesimus had been arrested by this time and was thrown into the same prison. As I said, this is the part of the story that is unknown. All we do know is that somehow a runaway fugitive and an imprisoned old apostle came in touch with each other.

By usual expectations, Paul would not even have taken notice of such a one, for in those days slaves were hardly regarded as human beings. Few free folk even noticed them beyond the function they performed. Or, had

Paul recognized Onesimus and discovered him to be both a thief and a fugitive, he could easily have responded to him in anger and condemnation.

Long before, however, Paul had begun to model his life after the pattern of Jesus of Nazareth. This was the One "who loved each one he met as if there were no other in all the world to love, and who loved all as he loved each." This is the way Paul had learned to live his life as well, which means there were no unimportant and insignificant individuals to him. Again, although the particulars are not clear, what the Risen Christ had done through Paul for Philemon, he did for Onesimus as well. The young slave experienced a powerful conversion, and as a result, became a very different kind of human being.

The name *Onesimus* literally means "useful," and in the letter that Paul would subsequently write, he makes a play on this fact, which suggests the impact Christ always makes on a person when he is allowed to come into their life. Paul said, "Onesimus used to be only useful in name, but now, he is useful by nature." Jesus Christ has a way of taking chaotic and disorganized lives and bringing them to effective and creative focus. "Old lives for new" — this is how the Christian way is often described. And so it was that Onesimus and Paul became very affectionately bonded to each other, and the young slave became a great help to Paul during his experience in prison.

And yet, for all the miracle of change that grace had brought to Onesimus, Paul knew quite well that the past could not be forgotten or avoided forever. Christianity does not invite us to take off the past like a coat and simply toss it aside without thought. Authentic Christian experience enables us to face up to our past, to make amends for it, and to proceed to live our lives in new directions.

The day came when Paul said words to Onesimus that must have struck terror to his heart. "You have to go back and submit yourself to Philemon, ask for his forgiveness, make amends for all you did." I say these words brought terror to Onesimus' heart, because runaway slaves in that day were treated with swift and consummate harshness. The whole fabric of ancient life rested on slavery, and extreme measures were taken to nip any kind of rebellion against it in the bud. In fact, the practice of crucifixion was invented by the Romans to keep would-be revolutionaries and runaway slaves in their place. Offenders were cruelly and slowly executed in high visibility to strike terror in the heart of anyone who might be pondering such behavior. Therefore, Onesimus could well have argued with Paul that he really must not have cared about him by asking him to risk such a terrible fate. And yet, Paul said, "No, this is what you have to do. One is never free for the future until one has honestly and openly faced up to the past."

Since he could not go with him, Paul did the next best thing. He wrote a letter to his friend Philemon, in which he asks a generous man to do an absolutely revolutionary thing; that is, to look on this one who was returning, not as the thief and runaway he had been, but as a human being for whom Christ had died and in whom he had done a saving work. Paul tells how Onesimus has become a part of his own heart, and he asks Philemon to step out of the culture in which he lived all his life, and to look at the situation from an entirely different vantage point — the way Jesus Christ would look at it.

In our Gospel of the morning, Jesus says, "If any one would come after me and does not hate his own father and mother, and wife, and children, he cannot be my disciple." I think one of the meanings of these harsh-sounding words is that we have to be willing to let go of the conditioning that was given to us in our heritage and allow Christ to give us new eyes, new values, new ways of perceiving what is right and wrong.

All of us are the prisoners of our own moment in history. We look back on the ancient world and the institution of slavery and judge it to be unspeakably evil. Yet two hundred years from now, people will undoubtedly look back on our era and see monstrous errors of which we are unconscious. One way of understanding Christian conversion is to say that we are constantly having to unlearn and relearn in light of Jesus Christ, to let go the things that we were taught by our culture because he is clearly calling us to new and better ways of being.

This is what the letter to Philemon was all about. Someone has said, "It is the seed that eventually split the rock of slavery." That is true. When human beings began to do what Paul asked Philemon, that is, to view slaves as more than possessions, but actually brothers and sisters in Christ, the time would come when the owner-slave relationship would have to give way to something more humane.

At any rate, this is the appeal that Paul makes to his friend, Philemon, and the chance he asked Onesimus to take. There was high risk on all sides of this revolutionary drama, and yet, the way it unfolded is exactly like the archetypal story from Chinese lore. This "Alchemist God" of ours, who in all things is at work, did with the Onesimus story what he has done again and again and again in history.

You see, there is the lovely sequel to this letter in the New Testament. Obviously, Philemon did rise to heights and did what Paul requested or this letter would certainly not have survived. The tradition is that he not only treated Onesimus as a brother in Christ, but he set him free and sent him back to the imprisoned apostle, who had said so clearly that he was useful to him and that he would have liked to have kept him by his side. Again,  the tradition is that Onesimus became one of Paul's most trusted and valued associates. The reason for believing this is that fifty years after this letter was written, the Bishop of Antioch, named Ignatius, wrote a letter to the Bishop of Ephesus, a letter that still exists — and do you know the name of that bishop? It is none other than Onesimus!

There is every reason to think that the slave who once stole money and fled into the night with no higher purpose than to lose himself among the hoards of Rome, eventually, by the grace of Christ, and the mercy of lots of other people, became one of the bishops of the early Church. The horse runs away and the people say, "We are sorry for your bad luck." And the old man is wise enough to say, "Bad luck, good luck — who is to know?" A slave runs away and eventually comes back, not with just twelve horses, but with all kinds of potential to do good in the world.

But that is not all. Another tradition is that Paul's letters were first collected and circulated by the Church in Ephesus. It was here that it was first recognized that these epistles had lasting and universal value, and this is how they eventually became a part of our New Testament. And who do you suppose was most responsible for collecting and distributing these letters? Most biblical scholars attribute this to the work of the bishop of that place — a man name Onesimus. And this would explain why amid all the letters that are addressed to churches, there would be included one personal letter. It was as if Onesimus was saying, "Let me tell you how I came to be. From one who had done an evil and despicable deed, here is what the forgiving grace of Jesus Christ can yet do." Had it not been for Onesimus, we might not have had the letters of Paul in our New Testament. And if he had not run away, he would have never met Paul. And if Paul had not seen him as a brother and not a slave, he would have never been converted. If he had not gone back to face his owner, he would have never really been free.

Do you see why I say that here is another variation on that universal theme "Good luck, bad luck — who is to say?" I am inspired by both of these stories to believe that the same pattern is also at work in my story and your story. Friends, we do not know enough to pass final judgment on the things that are happening to us. We do not have the capacity to eat of "the Tree of Knowledge of good and evil." That food is beyond us. Therefore, the wisdom of the old farmer, who dared to say in every moment, "Good luck, bad luck — who is to say?" is the proper stance for every one of us.

But for all we do not know, here is what we do know: "In all things, the seemingly good and the seemingly bad, God is at work for good!" Life is like a circus and every day is like those little cars that appear so tiny, yet, out of which emerge a thousand clowns. It is too early to come to a conclusion about any event. But it is not too early to live in hope, in faith, in confident openness. Our God is a Mystery, to be sure, but count on it — he means us good and in all things is at work to bring it to pass. Therefore, bet your life on it, stake your whole future on it. He loves us and means us good!

Notes
1. Carlos G. Valles, *Anthony de Mello*, (New York: Doubleday, 1987), p. 69.
2. Ibid., p 69.
3. Herb Gardner, *"A Thousand Clowns": A Comedy in Three Acts* (New York: S. French, 1962).

# COMMENT

As humans we have an insatiable need to explain things, to make sense of the world around us. We label people and events and put them into categories. We sort the good and the bad, according to *our* definitions. We seek meaningful coherence by making judgments about the things that happen to us. We keep convincing ourselves that the world makes sense according to our criteria and our interpretations of reality. We try to make the world conform to our ideas of coherence.

The problem is, it finally doesn't work. All too often, our explanations are highly presumptuous and fall short of ultimate coherence. At worst, our attempts to explain are often self serving and deny the mystery at the center of life. Exceptions which defy categorization keep coming along to challenge our neatly ordered world. And our judgments too often deny the radical freedom and mystery of God at work in the world and in our lives.

John Claypool's sermon "Good Luck, Bad Luck — Who Is to Say?" challenges our human propensity to explain things, while at the same time it proclaims the freedom and grace of God at work for good in our lives. This sermon is profound in thought but simple in its method. It tells two simple stories, that of a Chinese farmer and that of Onesimus, and from the two stories draws a series of profound conclusions representing "universal truth," in this case, the truth of the gospel.

Claypool's sermon is distinctive for at least two reasons. First, the point of the sermon, "We do not know enough to pass final judgment on the things that are happening to us," is a refreshing statement from the pulpit. How often does one hear this truth proclaimed in the simple, open way that Claypool does it? It is honest and direct. It cuts through all those explanations and "answers" we often assume preaching is about.

But at the same time, Claypool does not leave us without some answers: "But for all we do not know, here is what we do know: In all things, the seemingly good and the seemingly bad, God is at work for good!" That's a simple and refreshing proclamation of biblical faith. Distinctive in the sermon is the way in which Claypool has distilled a difficult subject into two or three memorable statements that proclaim the complexity and the simplicity at the heart of the Christian gospel.

Second, this sermon is distinctive because of its use of "story" to convey the truth of the gospel. This is narrative preaching at its best. The stories of the old Chinese farmer and of Onesimus carry the entire sermon. Claypool allows these archetypal stories to convey powerful truth simply in their telling, with limited interpretive or expositional comment along the way. The gospel is proclaimed here not through propositional statements about God, but through narrative. Narrative has the power to draw us into the world of the sermon and of the biblical text. Narrative invites us to identify our own story with the biblical story.

## POWER OF NARRATIVE

This sermon is not about proclaiming the gospel through a rational, doctrinal system of propositional statements. That's part of the point of the sermon: our "systems" finally fall short of expressing the fullness of the Divine reality. Narrative is the primary literary type found throughout the Scriptures. "Story" is God's way of revealing himself. The narratives of Scripture remind us that God meets us in history and in our lives and speaks to us through the events and experiences that make up our stories. Doctrinal theology, then, is always a "secondary" language to express the "primary" truth of the story. Theology exists to serve the story.

Claypool's emphasis on story in this sermon is a valuable reminder of the power of narrative to speak truth home to the heart of the listener. Toward the end of the sermon, Claypool makes the connection among the Chinese farmer, Onesimus, and us in a very quiet, understated way: "I am inspired by both of these stories to believe that the same pattern is also at work in my story and your story. Friends, we do not know enough to pass final judgment on the things that are happening to us.... But...here is what we do know...." These statements invite us to see that our stories bear some of the same truths as those of the farmer and of Onesimus, and that ulti-mately we are also part of God's story. God is at work for good in our sto-ries as well.

## STRUCTURE

Notice the simple structure of this sermon. After an introductory comment about archetypal stories, Claypool tells the story of the Chinese farmer and draws two conclusions from it by way of Anthony de Mello. Then he intro-duces Herb Gardner's delightful image of "a thousand clowns" and turns to the story of Onesimus for the remainder of the sermon. In Onesimus's story, Claypool explores de Mello's two conclusions, relates Onesimus to the farmer, and finally ties it all to us in the conclusion. It's a simple but tightly woven structure that brings the sermon together at the end and invites us to believe ever more deeply that "God loves us and means us good!"

## TEXT AND PROCLAMATION

The opening story of the old farmer and his wisdom, "Bad luck, good luck—who is to say" prepares us to  hear the biblical text of Philemon in a new way. Anthony de Mello's two conclusions about the story of the farmer give us a unique interpretive framework for hearing the story of Onesimus. De Mello's two points become the basis for the proclamation of the gospel from Philemon. Claypool demonstrates how Onesimus's story reveals two great truths: 1) We as humans are in no position to make final judgments on the things that happen to us; and 2) God is at work for good in our lives as the great Alchemist who takes the worst and brings out of it the best.

In preaching, as in all public speaking, transition points are crucial. For example, observe in this sermon the transition Claypool makes to the bib-lical text. He has told the farmer story and has related de Mello's two points. He then uses the image of the "thousand clowns" and Gardner's quote, "Every day is a little car filled with a thousand clowns — learn to be hum-ble and a friend of mystery and who knows how you will be surprised?" It

COMMENT

is at this point that Claypool makes the strategic transition to the biblical text while at the same time summarizing the entire thesis of his sermon. Notice how succinctly he says it, using the image of the little car with a thousand clowns to make the transition...

C O M M E N T

> *Here is a beautiful image of that "knowing and not knowing" that is the essence of faith. We can have confidence in this One who in all things is at work for good at the same time that we do not understand complete- ly how it is all going to work out. "Do not jump to premature conclu- sions about either good or evil" seems to be the import of this story [Chinese farmer], and right in the center of our Scripture lessons this morning is a story that proves de Mello's point.*

Here Claypool gathers up everything in the sermon to this point, gives us his thesis, and moves to the biblical story. In telling the story of Onesimus, the preacher proclaims that faith is about "knowing and not knowing," but in all things we can have confidence that God loves us and is working for good.

As Claypool relates Onesimus's story, notice how he pauses periodi- cally for interpretive reflection which becomes proclamation of the gospel. For example, in speaking of the word play in Philemon on the name *Onesimus* ("useful"), Claypool makes this point: "Jesus Christ has a way of taking chaotic and disorganized lives and bringing them to effective and creative focus."

Or again, in Paul's challenge to Philemon to "step out of the culture" and look at Onesimus's situation in a different light, Claypool notes Jesus' words in Luke 24:25 about "hating father and mother." We are called to let go of our cultural conditioning and "allow Christ to give us new eyes, new values, new ways of perceiving what is right and wrong." Paul is asking Philemon to view Onesimus the slave as more than a possession. "One way of understanding Christian conversion," the preacher proclaims, "is to say that we are constantly having to unlearn and relearn in light of Jesus Christ, to let go the things that we were taught by our culture because [God] is clearly calling us to new and better ways of being."

Here Claypool is allowing the text to proclaim important and surprising truths. God is the God of the unexpected, the unconventional. We cannot assume that the things that happen to us, or the calling of God in our lives, will follow expected routines and conventions. God is always doing a new thing. The God of freedom and mystery calls us to take risks as Philemon and Onesimus were called to risk. Ours is not to presume or to make final judgments about life or about God. We are called to listen and to respond to the call of God in our lives.

One of the powerful moments in this sermon is toward the end of the story of Onesimus when the preacher brings together Onesimus and the Chinese farmer. "The horse runs away and the people say, 'We are sorry for your bad luck.' And the old man is wise enough to say, 'Bad luck, good luck — who is to know?' A slave runs away and eventually comes back, not with just twelve horses, but with all kinds of potential to do good in the world...."

Onesimus — bishop and preserver of Paul's letter — exemplifies God's freedom and love at work in human circumstances to bring about good.

## NEED AND RESPONSE

In the face of our human need and propensity to seek explanations and make judgments at every turn about the events of life, this sermon proclaims there is much we cannot know. But there is also one great truth we can know: "God is at work for good." The sermon is finally about the essence of faith, about "knowing and not knowing."

In the final lines Claypool says it all and invites us to respond in faith: "It is too early to come to a conclusion about any event. But it is not too early to live in hope, in faith, in confident openness. Our God is a Mystery, to be sure, but count on it — he means us good and in all things is at work to bring it to pass." Here text and proclamation converge in the call to respond to the gospel in faith. The final word is that we can stake our future on it: "God loves us and means us good!" Having heard the good news, we are invited to believe it and respond joyfully with our lives.

## SUGGESTIONS

- In the near future, preach a biblical text by building your sermon around one illustrative story, as Claypool has done with the story of the Chinese farmer. Let your biblical text and illustrative story interpret each other. How can you allow the narratives to proclaim the gospel by simply telling the stories?

- Develop your own sermon around the basic theme of faith as "knowing and not knowing," and God's mysterious ways of working. What biblical texts might you preach? Consider passages such as Genesis 50:20 and the story of Joseph, the story of Job, or perhaps Romans 8:26–39. How could you draw upon Jesus' story of suffering, death, and resurrection in the gospels to preach on these themes?

- Can you think of some other "archetypal stories" that convey universal truth and can be used as vehicles to draw listeners in to hear the gospel in a new way? Watch for such stories and think about using them as you preach!

*Gary W. Klingsporn*

# Shared Any Good Yokes Lately?

MATTHEW 11:28–30

REV. RICHARD A. DAVIS
HOPE PRESBYTERIAN CHURCH
RICHFIELD, MINNESOTA

# SHARED ANY GOOD YOKES LATELY?

## MATTHEW 11:28–30

A s clergy, I fall into the category of being self-employed. That means Mr. FICA and I are very well acquainted. I send Mr. FICA large sums of money every three months, and usually, come tax time, I have to send him even more money. I recently read that an American who is self-employed works until May 6 every year before he works for himself. Over four months of my annual work year is spent laboring to pay the taxman. How depressing is that? In response, the politicians present me with their version of the gospel. It usually sounds something like this: "Vote for me, all you who are weary and tax-burdened, and I will give you a big tax break." While I can't recall that promise ever being fulfilled in my lifetime, it hasn't in the least diminished the enthusiasm of the promise-makers.

But politicians don't have a monopoly on ideas for lessening my financial burdens. There's a long list of others who continually try to seduce me with their particular gospel. Mystic Lake Casino offers me a windfall if I come out there. Tony Robbins and the other evangelists of self-improvement are continually calling me to the altar of wealth and success. I receive several pounds of mail every month from publishing houses, real estate developers, and various slick hucksters scheming to make me a millionaire. I sometimes wonder how I've managed to evade opulence for so long. Never have there been so many working so hard to make me a tycoon, but to my credit, thus far, I've done nothing but frustrate them. Try as they might, I've held my own and resisted their abundant blessings. I remain a paragon of indebtedness.

Each year I find myself spending more time on my financial obligations — more time paying bills, planning budgets, figuring taxes and generally trying to keep my head above water. I have an instant cash card and the new check card. I'm into direct deposit and automatic payments. I've got one computer at work and two at home equipped with state-of-the-art financial software like Quicken and TurboTax. I'm a '90s guy. I'm phonin' and faxin', spendin' and sendin', and flyin' and tryin'. I'm hooked up, booted up, revved up, psyched up, and — to be honest with you — FED UP.

The most exasperating thing about modern living is that all of those gizmos designed to make my life easier and less burdensome have done just the opposite. You don't have to be a rocket scientist to see what the age of technology and information is doing to us. A shorter work week? It's proven to be a false promise. Financial security? Another elusive butterfly. Never has the line between leisure time and work time been so thin. We now have telephones by the toilets and cellular phones for rent on the golf course. Students learn in sound bytes. We buy dinner at the gas station. We speak to our kids through an answering machine. Ain't it great? Are we or are we not having some fun now?

Into our busy lives comes a sound byte from Jesus: "Come to me, all you who are weary and burdened, and I will give you rest." Man, does that sound good to me! Into the din of pitches I receive every day comes this offer from the Son of God. *Come to me, all you who are fatigued and overwhelmed. Come to me, all you who are exhausted and weighed down beneath your burdens.... Come to me, all you who are just barely coping and need a break.* No matter how it's translated, it's pretty attractive, isn't it? Jesus offers relief to tired people. He steps right up to compete with Holiday Cruise Lines, Slumberland mattresses and Ramada Inn, and he offers us rest. Any takers? Speaking as one who more often than not feels burned out, I'm ready to study this passage. If you feel weary or burdened, you're welcome to join me. And, if you can't relate, you're welcome to tune out and spend the rest of the hour counting your blessings.

*"Come to me, all you who are weary and burdened, and I will give you rest."* Those first three words are at the very least audacious. Jesus doesn't say, "Come to God." It seems to me that would be a little less brazen. It's one thing to counsel someone who is hurting that he or she needs God, but it's quite another thing to say, "I'm the one who can really take care of your troubles." Unless, of course, you can really deliver. As we've seen previously in Matthew, Jesus is supremely confident of his divine capacity. No false modesty here. Jesus puts himself forward as God with skin on. He himself is the one and only authorized representative of God. Whatever it is that troubles us, ails us, or overwhelms us, Jesus says he has the wherewithal to handle it. Basic Christian doctrine #1: If you need to get to God, come to Jesus. So simple, but so provocative.

Next, notice that Jesus offers his help only to certain individuals, people who are weary and burdened. People having a hard time of it — those are the ones he wants. As one who's called to minister in his name, I sometimes wish he hadn't sent invitations to these folks. It means I'm called to work in a hospital. This conclusion didn't escape Martin Luther either; he noted that what makes this invitation so strange is that Jesus is, in effect, saying, "My kingdom is a hospital for invalids." Taken one step further, it suggests that people who are totally self-reliant don't fit very well in church. Lest we get too defensive when someone suggests that "religion is an opiate for the masses" as Karl Marx said, or a crutch for weak people, consider Jesus' invitation. He's calling for only the dysfunctional people in society to join him. People in pain may need an opiate to ease their misery. People with broken legs need crutches. And Jesus says, "Bring 'em to me, and I'll take care of 'em."

Consider how different the Christian church might look if Jesus had said, "Come to me, all you who have it all together." One thing you'd notice right away is the church would be empty, because there are only two kinds of people in society — those who admit their shortcomings and those who are liars. Jesus issues a general invitation to the sickies and the burnouts.

You should know that before you consider coming back next Sunday. You're in the company of a bunch of weaklings and losers here each week.

If, on the other hand, you find everyday life to be a bit much, Jesus is for you. If you're sick and tired of being sick and tired, this is for you. If you're depressed or discouraged or fed up or wiped out, you qualify for membership. Now that you know whether or not you belong in the company of Jesus, consider what he offers you. "I will give you rest." In the company of Christ, you can expect to find refreshment and rejuvenation, but he gives it in a most unusual way. Instead of giving you an easy chair and a footstool, he offers you a YOKE! Gee, you might think a two-week vacation in the Caribbean would be a bit more to your liking, but Jesus says, "Take my yoke upon you and *learn from me.*" This is the most remarkable twist in this whole passage. If someone is worn out, why on earth would you offer him another load to carry?

I wonder if Jesus used any visual aids with this teaching. After all, he'd been trained as a carpenter, so without a doubt he knew all about yokes. He and his father probably fashioned dozens of them in their workshop. I wonder if Jesus pointed to a yoke on an ox in a nearby field as he spoke these words. Or I wonder if he saw one sitting nearby. There were two kinds of yokes in Christ's day: a single yoke and a double yoke. Based on the context, I can't help but think Jesus was talking about a double yoke here, one made to harness two animals side by side. I think this because he encouraged us to learn from him once his yoke is on us, and also he says his yoke is easy and his burden is light. The best form of learning is to work right alongside a good teacher. If someone asks me to help move a piano and I'm already tired, you can bet I'm going to maneuver to be beside the biggest and brawniest brute in the bunch. That's sure to make my job easier and my burden lighter.

I think Jesus was inviting us to step into a double yoke right beside him. I can't imagine he would throw a back-breaking load on my shoulders and set me to plowing while he leaned on the fence and shouted out encouragement. I think the only reason Jesus' burden feels light is because he's right beside us bearing most of the weight. And watching how gracefully he shoulders that burden, we learn how to bear it effectively ourselves.

I also find it striking that Jesus admits to being gentle and humble of heart. Once again, if you're looking for someone to bear a burden for you, don't you think you'd look for someone who eats glass and spits fire? The words *gentle* and *humble* don't seem to sit too well with the word *yoke,* but here you have it. We must be careful not to miss the message here. Jesus turns the wisdom of the world upside down, and he reverses the secular solutions to our problems. When stress falls upon us, our carnal inclination is the fight-or-flight syndrome. When we feel weary and burdened, many of us long to take flight. We want a restful escape. We dream of a hammock beside a calm lake or an unending stint of R&R. We crave relief from all responsibility. But Jesus has something to say to this. His idea of "rest" is to get us involved in field work. Just when we feel most like disengaging, Jesus tells us to pick up a new burden, *his* burden, and to take action. However, when those same life pressures drive others of us to lash out at life and fight back with a vengeance, Jesus says to us, "No, learn from me, for I am gentle and humble, not pugnacious and aggressive."

From a worldly point of view, this passage is absolutely ridiculous. The very idea that yoking myself to some gentle and humble teacher who died on a cross is going to help anything — whew, it's beyond my reasoning. And yet, look what's promised to those who have faith in this method. "You will find rest in your souls." The Greek word for "soul" here is *psyche.* If you bring your stress and weariness to Jesus, he promises to calm your psyche. He doesn't once say your problems will be taken away. He doesn't promise to relieve your schedule. He doesn't once say he'll take your pain and trouble away. But he guarantees that your state of mind — your psyche — will be healed and restored. While the world promises to relieve our stress by piling labor-saving devices on us — devices that only compound our predicament — Jesus takes another way. He doesn't propose to alter our outward world, to rearrange our context; he promises to transform our inner person and give us genuine peace in the midst of a chaotic, threatening world.

Only Jesus has both the authority and the power to change our inner condition. Politicians, economists, sociologists, scientists and others are taking their best shots at trying to fix our outward predicament, and, may I add, with questionable success. And here comes Jesus offering to lighten our load with his yoke. Trying to rid ourselves of life's circumstantial burdens — and those burdens are considerable — will never work. At best, it will only offer a brief and partial reprieve. The only real solution to our inner weariness is to take on one more burden, the yoke of Jesus Christ. "For [his] yoke is easy and [his] burden is light." How can the yoke of Jesus be considered light? Well, try this. If you think godly and moral living is a heavy weight to bear, try living with acts of immorality on your conscience. Which is the heavier burden? If you think the demand of loving others is heavy, try living in a state of lovelessness. If you think God's call for generous giving is too demanding, try keeping hold of every dollar and every possession you've got. If righteousness is too intimidating for you, see if godless living helps you sleep at night. Once you take up the yoke of Jesus, compared to all the other yokes you've carried, I think you'll see just how light it is.

As I finished writing my sermon on Friday, I emerged from my office to find a fresh fax waiting for me which had been sent over by a friend and brother in Christ. Surprise! Surprise! The subject for the fax was the yoke of Jesus. It was a chapter from *The Pursuit of God* by A. W. Tozer, the late great Christian theologian and devotional author. If you've never read Tozer, run out and pick up anything he's written. The timing and content of the fax was heaven-sent, so I think God intended that I use these words in closing this morning. Listen to what Tozer has to say to weary and over-burdened Christians.

> *The heart of the world is breaking under this load of pride and pretense. There is no release from our burden apart from the meekness of Christ. Good, keen reasoning may help slightly, but so strong is this vise that if we push it down one place it will come up somewhere else. To men and women everywhere Jesus says, "Come unto me, and I will give you rest." The rest he offers is the rest of meekness, the blessed relief which comes*

*when we accept ourselves for what we are and cease to pretend. It will take some courage at first, but the needed grace will come as we learn that we are sharing this new and easy yoke with the strong Son of God himself. He calls it "my yoke," and he walks at one end while we walk at the other.*[1]

If you're one of those tired of walking it alone, consider becoming a yoke-mate with Christ. Amen.

Notes
1. A. W. Tozer, *The Pursuit of God,* (Harrisburg, Pa: Christian Publications, 1982), pp. 28–33.

# COMMENT

*"Mr. FICA and I are very well acquainted..."*

*"I remain a paragon of indebtedness..."*

*"We now have telephones by the toilets and cellular phones for rent on the golf course.... We buy dinner at the gas station. We speak to our kids through an answering machine."*

*"Vote for me, all you who are weary and tax-burdened, and I will give you a big tax break..."*

*"Ain't it great? Are we or are we not having some fun now?"*

What's distinctive about this sermon and makes it work so well is the delightful, humorous way in which Richard Davis addresses the paradoxes in modern life and in the biblical text, Matthew 11:28–30.

As the above lines indicate, Davis invites us to look at our lives and see the humor and the absurdity of telephones in toilets and on golf courses, and the thousands of other gizmos designed to make life easier. This technology promises an easier, much more wonderful life. But the opposite is happening. People seem more burdened and stressed out than ever. "I'm phonin' and faxin', spendin' and sendin', flyin' and tryin'," Davis says. "I'm hooked up, booted up, revved up, psyched up, and — to be honest with you — FED UP."

Who cannot identify with those feelings? Davis is calling attention to one of the great paradoxes of the technology and information age. In the opening paragraphs of this sermon he anticipates the text and prepares us for Jesus' words about "rest" by tapping into where most of us live each day: "Ain't it great? Are we or are we not having some fun now?"

## PROBLEM

The opening four paragraphs of the sermon ask us to identify with the question or problem Davis addresses. These paragraphs are light and whimsical, but they powerfully draw us in to identify with his frustration. The need that the sermon will address is just the "fed-up" weariness with life and with meaning precisely amid all the material and worldly promises of permanent relief and solutions.

Davis seizes upon the irony and paradox of daily life to prepare us for a deeper truth. Alluding to some politicians' "version of the gospel," the line "Vote for me, all you who are weary and tax-burdened, and I will give you a big tax break" obviously paraphrases Jesus' words and prepares us for the contrast between the empty, false offers of the world and the full promises of true rest in Jesus.

The issue is simply the burden and weariness of life in the modern age which manifests itself everywhere. The world's consumer-driven and consumer-oriented "false promises" entice us to "buy this or that" so that we may be relieved or have a happier life. Not only do these things fail to satisfy or relieve, they increase the burden. But Davis does not assault us with somber, guilt-laden pronouncements or doomsday rhetoric. Instead, he laughs at himself and asks us to laugh with him and ourselves, while taking the question seriously.

So there is the paradox and the need. Where do we turn?

## PROCLAMATION

Davis introduces his text at the beginning of the fifth paragraph: "Into our busy lives comes this word, a kind of sound byte from Jesus: 'Come to me, all you who are weary and burdened, and I will give you rest.'" Throughout the remainder of the sermon, he lets the text proclaim its one simple truth: "Jesus offers rest to tired people." True rest. Lasting rest. This is an excellent example of a sermon introducing a question or need and then letting the biblical text speak for itself to address that need.

Notice in the sermon how Davis's proclamation section works through Matthew 11:28–30 with a brief but not heavy-handed exegesis of each phrase of Jesus' saying. Davis has devoted a short paragraph to each of the seven phrases:

C O M M E N T

"Come to me"

"All you who are weary and burdened"

"I will give you rest"

"Take my yoke and learn from me"

"I am gentle and humble in heart"

"You will find rest for your souls"

"For my yoke is easy and my burden light."

*Come to Jesus.* The invitation is precisely for sick, weary people. Jesus will give rest. But Jesus offers a yoke. Here Davis addresses the paradox of stepping into the "double yoke" beside Jesus. This "rest" is not passive. It is the active life of discipleship, picking up a new "burden" and getting involved. This yoke paradoxically brings true rest for the soul! The only real solution to the inner weariness and burdens of our lives is to take on the yoke of Jesus Christ, whose yoke is easy and whose burden is light.

When developing a sermon, it is good at some point to try to state the thesis or point of what the text proclaims in one or two sentences. In this sermon, a good statement of the thesis appears in the last two sentences of the fifth paragraph before the end of the chapter: "While the world promises to relieve our stress by piling labor-saving devices on us — devices that only compound our predicament — Jesus takes another way. He doesn't propose to alter our outward world, to rearrange our context; he promises to transform our inner person and give us genuine peace in the midst of a chaotic, threatening world." Well said. Almost every sermon should have some kind of succinct statement of what the sermon is all about.

## RESPONSE

Since Jesus' words in this text are by their very nature an invitation, the entire proclamation section is an invitation to the listener to find rest in Jesus by identifying with him in faith, committing one's life to him, and learning what it means to take on Jesus' yoke. Notice how Davis says this right at the beginning of his exposition: *"Come to me....* Pretty attractive, isn't it? Jesus offers relief to tired people.... Any takers? If you feel weary or burdened, you're welcome to join me."

Observe how Davis quietly says this is an invitation to join him on the journey with Jesus. In effect, he says to the listener, "Just because I'm a minister doesn't mean I have it all together. Far from it. I'm fed up and frustrated [opening three paragraphs]. I need Jesus' rest day by day. Join me, if you need it too!" That's an ideal model for the posture of the preacher: companion, fellow journeyer. "We are all beggars together," as the preacher P. T. Forsythe once said.

The closing line of the sermon repeats the same invitation heard throughout the sermon: "If you're one of those tired of walking it alone, consider becoming a yoke-mate with Christ." That's important. It's the last line for the hearer to reflect upon. It gathers up the need (weariness) which has been addressed by the proclamation (Jesus' words), issuing in the invitation ("Come to me").

One of the most basic truisms in public speaking or other forms of communication is that a good speech or written piece should have an introduction, a body, and a conclusion. This sermon demonstrates that well. The introduction states the problem. The body dominates the sermon and proclaims the good news of the gospel to address that need. And the conclusion (with the quote from A. W. Tozer) reiterates the invitation throughout the sermon to "come, find rest in Jesus."

In the beginning of the sermon Davis has pointed to the frustrated irony of modern life: "Ain't it great? Are we or are we not having some fun now?" The implied answer is "No!" But at the end, having heard the beautiful promise of Jesus, one can say in response to the proclaimed Word, "Yes, it is great! Yes, we can have some fun! As yoke-mates with Christ!"

## SUGGESTIONS

- Study the opening four paragraphs of this sermon and reflect on how such an introduction prepares the listener for the biblical text. Think about how you can emulate this model.
- What are some of the false promises or "other gospels" our world offers us to relieve our burdens and weariness? Make a list and think

about another biblical text which would address this issue. Develop your own sermon on this subject.

• Identify other examples of paradox in Jesus' teaching in the gospels or in Paul's writings. Explore some of these in a series of sermons.

*Gary W. Klingsporn*

# "$3 WORTH OF GOD, PLEASE"

MATTHEW 14:28–29

DR. GARY W. KLINGSPORN
COLONIAL CHURCH
EDINA, MINNESOTA

# "$3 WORTH OF GOD, PLEASE"

## MATTHEW 14:28–29

O ne Saturday evening a little over two years ago, my wife Debra and I were driving down Franklin Avenue in Waco, Texas, where we were living at the time. Suddenly Debra cried out, "G.K.! G.K.! Let's turn around and go back. There was a cute little station wagon on that used car lot back there."

Now, I've learned in eight years of marriage that those impulsive U-turns in the middle of the road are not minor events. They are rather of critical importance to the peace and tranquility of our marriage. So I think it was only with a minor protest that I quickly whipped the car around, dashed back up Franklin Avenue, and turned in by the used car lot. There she pointed it out to me — a gray Pontiac Sunbird station wagon.

You see, I hadn't even noticed the car lot, and she had already picked out the car! It was obvious that she had fallen in love with this little vehicle immediately. We got out and looked at it and kicked the tires a bit. It seemed to us that it was in good condition — the mileage was low, the price reasonable. But the dealer was closed. It was a Saturday evening. So Debra said: "Let's come back and drive it first thing on Monday morning." And I said, "Well, maybe so."

You see, Debra was in the market for a new second car, but I was not. The old red Chevrolet Vega was good enough for me. She had driven it just out of college years before, and I was still driving it. I began listing all the reasons to her that we really ought not to consider buying a car just then. The strongest among my arguments was that "the Vega still runs." "Sure, the muffler is loud and about to fall off. That's right, honey; the air conditioner doesn't work in 108-degree heat in the summertime. And the radio doesn't work, but I'm the one driving it, and that's all right with me."

"Well, yes, honey, it is hard to start on cold mornings. I know that. But just don't drive it. You drive the other car. Yes, you do have to pump the brakes a little bit sometimes when you come to a stop sign. I'll try to do something about that. But I'll keep on driving it because, you know, I've grown attached to that old car, and we really can't afford a Pontiac station wagon." And then the zinger came. "Yes, honey," she said, "but with the baby on the way (Debra was pregnant), we need a dependable second car in case we need to take the baby out in an emergency in the middle of the night."

Somehow or other, I don't know how, I managed to suppress this project for the moment. We left the car lot that night, and we did not return on Monday morning. But for the next two or three weeks, every now and then, Debra would drop these little hints. Some of you men know what I'm talking about. "That sure was a nice little car." "G.K., I think that car has our name on it." "I drove by the car lot today, and you know what? It was still there."

And one day the truth came out that she had even stopped by and talked to the dealer. I knew we had a problem on our hands. And one day at the end of lunch Debra said, "You know, we have enough time. Let's go drive that little car. Come on, G.K." And so I finally caved in.

We went, and we drove it. She liked it a lot more, and you know what? I began to like it! It was a neat little car. And then when I knew that things had heated up to a fever pitch, I suddenly decided it was time to start checking all the other used car lots in town. You know, comparison shopping. I mean, this was the only car we'd looked at. So Debra agreed, but I could tell her heart wasn't into comparison shopping. I would read the classified ads and we would drive by other car lots. But the gray Pontiac station wagon was always there at the top of her loves.

And so after much looking, and much long-suffering on my dear wife's part, finally three or four weeks later, we went in and we bought that gray Pontiac station wagon. It took us over nine weeks to buy that car. Debra would have bought it in a day.

You know the disgusting part about all of this? She was right about that car from the very beginning. We found no better buy, and every now and then I say to her, "Deb, do you mind if I drive the Pontiac today? It's a great little car. I love the way it handles, and I'm so glad WE bought it."

Debra and I learned very early on in our relationship that we have very different personality types. In many ways we are exact opposites. She is a highly intuitive, spontaneous risk-taker. And I am the cautious, analytical, play-it-safe type. I approach things like you'd analyze an academic problem. I don't rush in. But she makes up her mind quickly. She's in touch with her emotions and knows exactly what she feels. It takes me a few days sometimes to decide whether I'm feeling anything at all, let alone what it is!

It's that analytical streak in me that took me off to graduate school, I guess. I have to examine all the options and wear a matter out in my mind before I can commit to it with my heart. Debra is ready to go out to a restaurant on the spur of a moment in the evening. She's ready to go over to someone's home just like that. But I have to plan to be spontaneous. You know, I have to plan it for next Thursday. And I have to put it on my calendar: "Be spontaneous. Have some fun today. Play." And then I can do it.

Not Debra. She knew that she and I were going to be married six months before I had figured it out. And she knew that we were coming here to Colonial Church a number of days before I knew it. Aren't they disgusting, these intuitive, spontaneous people? They're always out ahead of us cautious analyticals. It's almost more than I can take.

"Lord, if it is you, bid me come to you." "Come." So Peter got out of the boat and walked on the water and came to Jesus. And there is no question whatsoever in my mind with whom I identify out there that night on that storm-tossed sea. I'm in the boat with the disciples. I'm hanging on for dear life, clutching the mast and the wooden beams with all my might.

And you know who Peter reminds me of? You guessed it. Debra, my dear Debra. The risk-taker. Always ready to pull a U-turn in the middle of the road. Peter, ready to get down out of the boat and step into the unknown, drawn to embrace a new experience immediately. I think, drawn to his Lord. "Lord, if it is you, bid me come to you on the water." The others and I are back there in the boat analyzing the situation and shouting, "Peter, you're crazy! Get back in the boat." But out there in the darkness, in the middle of the lake with the wind howling, the lightning splitting the night, the thunder rolling and the waves swelling, Peter, with eager resolve on his face, steps down onto the swirling foam. And in that moment Matthew gives us a picture of faith.

Matthew gives to the early church, the church in all ages, and to us this morning, a kind of crazy picture of faith. It is faith not as we often think of it, not something that is safe and secure and cautious, careful and analytical, but here faith that is willing to risk and to move out.

Oh, but you see, *risk* is to me a word for the stock market. It's a word for corporate mergers and acquisitions. The high rollers. It's a word for space shuttle launchings. And experimental surgeries. That's where the risk is, not in my ordinary everyday life.

And please don't ask me about risk when it comes to faith. I'm doing all I can to minimize risk in my home and in my business and in my faith. I want to come to church, and I want to seek a haven of rest here, a risk-free zone. A place of comfort and reassurance where I can find salvation. After all, doesn't *salvation* mean to be saved? And isn't that somehow related to being safe? Safe in the boat? Certainty? Theological absolutes? Something that I can know beyond doubt. A place where I can be saved from the rest of the world.

Wilbur Rees describes that risk-free faith when he writes: "I would like to buy $3 worth of God, please. Not enough to explode my soul, or disturb my sleep. But just enough to equal a cup of warm milk, or a snooze in the sunshine. I don't want enough of him to make me love a black man, or pick beets with a migrant worker. No, I want ecstasy and not transformation. I want the warmth of the womb, not a new birth. I want a pound of Eternal in a paper bag. I would like to buy just $3 worth of God, please."[1]

That's it, isn't it? We want faith to be safe. We want God the Comforter, the Encourager, the Reassurer. And God knows we need all of those things. But too often, we want the cup of warm milk and the snooze in the sunshine. Sometimes we don't want enough of God to make us nervous, to challenge our prejudices, to change us and move us on to a new stage in the journey of faith. No, we want a comfortable God. It is within us to stay clutched to the beam back there in the boat with God at a safe distance. It's especially true of us cautious, analytical types.

But Matthew holds a different picture up before us: Peter and the disciples on storm-tossed seas, and Peter stepping out over the edge onto the water in that crazy U-turn in the middle of the road. "Lord, bid me come to you on the water." And Jesus answered, "Come." So Peter got out of the boat and walked on the water to Jesus. And that makes me very, very nervous. Peter is a controversial figure. We don't know quite what to do with this man. Read the literature on this passage, and you will find some trying to figure him out. "Peter, you're impulsive. You leap before you look. You're reckless. You're a show-off. You act without thinking. Foolish. Irrational. Irresponsible."

And I suggest to you this morning that faith sometimes looks that way. Faith sometimes looks foolish, irresponsible to those for whom faith is cautious and analytical, the risk-free comfort zone, the $3 worth of God, the cup of milk, the nap in the sunshine. You see, Peter is a man of the sea. He knows that you can float a boat on the water and you can catch fish from the sea. But you don't walk on the sea. And yet Peter here has one word to act upon, the word *Come*. He is willing to let go and to risk, because he is drawn to Jesus. I don't think he's just showboating; I think he wants more of this one who teaches and heals and loves, who mystifies him. I think he wants more than just $3 worth of God.

Peter is joined by the centuries of saints and martyrs who in faith at some point or another were willing to risk just like that. Abraham who packs his mules and goes 500 miles west, not knowing for sure where or why; Moses who after so many objections stands in the presence of the great Pharaoh of Egypt; Jeremiah the weeping prophet who knows his message will not be popular; Paul and Augustine and Luther and Calvin and Martin Luther King, Jr., and Mother Teresa — all of them together risking, stepping out at one time or another, willing to be open and vulnerable.

So it is for you and for me this morning. To have faith and hope in a sinful and painful world, is to risk disappointment and disillusionment when the world does not suddenly change and become more loving and nonviolent. To believe in the transforming power of Jesus Christ in a day of skepticism and materialism is to risk being called foolish, naive, shallow-minded idealists.

C. S. Lewis once said of himself, "I am a safety-first creature." I am cautious and careful. "But if I am sure of anything, I am sure that Jesus' teaching was never meant to confirm my preference for safe investments and limited liabilities." There is no safe investment, Lewis says. To have faith, to love at all, is to make ourselves vulnerable. "Love anything and your heart will certainly be wrung and possibly be broken."[2]

But you see, the fear of risk often paralyzes me into doing nothing. And I miss the vision of faith and the richness of life that God offers me in the faith. But Jesus says elsewhere in the Gospels, "Those who want to save their life will lose it; and those who lose their life, give it away, and plunge in for my sake and the gospel's, will save it...will find true life."

So how about you this morning? Are you cautious and analytical? Or are you willing to risk? Do you identify more with the disciples and me in the boat, or with Peter? Where in your life is God calling you to risk? Is it in some relationships at home? Perhaps it's some level of communication in your marriage relationship, some conflict or misunderstanding at home or at work that needs you to take the initiative to resolve it. Is this perhaps needed in relationships with your children, or children with your parents?

Are you being called to risk in your relationship with God, to risk coming to faith in Jesus Christ, moving away from $3 worth of God into more of God and giving more of yourself to God? Is ours a God of $3? Or a God who calls us in faith to be transformed, to be deepened, and to grow in prayer and meditation, in study and fellowship as a church together?

Where in Colonial Church are we being called to risk? For the unity of the church at large it's going to mean risk as we dialogue with one another. It's going to mean stepping out like Peter at times, uncertain, into the unknown.

One thing more. Let's all be prepared for what follows when we move to a new and deeper level of faith. Because I know some of you are thinking about the rest of the story here...when we desire to have more of God, to give God more of ourselves, when we risk....

When Peter saw the wind, he was afraid. And beginning to sink, he cried out, "Lord, save me." And Jesus immediately reached out his hand and caught Peter, saying to him, "O man of little faith, why did you doubt?" Why did you waver and go in two directions at once? In Matthew's portrait, doubt now becomes a part of the faith experience itself. Peter the man of risk becomes also Peter the man of doubt and hesitation. He hesitates because he takes his eyes off Jesus. He looks at the wind, his inadequacies overtake him, and he starts to go under. And that will surely happen to you and me as well.

That faltering is itself a very part of the creative risk-taking faith experience, where faith is better understood as a process than an object we possess. Frederick Buechner says that faith is "on-again, off-again rather than once for all." "Faith is not always being sure where you are going, but going there anyway."[3] The moments of uncertainty and inadequacy will come. Being called by Jesus Christ to come is being called to grow and to deepen, to stretch and to be transformed, to lose our lives for his sake in the Kingdom. Jesus at once stretches out his hand and catches Peter. He lifts him up and restores him. And when they get into the boat, the wind ceases and all of those in the boat worship him. With the early church together, Matthew and those in the boat confess, saying, "Truly, you are the Son of God."

The good news of the gospel this morning is simply this. In a life that's filled with storms and fear, in a world of darkness, God is present to us in Jesus Christ and bids us come. He says, "Take heart, it is I; have no fear.

Come." God bids us, like Peter, to step out in faith. Bids us no longer settle for $3 worth of God, a pound of Eternal in a paper bag. But rather,
"Come and be transformed." And when we falter God is there, always
there, to catch hold of us so that nothing can pull us under.

Where are we this morning? Are we on the periphery of faith?
Cautious and analytical? Are we keeping God at arm's length? Are we
examining all the options and comparison shopping, on and on and on,
before finally deciding that it's safe and reasonable to believe just a little bit
in God? Is ours a safe, entertaining God, Sunday after Sunday? Is ours an
intellectual God, nice to think about, but not really involved in our lives?

Or is God a calling and transforming God, who bids us make U-turns
in the middle of the road? Peter got out of the boat, walked on the water,
and came to Jesus. I wonder if you and I will do the same today and tomor-
row and whenever he calls. I wonder if we will dabble in our faith, settle
for a warm cup of milk, or give ourselves to God.

"Those who want to save their life will lose it, and those who lose their
life for my sake, and for the sake of the gospel, will save it," will find true
life.

*O Lord of life, you bid us come, and step out, and risk. Give us faith and
grace to do it…today. Amen.*

Notes

1. Quoted in Tim Hansel, *When I Relax I Feel Guilty* (Elgin, IL: David C. Cook Publishing
   Co., 1979), p. 49.
2. C. S. Lewis, *The Four Loves* (New York: Harcourt Brace Jovanovich, 1960), pp. 168–69.
3. Frederick Buechner, *Wishful Thinking: A Theological ABC* (New York: Harper & Row,
   1973), p. 25.

## COMMENT

Why spend nearly one-third of a sermon telling the story of something as seemingly trivial as a husband and wife buying a used car? If preaching is about the deep and holy things of God, why spend precious time in a sermon kicking tires on a car lot and hearing about the idiosyncracies of a husband who doesn't want to buy? Why not just start this sermon by saying, "In the fourteenth chapter of Matthew there's a story about Peter, Jesus, and the disciples on the Sea of Galilee..."?

Gary Klingsporn's sermon "$3 Worth of God, Please" raises interesting questions about the nature and function of the "introduction" in a sermon. How short or how long should an introduction be? What should its purpose be? How should the introduction relate to the rest of the sermon? Should it be a nice little joke to break the ice, a cute story or quote, often unrelated to the remainder of the sermon? Should an introduction get right to the point of the sermon and present the thesis? Or, can introductions engage listeners, lead them along and play with them, perhaps even "entertain," at the same time they begin to preach the serious content of the sermon?

The answer to these questions will vary from sermon to sermon and preacher to preacher. There is no one "correct" formula. But it is important each time we preach to ask ourselves about introductions and to be very intentional about the decisions we make in using the opening moments of a sermon. The opening is crucial. We either gain hearers or lose them. Often hearers will decide either to listen or to check out of the sermon right there. While opinions vary widely on the use of introductions, most who preach agree that a good opening is critical.

### THE OPENING

Klingsporn's sermon is distinctive in the way in which the extended opening story, or introduction, prepares us for the biblical text and proclamation. But the opening story doesn't just anticipate the story of Peter on the sea. The story of buying the car becomes a parable which helps us later to understand and experience the story of Peter in a new way. In this sense, the opening story is no longer "just an introduction." By anticipating the biblical text, it already begins to interpret and proclaim the meaning of the text.

Early in the sermon we as listeners do not know what the preacher is doing with this used car story. That's part of its effectiveness. When we finally reach the story of Peter, we're ready to hear it against the backdrop of the first story or parable. So the story leads us along in a way that helps us to see the biblical story in a new way.

With the opening story in the first one-third of this sermon Klingsporn has done something akin to Jesus' use of parable. It's as if Klingsporn is saying, "The Kingdom of God is like a man and a woman who drove past a used car lot one night, and...." The parable is about the meaning of faith. In the sermon it is set alongside the story of Peter walking on the sea, which is also a story about the meaning of faith. The car story helps us interpret the Peter story. The sermon introduction flows into the biblical text and its proclamation.

## TEXT & PROCLAMATION

This sermon is effective because it is personal in nature, universal in its truth, and incarnational in its understanding of biblical faith.

1. *Personal.* This sermon brims with the power of personal experience. It begins with the very personal and practical illustration of the personality differences between Klingsporn and his wife, and continues the theme throughout the sermon as the preacher invites us to identify with some very common human experiences.

The opening scene is a winsome and compelling way to gain and hold the listener's attention, because hearers can immediately identify with both the situation and the types of personalities involved. Buying a car is a common experience in most American households. Who has not felt some of the same emotions and encountered some of the same experiences described here? The story is down to earth. The preacher lets us know something of who he is and who his wife is!

This sermon was originally preached during Klingsporn's first year at a church numbering over three thousand members. In a church that size, people often find it difficult to know their ministers or feel close to them. Large congregations can feel very impersonal. In this sermon Klingsporn has let people know some things about his personality in a way that many of them can begin to know him. We get to know the preacher as "Gary" (or "G.K."). And we also get to know a little about who Debra is. It is good for the preacher to talk about himself and Debra in a lighthearted, humorous way in the pulpit. It helps overcome the distance between the people and the minister at the same time that it helps the preacher enter into the biblical story in a creative way.

Our people want to know us. We can let them into our lives, not in excessive or inappropriate ways of "bearing all" and revealing too much, but in dignified, appropriate ways that enable them to identify with us as human beings. Done appropriately, there is a power in the personal in preaching.

2. *Universal.* In the opening story and throughout, this sermon captures an element of universal human experience alongside proclaiming biblical truth in a way that has universal application. We can identify with Gary and Debra in terms of personality types. The world is filled with some people who are analyticals, and other people who are spontaneous, intuitive types! And because of that, we can perhaps identify better with either Peter who splashes out onto the water, or the other disciples who stay behind in the boat.

The preacher is wise to describe in some detail both his wife's spontaneous qualities and his own analytical bent. This shows a sensitivity to the fact that both types will be present in the congregation. It invites the listener to say, "Hey — I'm like that, too. This speaker knows 'where I'm at.' He's speaking to me where I live." Many in the congregation will identify with Debra. Others will identify with Gary. Who hasn't encountered these differences in people and personality types in families, in the workplace, at school, or in the church? There is a universal quality here that draws us into the sermon.

But notice, the purpose of this personality theme in the sermon is not to engage in an entertaining Myers-Briggs exercise: "So what type are you?" The whole point is to drive toward the biblical text and the issue of faith. What at first looks trivial — a husband and wife buying a car — later in the sermon helps us think about the varieties of faith experience and the meaning of faith itself. The real questions become, "What type person are you when it comes to the issue of faith?" "How difficult is it for you to believe the gospel and to act in living it out?" These are universal questions that should be asked in every gathering of those who seek to follow Christ.

Notice in this sermon that Klingsporn casts himself as the foil or protagonist of the story, rather than his wife — and not just to avoid an argument with her on the way home from church! The whole point of the story and the sermon is that faith is more likely won by those who are willing, like Debra, to risk — to step out into the deep. Klingsporn seeks to challenge people who have difficulty doing that. He will not allow the hyperanalytical among us simply to identify with him. He wants to invite us to change, and to approach life from a more risking, faith-full potential. He speaks especially to those who, like himself, demand to know for certain, after considerable study and analysis. He wants us to hear Jesus' words in a new way: "Those who want to save their life will lose it, and those who lose their life for my sake, and for the sake of the gospel, will save it" (Mark 8:35).

3. *Incarnational.* Klingsporn is not content with merely challenging the overly cautious to take risks. He deals realistically with one reason so many of us hesitate to do so: like Peter, we might sink. It would have been easy to dwell exclusively on the part of the biblical story that portrays Peter walking victoriously atop the water. But the preacher knows that reluctant risk-takers are aware of the "rest of the story" — Peter sinks. Making explicit reference to this fact is critical to handling the text and the subject with integrity. The preacher isn't covering up an essential point of the story, nor is he ignoring people's real concerns. Instead, he confesses that in Peter's case "doubt becomes a part of the faith experience itself."

Faith does involve danger, risk, and unknown outcomes. Now, how-

C O M M E N T

ever, with doubt out in the open alongside faith, even as a part of faith, the preacher has given us the full picture of the text and of faith.

We are familiar with the heroic "leap of faith" which is an essential part of risk-taking. Although this is the core of Klingsporn's message, note that he is not urging us to leap into nothingness. He reminds us that no sooner does Peter sink than the Lord himself reaches out to save him. Sometimes in preaching we call people to feats of faith that seem impossible. We easily fail to acknowledge that faith itself is a gift. Christ alone provides the resources to live out our faith.

The preacher allows the text to proclaim the good news of the gospel in a simple way: "In a life that's filled with storms and fear, in a world of darkness, God is present to us in Jesus Christ and bids us come.... And when we falter, God is there...to catch hold of us so that nothing can pull us under." The sermon invites us truly to believe that, and to risk stepping out in faith in a whole new way. Here biblical truth is incarnational. God is here with us to see us through.

## RESPONSE

Toward the end of the sermon the preacher asks, "Are you willing to risk [in faith]? Do you identify more with the disciples and me in the boat, or with Peter? Where in your life is God calling you to risk? Is it in some relationships at home? Is ours a $3 God?" These questions challenge us to change.

And notice how the questions move from the personal to the corporate — from risking in personal faith and relationships to the situation facing the church: "Where...are we being called to risk?...Is ours a safe, entertaining God, Sunday after Sunday?" In response to the parable of the car and the story of Peter, we are reminded in the closing line that God bids each of us "Come, and step out, and risk." But then we are reminded of the promise of God's empowerment: "Give us faith and grace to do it...today." The sermon has moved from the proclamation of the text and has left us to consider the meaning of Christ's own word in our lives: "Come!"

## SUGGESTIONS

- Spend some time going through this volume of *The Library of Distinctive Sermons* looking just at the opening paragraphs of each sermon to observe how various preachers have chosen to introduce different sermons. What openings do you like most or do you feel are most effective? Why? What can you learn from reflecting on these various introductions?

- How can you let your people get to know you better in appropriate ways from the pulpit? What stories can you tell that they can identify with? Perhaps you're already doing this regularly. If not, reflect on how you can do more of it.

- With what need for change or risk would you like to challenge your hearers? Have you personally had to make any of the changes you perceive would be healthy for your congregation to make? How can you use your own experiences to help others identify with the need for change?

- Develop a different kind of sermon on this same biblical story, but focus attention on Matthew 14:33, "And those in the boat worshiped him, saying, 'Truly you are the Son of God.'"

*Ron Durham*

# WHAT CREATES HAPPINESS?

PSALM 126:1–3

GALATIANS 5:22–23

REV. DR. SCOTT WALKER

FIRST BAPTIST CHURCH

WACO, TEXAS

# WHAT CREATES HAPPINESS?

PSALM 126:1–3

GALATIANS 5:22–23

Recently, I sat in our den and watched my seven-year-old daughter, Jodi, reading a child's biography of Helen Keller (1880–1969). Keller was made blind and deaf by disease when she was nineteen months old. Imprisoned in a world of darkness and loneliness, this little girl faced a bleak and painful future. When I watched Jodi interact with Helen Keller's plight, I felt a father's sadness as my daughter came face to face with the tragedy of life. Happiness can so easily be ripped away from each of us.

Yet, the greater story is that Helen Keller refused to be conquered by her physical handicaps and grew to become a popular writer, speaker, and internationally beloved figure. Rather than being a defeated and tormented woman, she was characterized by happiness.

In a book entitled *Optimism*, Helen Keller states, "no matter how dull, or mean, or how wise a man is, he feels that happiness is his indisputable right."[1] Keller claimed her right to be happy and experienced life's fullness.

As Helen Keller perceived, if there is a universal striving among men and women, it is to experience happiness. Ask any man or woman of any culture, generation, or educational level what they want to achieve in life, and they will invariably reply, "I just want to be happy!"

Yet, happiness is elusive and frequently escapes us all. Reflecting on this, the nineteenth-century English philosopher John Stuart Mill, cryptically said, "Ask yourself whether you are happy, and you will cease to be so."[2] Mill correctly recognized that happiness cannot be a goal in and of itself. Rather, happiness must be the by-product — the natural result — of a life lived in proper balance and harmony.

Put another way, happiness is like the rainbow. As children looking for a pot of gold soon realize, the rainbow cannot be discovered, grasped, captured, or created. Rather, the rainbow is the result of certain atmospheric conditions uniquely combining to create color, beauty, and God's visible promise of security. Likewise, happiness is the result of certain emotional and spiritual conditions coalescing in our lives. What are some of these necessary conditions for happiness?

Recently I read a book on the subject of developing emotional and spiritual health in the adult years. The author, Elizabeth Hurlock, states: "Three things are essential to happiness, or a state of well-being and contentment: acceptance, affection and achievement, often called the 'three A's of happiness.' If they are present, the individual can accept himself, makes reasonably good adjustments to life, and is satisfied and contented."[3]

Today I would like us to reflect on these "three A's" — acceptance, affection, and achievement — and see how vital they are to the health and happiness of the individual Christian as well as to the health of the church.

## ACCEPTANCE

The first vital ingredient of happiness is acceptance. Men and women long to feel accepted into the relational unity of family, friendship, marriage, and a religious community. Yet Scripture tells us that the deepest problem which confronts each of us is an abiding sense of separation and alienation from ourselves, from others, and from God. Genesis makes clear that we are the children of tragic relational divorce and that we are cast off, forever wandering east of Eden. This haunting loneliness saps the presence of happiness from our lives.

True happiness and contentment can only be found when this relational chasm is spanned, when we somehow reach beyond ourselves to feel the heartbeat and understand the thoughts of someone else. We were created to live within a world of relational intimacy. And we are immensely unhappy when we live alone in the midst of a crowd.

Recently, I found this to be true within the life of our church. A family moved into our community several months ago. They have been sincerely looking for a church home, a community of faith. After much deliberation and prayer, they narrowed their choices to two churches.

The first church greatly impressed them. This church had the strongest education program, the most dynamic worship, the healthiest youth program, beautiful facilities, and was located closest to their home. They liked the pastor and the staff. They visited the church many times and formed a favorable impression.

However, they chose to join the second church for one significant reason. Through their neighborhood and their work, they had developed some meaningful friendships with a few couples who attended the second church. Though this church lacked many things which the first church possessed, the warmth of friendship drew them to the second church. They felt accepted within its fellowship. They sensed correctly that the one primary thing which would make them truly happy was warm Christian relationships. They chose friendship over programs and facilities.

We must realize, as individuals and as a church, that the first key ingredient to happiness is a feeling of acceptance. We must place high priority on building and maintaining quality Christian friendships that bridge the chasm of our loneliness and separation.

## AFFECTION

The second element of happiness is affection. Building on the first requirement of acceptance, affection is the visual or emotional demonstration of our acceptance of one another.

For instance, there are many marriages and families where people know that they are accepted. However, within these family systems very little display of verbal, emotional, or physical affection is experienced. As a result, the feeling of acceptance, of being loved and appreciated, is made weak and anemic by the lack of affection.

Recently I was standing in a neighbor's yard when a pick-up truck came roaring down the driveway. Screeching to a halt, my neighbor's two teenage sons came bounding out of the truck and strode across the yard to where their father and I were talking. Big, strapping boys who exude masculinity, their finely honed muscles were glistening with sweat from basketball practice. Grinning, each boy grabbed his father in a big bear hug and tried to lift his stout, middle-aged, college-football-player frame off the ground. Then, amidst laughter, they gave me a big handshake and flashed grins that said, "We like you. Glad you came over!" I was suddenly filled with happiness. Their warm affection made me glad to be alive. The world was a brighter place to be.

How important it is in our marriages, families, and friendships to show affection to each other. And how important the element of affection is within the life of the Christian church.

I believe the spiritual health of a congregation is often seen in how warm and affectionate church members are with each other. When I walk into a church fellowship hall and laughter is in the air, when hands are being shaken, backs are being slapped, friends are being embraced, and smiles abound and are contagious, then I know that the Spirit of the Lord is in that place.

Acceptance is not adequately felt without affection. And without acceptance and affection combining together, there can be no mystical appearance of the rainbow of happiness.

## ACHIEVEMENT

Finally, people experience happiness when they feel a sense of achievement flowing from their lives. We become happy when we know we are involved in something worthwhile; that the labor of our lives has ultimate meaning.

I am reminded of the French existentialist Albert Camus, who lived through the horrors of World War II, nearly losing his life as a member of the French underground resistance. Reflecting on these days years later,

Camus said that giving his life for his country would have been a little thing, and he would do so gladly. But the pain that he could not bear was to live his life without meaning; without some ultimate sense of worth and purpose and achievement. For the human soul to be happy, there must be a sense of contribution and fulfillment.

And so it is with the corporate church. Happy churches are faith communities where people do more than just sit quietly in worship, or attend a Sunday School class, or serve on a committee. Rather, congregations filled with happiness are always engaged in forms of ministry that are seen as worthwhile and important. When congregations begin to help the poor, feed the hungry, visit the sick, lift up the downtrodden, give shelter to the homeless, and tell the good news of the Gospel in a hundred different and effective ways, then suddenly Christians are filled with the happiness that comes from achievement and worthy contribution.

Centuries ago, the Apostle Paul wrote to the church at Galatia, "But the fruit of the Spirit is love, joy, peace, patience, kindness, goodness, faithfulness, gentleness, self-control; against such things there is no law" (Gal. 5:22–23).

I believe Paul is saying that God intends for us to be happy people, and that when the Spirit of God is filling us, then we are satisfied. As such, it is God's will that we accept each other as brothers and sisters, that we show each other warm affection, and that we lead our lives to achieve great things for the Kingdom of God. This is the secret of happiness, the rainbow of our fondest dreams.

Notes

1. Helen Keller, *Optimism* (New York: T.Y. Crowell & Company, 1903), p. 1.
2. John Stuart Mill, *Autobiography* (New York: H. Holt, 1873), p. 2.
3. Elizabeth B. Hurlock, *Developmental Psychology*, Fourth Edition (New York: McGraw-Hill, Inc., 1975), p. 17.

# COMMENT

Preaching, good or bad, flows out of the multiple conversations going on in a minister's life. These conversations include the ongoing conversation with God in our spiritual lives. We preach what we have found to be true in our own lives. This need not simply be insights gathered during prayer, but "listening to our lives" as a whole. This is the "internal conversation" that is always transpiring with a God who "searchest out my path, and art acquainted with all my ways" (Psalm 139:3).

Then there is the pastoral conversation with the people of the congregation. What is noticed in our coming and going among them? Pastoral visitation, even in the largest of churches, is crucial for the conversation that must happen in the pulpit, else we are always merely quoting. This doesn't mean that we must actually *do* all of the visiting. It does require that we be moving among the people enough to feel and touch and see what is characteristic and what is unusual in their midst.

There is also the conversation that can only happen through the pastor's personal study and reading. Think of it, if you will, as a conversation with the centuries. Reading and study enable us to reflect on the wisdom of the ages as we prepare to speak. Good preaching grows out of the ongoing dialogue that takes place between the minister's mind and heart and the "great cloud of witnesses" through the ages.

Scott Walker's sermon "What Creates Happiness?" flows out of such conversations. A layperson in a former parish once came up to me and said, "Preacher, thank you for reading a lot. I don't, but it stimulates me to hear what you've been reading and thinking about." The listener always has a sense of anticipation that there may be an insight, a new perspective, an introduction to a new friend, when she comes to church on Sunday.

There is a danger to this conversation, of course. When unbalanced, it can mean that we only preach our own experiences, or let the congregation and its problems limit our preaching and always stake it to the Crisis of the Week. Or, we can never have an authentic word that is ours. Instead we will always be saying, "And as so and so said..."

Therefore, a person with only one friend will always find his perspective shaped by that single relationship. A pastor who reads, studies, and reflects has a breadth that cannot be had by the lazy and undisciplined sort who always depends on a wonderful experience to happen during a hospital visit to provide Sunday's sermonic insight.

It is obvious that Scott Walker reads and has read widely. The result of the reading is not obtrusive. It flows naturally into his sermons, as though he has been to visit many friends and come back to give us some spicy tidbits from the conversations. "What Creates Happiness?" cites Helen Keller, John Stuart Mill, and Albert Camus.

Walker also relays an insight that came from simply watching his child read a great book. He tells of the outcome of the efforts of two churches to reach out and bring into fellowship a person who was looking for a church family. He lets us watch a neighbor and his two sons bear-hug one another affectionately and without embarrassment or self-consciousness. The whole sermon is an ongoing conversation with his whole life.

## PROBLEM

There is one last partner in the conversation, and that is the world that we are trying to reach. If our reading fails to discern what is important from what is merely interesting, if it is only a digest or a fourth-grader's copied article from the encyclopedia and offers no insight, then it is useless.

Walker distills what he has read. The middle of this sermon consists of three simple points that struck him in a reading about emotional health. He relates this both to the universal hunger that he sees in our world to find happiness and to the passage of Scripture that he has selected for this day.

This "conversation with the world" is one of two theological options that the Christian church has chosen over the centuries. One option is called "kerygmatic," wherein the church declares the essence of the "faith which was once for all delivered to the saints" (Jude 1:3). The kerygmatic is concerned with clarifying the answers we have and remaining true to who we are.

The second way of conversing is called "apologetic." By this we mean an approach that "begins from below," where people are. We seek to make connection with the hungers, questions, and concerns of the world. An apologetic approach finds points of contact between the gospel and the world's needs. This approach demonstrates the relevance of the faith to the needs of people.

Both ways are found in the New Testament, so they are available approaches for different settings. Walker's approach is apologetic, as we can see from the structure of the sermon. He begins, not with the text or some abstract Bible truth for all time, but with a human longing.

The first part of the sermon is an exploration of the human search for happiness. Essentially, it is stated as a problem. The sermon begins with an apparent paradox. Happiness is what we all want, our deepest need, but it is also elusive and hard to find. How can we attain happiness? The listener also wants to know!

## TEXT

Next, Walker moves us to a new possibility — that happiness cannot be directly attained. It is, instead, the by-product of the configuration of certain "right conditions" in our lives. Here again, his insights are drawn not from a theology book, but from the writings of a psychologist who points us to "acceptance, affection, and achievement," which must be present in an emotional and spiritual balance for us to experience happiness.

Galatians says, "The fruit [singular] of the spirit," not "the fruits of the spirit." Walker has captured Paul's nuance in his shift to "conditions for happiness." In other words, to be faithful to this biblical word, we do not declare, "You ought to love people, be peaceable, be filled with joy, be patient, be kind, be good..." I remember seeing a televangelist once, his neck bulging, eyes wide and nostrils flaring as he slammed his fist down on a pulpit and thundered, "My friends, we've got to LOVE one another!" The incongruity caused me not to want to love, but to laugh.

The fruit of the spirit is a result: fruit. When we attend to the priorities of the kingdom, the fruit appears while we are busily about these weightier things like justice, mercy, witness, and stewardship.

Walker's structural method in this sermon is not to thunder the truth and then apply it. Instead, he begins where many people are: searching for happiness. He considers that, then talks about what actually leads to happiness. He convinces us that happiness cannot be attained. It is only the result of the right balance of priorities in our lives.

It is fitting to handle this text, not at the front end of the sermon, but as the "result" of our search. Form and content are the same.

## PROCLAMATION

The entire proclamation in this sermon is succinctly stated in the last two paragraphs, but it has a climactic effect. Walker's last paragraph powerfully summarizes the entire sermon but reweaves it with theological truth. God wants us to do more than be church people. God wants what we want: for us to be happy.

What we also discover is that we find what we want by wanting what God also wants: by doing the will of God. "This is the secret of happiness, the rainbow of our fondest dreams." We have come back now and answered a secular question with a universal truth. They are really the same.

The danger of apologetic approaches, of couse, is that they may reduce or distort the gospel. So our question is, "How is the gospel more than just self-help or good-will or psychological conditions?" This search for the kerygmatic "high ground" can also be a distortion, however. What is the gospel when not applied and connected to human needs? What is wrong with plain human longings? Must they be spiritualized before they can embody spiritual questions?

As theologians have reminded us, we are always on a continuum between identity and relevance, and we always move toward one at the expense of the other. If that is true, then, like Walker's sermon suggests, we had best seek balance between the two.

Another strength of this sermon is that Walker subtly shifts us away from the individualism of the search for happiness that pervades our society. He talks about the conditions for happiness in corporate as well as individual terms. It is found in the context of a believing community and not simply within ourselves.

## RESPONSE

I asked myself, "How would I feel after hearing this sermon?" First, it suggests rather than prescribes. Yet in the three conditions that he explores, Walker offers some definite ideas for the church. Be busy about things that matter. Work at being the kind of warm, accepting fellowship that will connect with people looking for happiness.

As listeners we are invited to see how important "how" we do church can be, rather than just "what" we do. One strength of this sermon is its simple and memorable structure:

- People want to be happy but don't know how.
- Happiness is a by-product of the right conditions in balance: acceptance, affection and achievement.
- When the Spirit of God fills us, these things happen in us and through us and among us.

A listener could go away and easily recall the sermon. There is plenty on which to hang one's hat. Generally I dislike alliterative sermons for one reason: they usually sound forced, like an adolescent writing a first term paper with an encyclopedia on one side and a thesaurus on the other. When I have heard preachers use this (especially the pretentious and bombastic "Let me show you how good I am" sermons at large gatherings), I forget the point and try to guess what "P" word the preacher will use next. I am off track.

Walker states where he is going. The way he says it is unobtrusive and natural, arising from a quote. The alliteration does not call attention to the cleverness of the preacher but to the profundity of the sermon's thought. A good lesson here for all of us!

Sermons can also ask us to reflect. That, too, is a response. I decided that I would go to lunch after hearing this, feeling uplifted but also thinking about my church and its climate, looking at my own comfort or discomfort with expressing affection. I might decide, "I am going to be more interested in that visitor who sat in front of me."

## SUGGESTIONS

- Analyze your typical schedule. Is there a balance in your own life among time with others, time with God, time with yourself, time with your family and time in the study? Do you read a healthy balance that includes nontheological reading?
- Do you have any relationships that are not related to the church? Do you ever converse with people who are "outside the gate"? Strike up some relationships "out there" and listen to what people are talking about
- You can also do this by reading in the popular realm. What themes do you see? I have always felt that novelists and poets rather than journalists are the best "seers" of what is happening "out there." Utilize the lists of top fiction that *Christianity Today* and *The Christian Century* put out each year and let them enrich your preaching.

*Gary Furr*

COMMENT

# THE PURPOSE OF WORSHIP

PSALM 95:1–7c

REV. DR. GEOFFREY V. GUNS
SECOND CALVARY BAPTIST CHURCH
NORFOLK, VIRGINIA

REV. DR. GEOFFREY V. GUNS

# THE PURPOSE OF WORSHIP

PSALM 95:1–7c

E rik Routley wrote in his study of Psalms that "the most precious achievement and duty of the Hebrew people was the worship of God."[1] It was through their worship that Israel remembered the experiences of their past. They remembered how God had brought them out of slavery in Egypt, how he had met their physical and spiritual needs, and how he had finally brought them into a land flowing with milk and honey.

In our study of worship we have learned that God is the object of our worship. Second, we have learned that God instituted the sabbath as the day of rest, but over time the sabbath became Israel's day of worship. As Christians we worship on Sunday, because it is the day of the Resurrection of our Christ. Third, we have learned that the place of worship has significance. Worship takes place within the context of a certain location, for example, the temple, the synagogue, the church building.

Since worship was central to Israel and continues to be so in the Christian church, we need to examine its purpose. The words of our text have been used for centuries as a "call to worship."

The call to worship has five major functions according to Franklin M. Segler: "The purpose of the call to worship is (1) to direct the minds of the congregation toward God, (2) to remove distractions from the attention of the congregation, (3) to call for participation of the congregation in all that transpires, (4) to call for a unity of all the people assembled, and (5) to create the proper attitude or atmosphere for worship. It may be compared with the call of an army officer, 'Attention.'"[2]

Let us hear again the words of the text:

> O come, let us sing unto the Lord: let us make a joyful noise to the rock of our salvation. Let us come before his presence with thanksgiving, and make a joyful noise unto him with psalms. For the Lord is a great God, and a great King above all gods. In his hand are the deep places of the earth: the strength of the hills is his also. The sea is his, and he made it, and his hands formed the dry land. O come, let us worship and bow down: let us kneel before the Lord our maker. For he is our God, and we are the people of his pasture, and the sheep of his hand.

This particular psalm has been classified as one of the "enthronement psalms." We are not sure when this psalm was written, nor are we certain who wrote it. Old Testament scholars have set forth several theories regarding authorship, date of writing, and the occasion of the psalm, but these need not detain us. There seems to be no clear consensus as to who is correct. However, we are sure of one thing: this particular psalm was used in Israel's corporate worship of Yahweh.

Psalm 95 has been divided into two parts. Part 1 is contained in verses 1–7c and part 2 in verses 7d–11. The first part is a call to celebration; part 2 is a call to repentance, "Harden not your heart...." I want to examine part 1 today. Clearly these words of the ancient psalmist provide us with keen spiritual insight as to the purpose of worship.

What then is the purpose of Christian worship? We will understand Christian worship only when we grasp the purpose of worship in the Hebrew tradition. For the Christian tradition of worship has been inherited from the Hebrew tradition.

## I. WORSHIP CREATES CHRISTIAN COMMUNITY

Notice that the psalmist calls for the entire community to come together. "O come, let us sing unto the Lord; let us make a joyful noise...; let us come before his presence…; let us worship and bow down…; let us kneel before the Lord…; we are the people of his pasture…." The emphasis in Hebrew worship was always upon the entire congregation of Israel that would gather to worship Yahweh at his sanctuary. God's covenant with Israel was not just a covenant with Abraham, Isaac, and Jacob, but with their descendants. God's covenant handed to Moses was not just for Moses and priests, but it was for all of Israel. It detailed how they were to live before him and how they were to live in community with one another.

Worship is a community event. One of the dangers of contemporary religious teaching is that it seeks to reduce faith and everything that relates to it to the individual level. All you need is a personal relationship with the Lord. All you need is your own sense of God. All you need is to be personally filled and empowered by the Holy Spirit. There is a tendency to want to take the corporate or community aspect out of religion and worship.

When we remove the community aspect from worship, then we can take the community aspect out of all life. We need not feel a sense of responsibility for anything that happens in the community if it does not have a personal impact upon our life. Yet, we must be reminded that we are indeed our brother's keeper. God has called us to live in community and fellowship with one another.

When we look at worship patterns in the New Testament church, it is clear that it was about *koinonia* ("fellowship"). Worship centered on the community's sharing together in the breaking of bread, prayers, and teaching. In the Acts of the Apostles (2:42) we clearly see this: "And they continued steadfastly in the apostles' doctrine [teaching] and fellowship, and in breaking of bread, and in prayers."

When we come together for worship, we become the living reality of the body of Christ in the world. Though we are individuals, yet we become that one body, united through his death and resurrection. "For as we have many members in one body, and all members have not the same office: So we, being many, are one body in Christ, and every one members one of another" (Rom. 12:4–5).

In our gathered worship each Sunday, the Holy Spirit ministers to the spirits of each of us, and builds and keeps the unity of the Spirit in the bond of peace. In worship we are drawn closer to one another. In worship we are strengthened by one another. In worship we are encouraged by one another. In worship we are taught by one another. In worship we are accepted by one another. In worship we help one another. In worship we come to love one another. In worship we come to see each other, human beings, created in the image of God. In worship we are inspired by one another. In worship we are reminded that though we may be different, though we come from different economic, educational, social, ethnic, and racial backgrounds, we are all one in Jesus Christ.

In Ephesians 4:4–6 Paul reminds us that "there is one body, and one Spirit,…one hope of [our] calling; one Lord, one faith, one baptism, one God and Father of all, who is above all, and through all, and in you all." Worship is central to our community life. Without it we would dry up spiritually. Without it we would not love like we do. Without it we would not serve like we do. Without community worship I would not be as spiritually strong as I am now. Worship builds Christian community.

## II. WORSHIP CELEBRATES THE GOODNESS OF GOD

Notice again the text and its celebrative nature. Let us come singing unto the Lord. All singing is for the ears of God. It's not intended to impress the congregation, but to impress and celebrate God. The KJV uses the words "joyful noise" twice. However, those words fail to do justice to what the psalmist really meant. The Hebrew has in it the thought of a "joyous shout," a cry of jubilation. It is not a quiet sound, but a thunderous, loud, roaring shout of "Hallelujah" to God. In Luke 19:37–38 when Jesus entered triumphantly into Jerusalem on that first Palm Sunday, his disciples cried with loud voices of praise. They celebrated God's great act of deliverance in the Messiah.

Hebrew worship, as it is manifested in the Old Testament, was demonstrative. That is to say, it was joy in action. When they had crossed safely to the other side of the Red Sea and Pharaoh's army had been drowned, Israel celebrated God's victory. In Exodus 15:20–21, "And Miriam the prophetess, the sister of Aaron, took a timbrel in her hand; and all the women went out after her with timbrels and with dances. And Miriam answered them, Sing ye to the Lord, for he hath triumphed gloriously; the horse and his rider hath he thrown into the sea." Now look at 2 Samuel 6:14–15. In this passage King David brought the ark of the covenant up from the house of Obed-edom. The Word says, "And David danced before the Lord with all his might; and David was girded with a linen ephod. So David and all the house of Israel brought up the ark of the Lord with shouting, and with the sound of the trumpet." Israel celebrated God's gracious kindness.

Robert E. Webber wrote that "a celebration, whether it be a birthday, anniversary, or a national event, has three main characteristics. A celebration remembers a past event. A celebration makes the past event contemporaneous. Past events are remembered and celebrated through story, song, drama, and feasting."[3] If we take that definition, then it becomes clear for the demonstrative, joyful action of Hebrew worship.

Israel celebrated God's deliverance of them from the harsh, cruel, ruthless, merciless, and heartless hand of Pharaoh. They remembered when they were nobodies and God made them his own covenant people. They remembered when they were in the desert and he brought water out of the dry places. They remembered when they were sent manna from heaven each new day. They remembered how he went before them in a cloud by day and a pillar of fire by night. They remembered how he fought their battles and saved them from the hands of their enemies. They remembered God.

Notice further, that worship celebrates the past as a living event. Just as God had delivered them in the past, when they gathered it was as though the event were happening right then. Worship made the Exodus a contemporaneous event. Every occasion of worship was an opportunity to celebrate the event of the Exodus. It was like our repeatable reminder of the Lord's Supper. Every time we celebrate the Lord's Supper it is as though you and I are right there in the Upper Room with Jesus and his disciples.

Israel remembered God through their stories, their songs, their dances. Worship was never an event without emotional attachment to the past and present.

Whenever we come to worship we come to celebrate as well. Worship is not intended to be a quiet, regal, dignified event where the Spirit of God is kept locked up in our hearts. Rather, it is a joyful celebration of God's salvation and deliverance. All of us have some reason to celebrate something that God has done in our lives. It may be a victory over defeatism or over spiritual shyness. We may have been delivered from some dreadful situation. For some of us, it's been deliverance from enemies. Deliverance from poverty. Deliverance from ignorance. Deliverance from frustration. Deliverance from a party spirit. Deliverance from temptation. Deliverance from substance abuse. Deliverance from a failed marriage. Deliverance from senseless spending habits. Deliverance from fears and anxiety. Deliverance from sexual deviousness. Deliverance from venomous speech. But most of all, each of us can celebrate being delivered from the hand of spiritual and eternal death. God has set us free!

Therefore, when we come to this place on Sunday, it's not a funeral. It's not a morbid gathering of morbid people, but a gathering of vibrant, animated, dynamic, lively, spirited, intense and red-hot people who understand that it was God's grace that woke them up this morning. It was grace that kept them all week long. It was grace that brought them to the house of worship. Worship is for celebrating the goodness and grace of God. It is for celebrating what he has done in the past and what he is doing right now. And if you want to shout, then shout. If you want to run, then run. If you want to dance, then dance. If you want to cry, then cry. If you want to hold up your hands, then hold them up. If you want to jump up and down, then jump up and down. If you want to wave your arms, then wave your arms. Just celebrate!

### III. GOD IS THE CENTER OF ALL WORSHIP

Everything in worship focuses on God. Our songs are for the Lord, our joyful noise is for the rock of our salvation. We come before his presence. We sing our psalms to him. We come to worship and bow down and to kneel before him. For he is God and we are the people of his pasture and the sheep of his hand.

God is the center of worship because he is worthy of all the praise and the honor. The Lord is a great God, and a great King above all gods. He is God, and beside him there is none other. He is God over all of creation. He is the Ruler of the entire cosmos. In his hands are the deep places of the earth. The very strength of the hills is his.

We are told in Psalm 100: "Make a joyful noise unto the Lord.... Serve the Lord with gladness.... Enter into his gates with thanksgiving, and into his courts with praise: be thankful unto him, and bless his name." And that's what we have come to worship to do. We have come to bless the name of the Lord. The Lord our God is worthy, not because of what we want him to do, but because of what he has already done. Our God is a great God. We serve a God who can do anything but fail. He can comfort lonely hearts. He changes difficult situations. He changes adverse circumstances. He can open blinded eyes, and he can unstop deaf ears. He can heal diseased bodies. He can mend broken relationships. He can move our mountains. He can conquer our worst enemies. He can fix every problem. He can guide every footstep. He can heal our deepest hurts. He can forgive our worst sins. He can lift our heaviest burden. He can calm our worst storms. He can satisfy our deepest hunger.

I don't know how you feel about it, but I need to worship. I need to feel the fire of worship. I need to feel the power of worship. I need to feel the energy of saints in praise. I need worship. Something happens to me in worship. I get stronger in worship. In worship I am filled with the Holy Spirit. In worship I see God.

*All hail the power of Jesus' name!*
*Let angels prostrate fall,*
*Bring forth the royal diadem,*
*And crown Him Lord of all.*

Notes
1. Erik Routley, *Exploring the Psalms* (Philadelphia: Westminster Press, 1975), p. 17.
2. Franklin M. Segler, *Christian Worship: Its Theology and Practice* (Nashville: Broadman Press, 1967), p. 155.
3. Robert E. Webber, *Worship Old and New* (Grand Rapids: Zondervan, 1994), p. 28.

# COMMENT

Good preaching should teach as well as proclaim and inspire. Geoffrey Guns's sermon "The Purpose of Worship" is a fine example of a "didactic sermon," one that teaches the Christian faith.

This sermon examines the purpose of Christian worship. It was originally preached as part of a larger series of sermons comprising a study of worship. The sermon instructs the listener about the meaning of worship. It proclaims the good news of the gospel. And it inspires the listener to a more active and vital worship as a celebration of God's goodness.

Also distinctive of this sermon is an important theological emphasis it makes: "God is the center of all worship." In theory, we may take this point for granted and assume that its truth undergirds all our worship. In practice, however, there may be significant reasons to take another look at our worship and ask: "Is God really at the center of all our worship?"

A sermon like this challenges us to ask how much of our worship focuses on our own human needs for self-fulfillment, emotional well-being, answers to prayer, and individualized spiritual renewal. When Guns proclaims that "everything in worship focuses on God," he makes a profound theological statement that may challenge many of our contemporary assumptions and practices regarding worship. In this sense, the sermon invites us to some important theological reflection on just how "God-centered" or "human-centered" our worship and faith expressions are, particularly in the context of the church in North America in the late twentieth century.

## STRUCTURE

Look at the sermon again and observe its clear structure. The sermon may be outlined as follows:

I. Introduction. This section introduces the purpose of the sermon and sets it in the context of an ongoing series of sermons. It states the *Text* and the *Need*, the question of the sermon.

II. Body. This section consists of the *Proclamation* of the text in three points.

III. Conclusion. Finally, one paragraph focuses on invitation and *Response*.

## NEED

The question Guns addresses is, What is worship? Why do we do it? His concern is that many people attend worship but never reflect on its meaning and importance in the life of the faith community and the individual believer. If a Christian congregation is to grow spiritually both as community and as individuals, a proper understanding and appreciation of worship is critical. Guns therefore seeks to address the need to grow spiritually through a deeper understanding and experience of worship.

Notice how clearly Guns states the question in the Introduction of his sermon: "Since worship was central to Israel and continues to be so in the Christian church, we need to examine its purpose.... What then is the purpose of Christian worship? We will understand Christian worship only when we grasp the purpose of worship in the Hebrew tradition...."

Note also in the second paragraph of the sermon how clearly he situates this particular sermon in the context of the larger series he had been preaching. In five short sentences he reviews for the congregation the subjects of the three previous sermons in the series (God as focus, the sabbath, the place of worship). Then, in the very next sentence, he introduces the subject of this sermon — the purpose of worship.

Guns gives us a good simple model for reviewing a sermon series. When you're preaching a series, toward the beginning of the sermon it's important to review the earlier sermons briefly — to refresh the listener's memory and to help the listener situate the present subject in the broader context of proclamation and teaching. When preaching a series, it is also helpful to print a list of the sermon titles or subjects for the entire series in the church bulletin or newsletter throughout the duration of the series.

COMMENT

## TEXT

Because the biblical text provides such an important basis for his entire sermon, Guns introduces the text in an early paragraph right at the beginning of the sermon. He chooses to read the text in its entirety because he wants to discuss it as a whole. Then he notes a few historical background features, e.g., that this is an "enthronement psalm" of uncertain date and authorship.

One temptation for preachers who love the historical background study of a text is to introduce too much background into the sermon. The information may be interesting and important to us as preachers, but is it critical to the main point of the sermon? We must always ask ourselves how important historical background information is to the point we are making in a sermon. If we give too much background, we can easily lose our listeners in all the dates and details or bore them into an early Sunday nap!

Guns is appropriately very sparing of background information in this sermon. Commentaries on Psalm 95 may have up to ten or twenty pages of background information about this psalm. Guns has touched on that in two short paragraphs. He needs to do no more.

But note that Guns acknowledges he has chosen to deal only with verses 1–7c of the psalm (a "call to celebration"). The remainder of the psalm (verses 7d–11, a "call to repentance") is outside the focus of this particular sermon. That is the kind of information important to acknowledge when we are dealing with part of a text and cannot address the entirety of it.

Guns has appropriately chosen Psalm 95:1–7c for this sermon because it is a "call to worship" celebrating God's kingship. As a call to worship in the life of ancient Israel, these verses give us some important insights into the meaning and purpose of worship.

With this text Guns is in effect saying: "What is worship? Why do we do it? The best place to find the answer to that is in Israel's worship as expressed in the Psalms." Notice also how he makes the connection between Hebrew and Christian worship by reminding us that as Christians we have inherited much of our worship from Hebrew worship.

In a day when Old Testament texts are too often avoided or neglected in our preaching, Guns is to be applauded for doing some vital preaching from the Old Testament. He is also to be commended for the appropriate way in which he has acknowledged the indebtedness of the Christian tradition to the Hebrew Old Testament tradition. In our study and theological reflection, we would all do well to continue working toward a proper understanding of the relationship between the Old and New Testaments.

## PROCLAMATION

In the body of his sermon (parts I–III) Guns lets his text, Psalm 95:1–7c, answer the question of the sermon. What is the purpose of worship? Worship is a celebration which (1) creates Christian community, (2) celebrates the goodness of God, and (3) focuses on God as the central reality of all life. This is finally a "three-point" sermon which teaches these three truths and calls people to a deeper experience of worship.

1. *Worship creates community.* Guns calls attention to the abundance of plural pronouns in the text ("we," "us," "our," a total of ten times in most English translations). The grammar of the text itself proclaims that worship is a community event. The text is about a covenant people in relationship with God: "We are the people of his pasture."

Here Guns makes an important point when he says, "One of the dangers of contemporary religious teaching is that it seeks to reduce faith and everything that relates to it to the individual level…." He cautions against the cultural predominance of radical individualism. He reminds us that both Hebrew and Christian worship and life were strongly communal in emphasis rather than centered on the individual.

Guns's quotations of Acts 2:42, Romans 12:4–5, and Ephesians 4:4–6 are well chosen to make the point that as Christians we are called to live in a fellowship (*koinonia*) in which we encourage, strengthen, support, and love one another. We would do well in our study, teaching, and preaching to explore this tension between the biblical emphasis on "community life" and our contemporary culture's emphasis on individual existence and its accompanying loss of community.

2. *Worship celebrates the goodness of God.* The celebrative nature of worship is prominent in Psalm 95:1–7c, says Guns. There are expressions of "singing," a "joyful noise" or "cry of jubilation," "thanksgiving," and "songs of praise" (vv. 1–2). Just as Israel in worship constantly celebrated God's acts of deliverance, we are called to celebrate God's goodness and salvation. This means remembering the past and making it come alive in the present. We all have deliverances to celebrate, says Guns. We all can celebrate the grace of God. And this kind of worship should be lively if it is truly a celebration.

3. *God is the center of all worship.* Here Guns focuses on the God-centered phrases prominent in the text. Worship is offered "to the Lord," "to the rock of our salvation." For "the Lord is a great God," "a great King." We are to bow down and "kneel before the Lord," for he is "our God." Worship celebrates God.

As we said above, this emphasis on God-centered worship is important in our day when some styles of worship can seem more like "entertainment" than worship directed to God. In worship do we sometimes feel like spectators at a concert, applauding the performers on stage? In our sermons do we spend more time talking about ourselves and our needs and problems, or about God? In our prayers and "personal testimonies" is the focus ultimately on us or on God? These are important questions to ask ourselves.

There is often a fine line between God-centered worship and worship that seeks to gratify or fulfill the self. Theologians call this the difference between faith or theology that is "theocentric" (centered on God) and that which is "anthropocentric" (centered on our human selves). Theocentric faith is true biblical faith. Anthropocentric faith is ultimately an expression of idolatry. We need to ponder the distinctions and continually evaluate our theology, our worship, and our service in order to let God be the center of all.

This is not, of course, to say that we humans do not derive benefits from worship. Guns acknowledges that as individuals and community we derive great benefits from worship. But these benefits are clearly secondary, a by-product of focusing on God. The healthy nurture and spiritual growth we experience through worship are derived ultimately from recognizing that God is the center of all worship.

RESPONSE

Because of the very nature of Psalm 95:1–7c as a "call to worship," both text and proclamation throughout the sermon function as an invitation to respond in joyous, celebrative worship. The whole sermon motivates us to act. The preacher calls us to take this understanding of worship and live it out each time we enter into worship.

Occasionally Guns draws specific attention to invitation and response. Near the end of part II of the sermon, for example, he says: "All of us have some reason to celebrate something that God has done in our lives." "Each of us can celebrate being delivered from the hand of...death." "If you want to shout, then shout." "Just celebrate!" These are the invitations to the listener to become more free and celebrative in worship.

Note also the sustained series of declarative statements toward the end of the sermon: "He can comfort lonely hearts. He changes difficult situations...," etc. These are powerful invitations to truly believe the good news of the Christian gospel and respond in faith. Guns then closes the sermon by saying, "I don't know how you feel about it, but I need worship...." In essence, he is asking us: "How do you feel about worship?" His series of "I need" statements (final paragraph) invites hearers to identify with him in their need for a God-centered worship that celebrates God's goodness and creates community.

"The Purpose of Worship" is a good example of a well-crafted sermon in which text and proclamation address a need and issue in an invitation to respond. The sermon teaches us about worship, proclaims the gospel, and challenges us all along the way to a renewed and joyful celebration. "O come, let us sing to the Lord; let us make a joyful noise to the rock of our salvation!"

SUGGESTIONS

- If you have not done a "didactic" sermon lately, try doing a sermon or a series that "teaches" on one or more of the great Christian doctrines: Revelation, Authority of Scripture, the Trinity, the Creation, Providence of God, Humanity in the Image of God, Person and Work of Jesus Christ, the Holy Spirit, the Church, the Sacraments (or Ordinances), Christian Hope.

- The Psalms are a great resource for preaching. Do a series of sermons from the Psalms. For example, you might take Psalm 145 (a hymn of praise), Psalm 13 (a lament), and Psalm 30 (a song of thanksgiving) and do a series of sermons tracing the contours of the life of faith. If you're not already familiar with it, I recommend Walter Brueggemann's *The Message of the Psalms: A Theological Commentary* (Augsburg, 1984) as an excellent resource.

- Do some reading and reflection on the issue of "theocentric" versus "anthropocentric" faith and practice as discussed above. How aware of this issue are you? How do you respond to the problem? How can you address the question in your own preaching and teaching?

*Gary W. Klingsporn*

# FINDING SPIRITUAL MEANING IN A SPIRITLESS WORLD

PSALM 1:1–3

REV. DR. JOHN KILLINGER
PROFESSOR OF RELIGION
SAMFORD UNIVERSITY
BIRMINGHAM, ALABAMA

# Finding Spiritual Meaning in a Spiritless World

PSALM 1:1–3

William Broyles, Jr., was senior editor of *Newsweek* magazine. It was a heady world of power, intrigue and creativity. He spent every day on the phone and in the company of the most influential people in the world. He helped to determine the public perception of events that were shaping history. He made hundreds of thousands of dollars a year. He was the idol of everybody who knew him. Almost every door in the world was open to him. Yet Broyles found it all increasingly empty. He awoke in the mornings with the taste of despair in his mouth. There *had* to be more to life than this, he was convinced. So one day he walked away from all of it. He cleaned out his desk and retired before he was forty. He began climbing mountains, trying to find something up there that was missing down below. When he thought he was in shape for it, he signed on for an expedition to climb Mount Aconcagua in South America, the tallest mountain in this hemisphere. It was a harrowing experience. In the freezing cold at night, they lay in their tiny tents high on the mountain's side listening to the wind and fearing they would be blown off. But Broyles found at those altitudes the clarity of thought he had been missing as an executive in New York.

Marcia Edelman was a doctor in Florida, and her husband was a civil engineer. When his company posted him to North Carolina, she decided to answer a nagging call she had been feeling for several years. Instead of remaining at her practice or opening another practice where her husband went, she entered seminary to learn more about her religious faith. When she finished her degree, she became a deacon in a local church and gave her time as a volunteer on the staff.

Janwillem van de Wetering was a Dutch businessman who lived all over the world. He was happily married and enjoyed a high style of living. But he was haunted all the time by the question of meaning: what did his life mean and what is life itself all about? He traveled to Kyoto, Japan, and spent a year in a Zen Buddhist monastery looking for answers. This only made him more restless. He continued to need great chunks of time away from his business to contemplate the deeper aspects of human existence. He returned to Kyoto. He spent several months in a Zen commune in the northwestern U.S. He began to write books, always probing and seeking. He now lives in Maine. He is still looking.

Are these people unusual today? No. They reflect the great spiritual unrest in our world, the sense that there must be something deeper and more meaningful in our culture than we have found. Our world has changed enormously in the last fifty years — probably more than it had changed in all the millennia before. New technology has altered everything — philosophies, institutions, the church, the family, the way we think about existence. And as the earth shifts, our sense of well-being, our trust in the traditional answers, our understanding of ourselves all shift with it. We hunger and thirst for meaning, for understanding, for a way to be, for a way to make a difference. And instinctively, because as Augustine said, our hearts are restless until they rest in God, we turn to spiritual journeys, pilgrimages of the heart, to discover what is missing in our lives. We know there is something deeper, and we know it has to do with discovering the divine spirit.

Listen again to the words of our text: *"Happy are those... [whose] delight is in the law of the Lord, and on his law they meditate day and night."* Do you see what it is talking about? We may have a negative sense of the law because of our Christian upbringing. It was lawyers who crucified Christ. Paul said the law kills and the spirit gives life. But those were the extreme cases. In general the law was considered beautiful and gracious, a gift of God for the fulfillment of the human spirit. Jesus himself loved it and said not a jot or a tittle would pass away from it because of anything he did.

People did meditate on the law day and night. They ate, slept, breathed the Torah. It was their source of inspiration and mysticism. God Almighty had given it to them. It was their connection, their link to divinity. It gave them meaning and stability for living. The person who meditated on the law day and night was like a tree planted by a stream of living water — a metaphor of abundance in a land where streams of living water were not plentiful. She would yield her fruit when she was supposed to, and her leaves would not dry up and fall away.

The truth has been there all along. The path is well marked. The way to spiritual depth and meaning is through meditation on what God has given us. It is through becoming an inward people in a world that is mostly outward, through continuing our journeys when others have stopped along the way. It is through restlessness and discontentment, through giving up whatever it takes to follow in the way. It is through praying and seeking a life of the spirit in a world that denies the spirit and insists that everything is material and immediate and usable now.

And think what you are missing if you have not followed this way, if you have resisted the urge and continued to find life only in the abundance of what you have or in the diversion of isolated pleasures. *You are missing the opportunity of relaxing and unburdening yourself in the presence of the Spirit at the heart of everything.*

Life is so difficult today, so demanding and crushing. Our schedules alone are enough to shorten our lifespans. I saw a man in the airport in Toledo running frantically down the halls screaming, "My datebook! My datebook! I've lost my datebook! If I don't find it, my life is ruined!" You know the feeling? Traffic is an enormous stress. Imagine if you could have shown our forebears a video of what you see in the stalled lines of automobiles every weekday morning — women trying to get their hair combed and their makeup on, men chattering away on car phones to set up appointments, children struggling with each other in the back seat, people gulping down coffee or eating sweet rolls, raising their cholesterol levels. Our ancestors would have been horrified! We come in at night and plop in front of the TV, too tired to do anything else. But TV doesn't help. All those sitcoms, medical shows, lawyer programs, and real-life dramas only add to our sense of emergency, our feeling that the world has come unglued and is flying in a million directions.

We need the presence of God, don't we? We need to be able to come into that presence every day and loosen our corset strings and go *boing-g-g!* all over the place. We need to let ourselves go where we can do it and not be hurt again, where we will be held and comforted, rocked and assured, gentled and loved. We need to be able to say, "I messed up again, God. I went out there with the best of intentions and I screwed it all up again." And to hear God say, "Shhh, that's all right, you're home now. Just relax and breathe deeply. Let's enjoy this time together."

*It's in the presence of God that we find ourselves again and know most deeply who we are and what life is about.* There is where we discover the integrity that seems to be lacking in the world around us, where we touch bottom and know we can stop treading water. Everything false drops away. Life stops spinning. We connect with the center and know what truth is. We feel love. Love is what it's all about, isn't it? Jesus said it is the sum of the law. Rabbi Hillel, one of the great orthodox rabbis of Jesus' day, said the same thing. So did the Apostle Paul: "Now abideth faith, hope, and love, but the greatest of these is love." So when the psalmist wrote about meditating on the law, he understood that that's what it all comes down to — love. In the end, love. At the bottom line, love.

I resonate to something W. Paul Jones wrote in his book *The Province Beyond the River.* Jones was a professor of theology who said he had never had a real experience of God. He had talked about God and written about God for years, but had not really felt God in his life. So he deliberately set out one summer to experience God. He checked himself into a monastery in Colorado for the entire summer, and spent his days going to mass, praying, working in the garden, reading, meditating, and waiting for God to become known in his life.

He was not disappointed. One day he was serving in the kitchen with one of the brothers, and admitted to the brother that he was highly educated but was only learning to pray. The brother was sympathetic, and began to try to help him. And somewhere "between the cauliflower and the squash," wrote Jones, "prayer became defined as experiencing God as he who knows all of my weirdness and weaknesses, and loves me anyhow; and our rejoicing together in that acceptance."[1] Prayer is experiencing God as the one who loves us in spite of our quirks and oddities, our problems and our foolishness. Jones's whole life was changed by this experience. He knew himself better than he had ever known himself, for he saw himself from God's vantage point. And he could finally accept who he was because he knew that God accepted him that way.

Love becomes most fully possible when you're relaxed in the arms of God, when you're breathing deeply in the spirit. It's when you're uptight and stressed out that you become irritated and flare up and lash out at others, isn't it? But when you're resting in the arms of God, when you have a sense of well-being clear to the bottom of your toes and you know the divine Spirit is there, holding you and rocking you, you can't be that way. You can't hate, you can't strike out, you can't even feel irritation. You're missing that if you're not living in prayer and meditation, not following the inward journey that leads to peace and fulfillment.

*And you're missing being caught up by the Holy Spirit and reoriented and reactivated for things you've never dreamed of!* I hesitate to take the sermon this far because I know most of us are completely unacquainted with the Holy Spirit in our day. If I were talking to Pentecostals or Holiness people, they would understand. But we have pretty much relegated the Spirit to those fringe elements of society, haven't we? We talk about God the Father and Christ the Son because we can do that safely and without threatening the status quo. They are the stuff of tradition. But when we talk about God the Holy Spirit we are talking about that aspect of our spiritual experience that unsettles people, that throws a hat on our Scrabble boards and messes up all the pieces, that makes us uncomfortable until we say, "All right, Lord, I've had it! I'll do what you want me to do!"

We are not really taking the history of the early Church and of Christianity seriously until we acknowledge the role of the divine Spirit in all of it and admit that the same Spirit is alive and ready to upend our existence right here, right now, in this place. Oh, we have conspired to pretend that the Spirit does not operate that way any more — that the Spirit does not take possession of people, that the Spirit doesn't come like heavenly fire upon us, that the Spirit doesn't make us babble in strange tongues, that the Spirit doesn't heal the sick and make the lame walk and raise the dead. But that is probably because we live so far from the center of the Spirit's power, because we have determined to walk around the fringes of the presence and not venture into the maelstrom at the heart of the divine Mystery.

We are so weak and anemic in our spirituality. One of the English theologians used to say of some people's sermons that "they didn't have enough gospel in them to save a titmouse!" It is the same with us and the Spirit. We have not begun to discover the depths and the heights. We haven't felt a *tenth* of the power of God in us. Maybe not a *hundredth* or a *thousandth* or a *millionth*.

My friend Dennis Covington has written a book about the snake handlers in Northern Alabama. It is called *Salvation on Sand Mountain.* Dennis went up there and visited in the homes of the Holiness people who were handling snakes. He ate at their dinner tables, played with their children, went to their services. He witnessed their deep conviction about the power of the Spirit that leads to their taking up those big, long, writhing serpents and waving them around. It changed Dennis's life. He was a writer, an academic, a teacher. He had been a Christian for years. He had assumed that those people were part of a lunatic fringe in society. But Dennis put his hand in the cage and took out a poisonous snake. Trembling, he held it aloft and prayed to God. And he will never again be the same. He discovered the baptism of the Holy Spirit.

Should I have kept quiet about this, muffled it, avoided the subject? I could have ended with the bit about relaxing in God's arms, finding our integrity, discovering love, and none of us would have been uncomfortable. I am not trying to make us uncomfortable, to throw dead cats in cathedrals.

We are too adult for that. What I want us to see and admit is that *we have not begun to plumb the depths of understanding and meaning in our faith; that we have barely begun the journey of the soul toward God, and we are cutting ourselves short if we pretend that we are Christians merely because we have been baptized and have made a confession of faith in Jesus Christ among those for whom this is normative.* There is so much more. The Mystery is so much deeper. The rewards are so much greater.

Carry our text in your heart this week. Think about it. *"Happy are those...[whose] delight is in the law of the Lord, and on his law they meditate day and night."* Not once a week. Not when it suits them. Not when the feeling happens to come over them. But "day and night." Constantly. Continually. Not as a burden, but out of delight. They are happy. They feel like trees planted by streams of living water, and they bear fruit when they are supposed to. That is, their lives are connected and in order. They have found out what it's all about. They have discovered how to live positively in a negative age. They're up to it. Are you?

> *Come, Holy Spirit of God, and draw us into the awful center of your power. Humble us, cleanse us, redirect us, empower us. Show us fear in a handful of dust and hope in a dry rock. Rescue us from shallowness and help us to breathe deeply, from eternity. In the name of the One who was ordained to die on a cross to show us the meaning of love and obedience. Amen.*

Notes
1. W. Paul Jones, *The Province Beyond the River* (New York: Paulist Press, 1981), p. 57.

# COMMENT

John Killinger's sermon, "Finding Spiritual Meaning in a Spiritless World," is distinctive in the way it draws the hearer in through the use of multiple stories, questions, and metaphors. He captures the emptiness experienced by many in our culture whose lives are centered in the pursuit of success and the trappings of affluence. What is unique is his analysis of contemporary culture which seeks to "find life only in the abundance of what you have or in the diversion of isolated pleasures." It is true that we live in a time of great spiritual unrest which cannot be quieted through the external things of our time. Our preoccupation with external and material things still leaves us with a deep thirst for meaning and a hunger for fulfillment.

Killinger invites us to consider an inward journey as an alternative. This is a spiritual journey which finds its rest in the God of the psalmist who points the way to refreshment and fulfillment through prayer and meditation on the Law. This sermon speaks not only to the seeker but to those already committed to the vitality and depth of their faith. In many ways what we have is a sermon within a sermon.

## NEED

The introduction to this sermon consists of a series of three stories which most of us would consider to be descriptions of men and women at the top of the game professionally. They have achieved educational and financial success, prestige and mobility. Yet they hunger and thirst for meaning in life. A fourth story is added, the story of a professor of theology, W. Paul Jones. Killinger here puts his finger on a significant need of our time, using Augustine's quote: "Our hearts are restless until they find rest in God."

The four stories point to the need for a relationship with a God who is present. Theologically, this hunger and seeking are signs of our separation from the One who created us. Sin, in its most fundamental form, manifests symptoms of loneliness, emptiness, and a spirit that seeks fulfillment. In his first of five questions Killinger asks if these people are unusual today. He answers his own question with a "no," and like a good fisherman who has tossed out the bait, he allows us to examine the reality of sin without offending.

It is easy to identify with this contemporary presentation of our situation in life. Who hasn't at some time had the nagging suspicion that there is more to life than the "happiness gods" of our time? With our assent Killinger leads us into an intuitive acknowledgement of our own brokenness and need for God.

## PROCLAMATION

"Happy are those...[whose] delight is in the law of the Lord, and on his law they meditate day and night" (Ps. 1:1–2). Although the text is a short two verses, it is powerfully brought into play in this sermon following the four stories of people's lives. Killinger spends a few moments bringing the listener into the Scripture passage. He becomes teacher and advocate for the Law, helping the hearer to contextualize the Hebrew concept of Law: Torah as instruction and a guide for living. He distinguishes Hebrew Torah ("teaching, instruction") from the commonly held Greek view of Law with its inherent sense of justice and punishment. In a few short sentences he leads us to Torah as the Path and Truth for God's people and undergirds his view by reminding us of the value of the Law to Jesus and to Paul.

The description of Law in this sermon provides a wonderful teaching moment for the average lay person. Killinger provides a new lens for understanding Scripture which complements his practical theology of grace. Then he weaves the remainder of the text into his sermon by telling us that the person who meditates on the Law is like "a tree planted by living water, which yields its fruit in its season and its leaves do not wither"...(v. 3). The suggestion is to become a person who moves inward in the search for meaning. Meditation and prayer open us to God's spirit that lives within. The Spirit waits to embrace and refresh our weary souls.

The good news proclaimed here is that there is an alternative to the frantic pace of the outward pursuit of life. The call is to be like a child

C O M M E N T

crawling into the lap of a parent for comfort. We can "relax and rest in the arms of God." The unconditional embrace and acceptance of God's love are being offered. Killinger has presented a path for experiencing a sense of "well-being clear to the bottom of your toes." God offers us rest, refreshment, and love for our souls and promises in season to use us in meaningful and productive ways.

Now for a surprise. The main point has been made. The audience has been reminded of the Source for resolving the search for meaning and fulfillment. Fed and comforted by the preacher's words, we might say, "How about an Amen?" Not so fast!

## INVITATION

Killinger has a second point. As he pushes out into deeper water, he wants us to join him. So he challenges us to consider stepping into the unknown depths of our relationship with God. His challenge is to deeper faith, deeper understanding and experience of all God has to offer. His brief section on the role of the Holy Spirit brings the follower of Christ face to face with his or her own hunger for a deeper relationship with Christ. The last story of Dennis Covington's experience with snake handling is provocative and discomforting. The challenge is to "plumb the depths of all God has to offer us." The invitation is to take the "leap of faith" because there is so much more available from our God.

This sermon is about *proclaiming* the comfort and depth of God's love. But the *invitation* is to transcend the comfort of faith. Killinger concludes by reviewing the text from Psalm 1 and encouraging consistent and continual commitment to meditating on the Scripture.

## STYLE

This sermon is more like a richly woven tapestry than a clear photograph or blueprint. Killinger weaves multiple threads into a beautiful but not crystal-clear work. He invites us to discover restoration, refreshment, and the embrace of God through the deepening of our faith. The threads woven into this tapestry are five stories, five questions, mostly of a rhetorical nature, and a few metaphors. Stories and metaphors capture and hold our attention. They also provide a variety of avenues for the listener to become an active participant in the sermon instead of a passive observer. The potential problem is pulling all the pieces together into a cohesive whole. This style foregoes crispness and linear clarity in favor of authenticity.

Killinger's sermon shows a vulnerability of heart and a compassion for his people that rings true. It has been said that "what comes deepest from the heart goes widest to the world." This is that kind of sermon. It is a tapestry whose beauty lies in the weaving of Scripture and story from the heart of the presenter.

## SUGGESTIONS

- Try stepping beyond the comfort zone of your people to authentically challenge them to deeper faith. How can you do that in your preaching? What biblical texts come to mind?
- Try using two or three different kinds of stories for the purpose of attracting the attention of the wide variety of people in your audience.
- Preach a sermon from what is deepest in your heart. Try working at authenticity and vulnerability more than just precision.
- Consider developing a sermon on one of the following texts containing imagery similar to Psalm 1: Jeremiah 17:5–8; Proverbs 3:13–18; Psalm 119:1–8.

*P. Hunter*

# HIDE AND SEEK: THE CELESTIAL GAME OF SPIRITUAL QUEST

JEREMIAH 29:13–14a

REV. DR. STEPHEN BRACHLOW
PROFESSOR OF CHURCH HISTORY AND
CHRISTIAN SPIRITUALITY
NORTH AMERICAN BAPTIST SEMINARY
SIOUX FALLS, SOUTH DAKOTA

REV. DR. STEPHEN BRACHLOW

# HIDE AND SEEK:
# THE CELESTIAL GAME
# OF SPIRITUAL QUEST

JEREMIAH 29:13–14a

J ean-Pierre de Caussade, an 18th-century French Catholic, wrote a little treasure of a book entitled *The Sacrament of the Present Moment*. About a third of the way into the text is this truly remarkable passage:

*God hides from us in order to raise souls up to that perfect faith which will discover [God] under every kind of disguise. For once they knew God's secret, disguise is useless. They say: "See [God]. There [God] is, behind the wall, looking through the trellis, in at the window!" O Divine Love, conceal yourself, mystify us, arouse and confuse us. Shatter all our illusions and plans so that we lose our way, and see neither path nor light until we have found you, where you are to be found and in your true form—in the peace of solitude, in prayer, in submission, in suffering, in succor given to another, and in flight from idle talk and worldly affairs. And, having tried all the known ways and means of pleasing you and not finding you any longer in any of them, we remain at a loss until, finally, the futility of all our efforts leads us at last to leave all to find you henceforth, you, yourself, everywhere and in all things....*[1]

My wife, Dixie, and I have two adult children, Andrew and Allison. When they were young, one of their favorite things to do as a family was to play hide and seek in our home by McKennan Park. When night came, and it was dark outside, we would turn off all the lights in the house. Then three of us would hide, while the one who was "it" had to shut their eyes, cover their ears, and count to fifty.

It was a great old house in which to play the game with little kids — plenty of rooms and closets both upstairs and down in the basement. Sometimes when Dixie or Andrew was "it," I would take Allison, our younger, to the basement to hide in what we knew was arguably the best spot in the house. There was this little space between the furnace and the concrete foundation wall into which we could just fit if we slipped ourselves in sideways. I must admit, it was pretty scary down there in the dark, with our backs up against the cold cinderblock wall, wispy spider webs clinging to our hair and clothing, our faces inches away from that old monster of a furnace that gave a huge shudder and groan every time it fired up in winter.

Then we would hear the alarm raised from somewhere upstairs: "Ready or not, here I come!" And the hunt was on. And what a thrill it was to stand there in the dark, holding our breath, trying to be absolutely silent. Two hearts — one younger, the other twenty-eight years older — both pounding equally as fast in the darkness. Each of us hoping not to make a move, knowing that someone out there was searching for us, upstairs and down, in closets, under beds and behind furniture...until we'd suddenly hear a blood-curdling shriek (usually two blood-curdling shrieks!) as Dixie or Andrew was discovered in whatever more obvious place they had chosen to hide. And so the lights would go on, and we'd all come out and laugh about how scared we had been and how much fun we'd had playing hide and seek.

The spiritual life is, as the text from Jeremiah 29 suggests, something like that, like a great celestial game of hide and seek, full of all the thrills and adventure of the game we played as kids. "If you seek me with all your heart, I will let you find me, says the Lord" (vv. 13b–14). Now, no metaphor of the faith is ever entirely adequate, but this one is, I think, suggestive of some intriguing ways of understanding the nature of our spiritual journey.

First, it suggests to me that the spiritual journey requires an element of playfulness. That's what I first loved about the de Caussade quote. That's what caught my attention: his sense of play in the spiritual life. It's almost whimsical. "For once they knew God's secret, disguise is useless. They say, 'See [God]. There [God] is, behind the wall, looking through the trellis, in at the window!'" How refreshing! What fun! The spiritual life as a game of divine playfulness.

The great scholastic theologian Thomas Aquinas believed that those of us who take our faith too seriously show a profound lack of trust in God, or, as he put it in a quaint medieval expression: "Unmitigated seriousness betokens a lack of virtue."[2] Sometimes I do think many of us live our Christianity with too much "unmitigated seriousness." What we may really need is to lighten up. To worry less. To let go and enjoy it more. To discover the playful side of God.

Second, if it's like the game we played as kids, then I suspect God enjoys it too. Apparently God does so by being the one who, at times, does the hiding, as the one who appears in disguise. "Truly, you are a God who hides himself," the prophet Isaiah wrote (Isa. 45:15). That's what Jacob discovered, much to his surprise, after sleeping in the wilderness with a rock for a pillow and dreaming about angels going up and down a ladder to heaven. Caught completely off guard, Jacob awoke from his dream, looked around at what he thought was desolate, God-forsaken land, and said, "Surely the Lord is in this place and I knew it not" (Gen. 28:16). And so God plays the game with us, and even seems to delight in taking us by surprise, in having us discover Christ, for example, when and where and in whom we would least expect to find him, so that we, too, find ourselves saying, "Surely God is in this place and I knew it not."

Third, like the game we played as kids, it seems that, for it to be any fun at all, there has to be a darkness, even if that darkness gets awful scary. I mean, how much fun would it be to play hide and seek with the lights on? And, as we all know, some days it can get awfully dark in the living of our lives. We sometimes find ourselves feeling quite lost, wandering through our days, with, it seems, no idea of where we are headed. Luther understood that. "Not knowing where you are going" and even "what you are seeking," Luther said, is a necessary ingredient of authentic spirituality. "Discipleship is not limited to what you can comprehend," Luther wrote. "Bewilderment," he said, "is the true comprehension. Not to know where you are going is the true knowledge.... You cannot find [your way] yourself," Luther concluded, "so you must let [God] lead you as though you were blind."[3]

And so we discover when the light of faith seems to go out, and we find ourselves bereft of any vision for the future, that all we may be able to do is put our trust in the One who says in Isaiah 42, "I will lead the blind by a road they do not know, by paths they have not known I will guide them" (v. 16). And so we may find out, quite unexpectedly, that we often do end up stumbling into some dark room of our lives we perhaps thought was empty and completely God-forsaken, only to find that God is there, as God is everywhere, waiting to be found. And we come to understand those words of grace afresh: "See? I told you so. 'When you seek me with all your heart, I will let you find me.'"

Finally, we come to the strange truth, the great surprise, the profound paradox of this celestial game. While we are called to seek, Scripture also makes it clear that, in contrast to the game we played as kids, it is God who actually does the finding. I like the way a Dutch Benedictine monastic community put it recently in their little rule for initiates: "You want to seek God with all your life, and love [God] with all your heart. But you would be wrong if you thought you could reach [God]. Your arms are too short, your eyes are too dim, Your heart and understanding too small. To seek God means first of all to let yourself be found by [God]."

So the rules of this game appear to go something like this: "seeking" is our task, "finding" is God's. The "finding" is God's promise to us, God's work for us, God's gift of grace in our seeking lives. Jean-Pierre de Caussade put it this way: Those who "truly seek this treasure...have nothing to fear. They can only fall under that almighty hand...which leads them towards the goal from which they are straying and puts them back on the path they have lost."[4] If we "seek" with all our heart, God promises that we will find our way home...where, when, or exactly how, we may not always know, but the promise is, "I will let you find me, says the Lord."

"So never let yourself lose heart," the Rule for the Dutch Benedictines concludes, "but go on seeking God in everything, in everybody...they are all pledges that you will finally meet [the One who seeks you]." Hallelujah! Amen.

Notes
1. Jean-Pierre de Caussade, *The Sacrament of the Present Moment,* trans. Kitty Muggeridge, (San Francisco: Harper & Row, 1989), pp. 18-19.
2. Quoted in Belden C. Lane, "Desert Catechesis: The Landscape and Theology of Early Christian Monasticism," *Anglican Theological Review,* 75(1993), p. 305.
3. Quoted in Dietrich Bonhoeffer, *Cost of Discipleship,* revised ed. (New York: Collier Books, 1963), p. 103.
4. Caussade, p. 30.

# COMMENT

One word that recurs throughout these sermon comments is "simplicity." Simplicity is a virtue in preaching that should be distinguished from "simplistic." Simplicity in preaching means that we are Masters of Clarity and not merely the Obvious.

Another word that is important in preaching is "authenticity" which, like simplicity, is often misunderstood. It is not the same as self-disclosure. To "reveal all" often can also be a form of narcissism or worse — a pathology derived from some cosmic need to make oneself understood or pitied. Some disclosures in this "let-it-all-hang-out" time of ours cry out to be "put back."

Authenticity is a reflection of personal integrity. Integrity means, literally, "wholeness." Authenticity is communicated both verbally and nonverbally, but in its essence means that who we are and what we say come close to each other. It does not mean that we are perfect. But it does imply that every good sermon has some real connection to the preacher's own being. Sermons do not drop down out of heaven. They well up from the depths of a human heart like a spring of living water.

I like this sermon! It tells me a lot about what this preacher reads, who he is, and what his own spiritual pilgrimage has been like. It is both simple and authentic, to such a degree that it can be deceptive to the reader. It is rich in images, careful in its theological assertions and true to the biblical text.

Structurally, Brachlow's sermon is very simple. He begins with reflection on a classical text in Christian spirituality about the hiddenness of God. Then he moves to a child's game (hide and seek) as a metaphor of the Christian life. The structure of the sermon takes the form of asking the question "What are the 'rules' of this game we play of searching for God?"

There are four "rules":
- an element of playfulness (not taking ourselves so seriously);
- God also participates in the game and hides himself;

- mystery and darkness are part of the game (that is, "not knowing" is essential to the process of spiritual knowing); and
- while we are called to seek God, it is God who actually does the finding.

## QUESTION

These "rules" are actually very complex assertions about spiritual reality. Why do we need to know the "rules"? Because we are often perplexed by the apparent elusiveness of God in our daily experience.

Despite all the confident assertions by religious leaders and institutions, finding and knowing God in real experience is a challenging task. Yet the hunger to find God is powerful. An intelligent and thoughtful person in the average church must negotiate the discrepancy between the faith assertions she or he hears from the pulpit and the sometimes disconnected experiences of daily life. These experiences often involve unexplained suffering, boredom, emptiness and stress. The task of noticing the footprints of a present God can be daunting.

This gulf between what we profess and what we really know is the human dilemma which Brachlow addresses. It decries the easy and superficial spirituality which too many ministers offer as a substitute. "Where is God in the midst of my life?" That is the question that so many ask.

## TEXT

The novice preacher might well look at Brachlow's effort and ask, "What text?" He never returns to the text, at least not in the sense that a seminarian is trained to do. No background, no exegesis, no hermeneutics. Yet this is a profoundly "biblical" sermon. Why?

A closer look at Jeremiah 29 reminds us that it is a letter addressed to people who have been offered a superficial solution to a profound problem. Written to the exiles held captive in Babylon, Jeremiah is advising them to disregard calls for a premature return to Jerusalem. Instead, he suggests that they accept their situation and make the best of it.

The exile is the pre-eminent experience of spiritual darkness in the Old Testament. In that catastrophic disruption, the Judeans lost every familiar symbol of the spiritual life: home, land, temple, and tradition. Where would they find God now? Jeremiah's answer was a stark challenge to their cultic experience: their God, he said, could be found, anywhere, even in the emptiness of a spiritual wilderness, in captivity, in failure and defeat.

Now Brachlow's method can be seen in a new light. A sermon can be biblical without being a history lesson or exposition. To be biblical means that the intent, the driving pulse of the text, must be consistent with the images and assertions of the sermon.

## PROCLAMATION

So Brachlow asserts a powerful message of grace. "If you seek me, says the Lord, I will let you find me." Grace is a great reversal that upends our comfortable and distorted systems of righteousness.

Once, at a denominational meeting, we viewed a new videotape that proclaimed that basically our society, once godly and righteous, was now taking the A-train to hell. An African-American friend leaned forward and whispered, "Gary, that's a Caucasion view of American history." That remark struck me with great force. It had never occurred to me how conditioned our evaluations of things can be.

There is a great tradition of lament in preaching that always has the same basic theme: "Things have never been this bad and they're probably going to get worse." The "jeremiad" has come to stand for "holy whining" about how bad things are and is often confused for "prophetic preaching." But that is not exactly fair to Jeremiah and the prophets. They often declared judgment not when things were bad, but when they seemed to be going well. When disaster came, these cantankerous souls began to proclaim hope. The word of grace comes not when all is well, but precisely when there seems to be no hope.

Many years ago, a writer named Robert Zeluff wrote a little book called *There's Algae in the Baptismal Font.* He told of looking back over fifteen years or so of preaching and discovering that he had only preached one basic sermon. It said, "Shape up, folks!" Over and over.

In the book of ministry, grace is often left until the appendix or shoved into the footnotes to say something like, "Oh, yeah, and if you mess up, God can redeem. *But don't mess up!*" And instead of surrender, we tighten up.

Grace is a "crossing over," a realization that we do not hold up the standards, slice the pie, or control the outcome. We humbly bear witness to the great and mysterious God who never abandons or forsakes the world.

Jeremiah (and Brachlow) call us to that reality. When all the forms and structures fall away, there is still Someone to whom our prayers go, Someone who is present to us if we call. That can be a terribly threatening message to the religious institutions and their self-interests.

## RESPONSE

So what sort of response can there be to grace? This can be tricky for the preacher, for it is all too easy to lapse into "Do this, and you shall live." The answer can be found in the difference between discovery and being found.

What Brachlow invites is a radical reorientation in which nothing changes and yet — because of our shift in perspective — *everything* changes. He asks us to open up and make room for God in our lives. It evokes the simplest and most basic reality of life, both spiritually and (according to Erik Erikson), psychologically: trust.

How? First, we can *give up,* by paying attention to what is already in our midst. Brachlow gives us a wonderful image of this when he tells of waiting in the basement next to the old furnace: "And what a thrill it was to stand there in the dark, holding our breath, trying to be absolutely silent. Two hearts — one younger, the other twenty-eight years older — both pounding equally as fast in the darkness. Each of us hoping not to make a move, knowing that someone out there was searching for us."

Here is the image of contemplative prayer: entering into silence and finding not emptiness, but a universe full of God. "Quit doing so much" doesn't sound like a response to a nation of activists. We are like the man who walked all over his house looking for his glasses, only to discover that they had been perched, all the time, on top of his head.

Second, we are invited to *lighten up*. If this sounds irreverent, we might heed the words of Thomas Merton, who once wrote in *The Sign of Jonas* that we cripple ourselves spiritually when we take ourselves too seriously. Instead, he advised, we ought to expect less of ourselves and expect everything from God on whom our lives depend!

This does not negate our quest for God; it puts it into proper perspective. Grace is "letting yourself be found." This is good news to people who are accustomed to striving to overcome every problem they face.

### SUGGESTIONS

- One of the great needs of present-day ministers runs contrary to the pressures of the job. We need to pull aside and attend to the task of personal spiritual growth for the sake of others. This can be started as simply as by reading the great spiritual classics. Immersing oneself in this literature enables the preacher to be in touch with the spiritual wisdom of the ages. There are many guides to this great wealth of literature. I would suggest just a few. They are:

  Foster, Richard J., and James Bryan Smith, eds., *Devotional Classics: Selected Readings for Individuals & Groups* (Harper San Francisco, 1990).

  Magill, Frank N., and Ian P. McGreal, eds., *Christian Spirituality: The Essential Guide to the Most Influential Spiritual Writing of the Christian Tradition* (San Francisco: Harper & Row, 1988).

  Maas, Robin, and Gabriel O'Donnell, eds., *Spiritual Traditions for the Contemporary Church* (Nashville: Abingdon Press, 1990).

  Willard, Dallas, *The Spirit of the Disciplines* (San Francisco: Harper & Row Publishers, 1988).

- Try taking a biblical text and creating a sermon that communicates the intention of that text without ever actually referring back to its historical circumstances. "Translate" it into a present image.

*Gary Furr*

# SECRETS OF THE HEART

PSALM 37

REV. D. STUART BRISCOE
ELMBROOK CHURCH
BROOKFIELD, WISCONSIN

# SECRETS OF THE HEART

PSALM 37

T he Bible says that God is more interested in the heart than in the externals of life. However, if we are honest about it, very often we are more interested in the image we project, frequently with a view to covering up what is really going on inside. That being the case, there is a fundamental difference between how God looks at humanity and the way we look at people and the way we look at ourselves. Image. Dressing for success. Conveying an impression. These are the things we tend to be interested in.

Probably most of us this past week have been shocked and saddened about the O. J. Simpson story. He was the quintessential success story in our American land of opportunity. Born in a tough ghetto neighborhood of San Francisco. In trouble as a kid. Fighting as a teenager. Heading for jail. Probation in his young adolescence. Fortunately, he could run. He was big and strong and elusive. Some coaches got hold of him and more or less knocked him into shape. Too lazy in school to make the grades to get into college even though he was such a superb athlete. But they got him into a junior college where he promptly broke records in football though he didn't do much academically. Eventually they got him into USC, where he became the All-American. As an All-Pro leading rusher he reached the Hall of Fame. There were movies, success as the urbane commentator for televised football, and the famous commercial where he runs through airports and encourages us to rent Hertz cars. In the process, he made millions. He was regarded by many people as a model for young people. The athlete. The strong man. The guy who made good.

Now we are hearing what he was really like. And it's a sad, sad story. The image was superb, the reality was something else.

We've got to be more concerned about heart, folks. God is. It is out of the heart that the issues of life happen. That is why the Bible mentions the heart almost a thousand times, dozens of those occasions in the Psalms. We've been looking at what goes on in the heart as we've been studying the Book of Psalms. Today we come to Psalm 37. Let me read the first eleven verses to you.

> *Do not fret* because of evil men,
>     or be envious of those who do wrong;
> for like the grass they shall soon wither,
>     like green plants they will soon die away.
>
> Trust in the Lord and do good;
>     dwell in the land and enjoy safe pasture.
> Delight yourself in the Lord
>     and he will give you the desires of your heart.
>
> Commit your way to the Lord;
>     trust in him and he will do this:
> He will make your righteousness shine like the dawn,
>     the justice of your cause like the noonday sun.
>
> Be still before the Lord and wait patiently for him;
>     *do not fret* when men succeed in their ways,
>     when they carry out their wicked schemes.
>
> Refrain from anger and turn from wrath;
>     *do not fret* — it leads only to evil.

For evil men will be cut off,
>but those who hope in the Lord will inherit the land.

A little while, and the wicked will be no more;
>though you look for them, they will not be found,
But the meek will inherit the land and enjoy great peace.
[italics mine]

It's a rule of biblical interpretation that if you find a phrase repeated in a context, in all probability that is what the context is about. Did you notice what is repeated in this passage? "Do not fret." "Do not fret." "Do not fret." *Fret* is not a word we often use. *Don't get frustrated* would probably apply more. Life *is* frustrating. Let's face it, many, many people have deep longings and aspirations in their hearts, but circumstances are such that they don't come to fruition. And then, what happens? These unfulfilled desires often engender frustration. The psalmist, however, tells us that we've got to be able to handle life's frustrations, even though our longing heart may not find satisfaction. Why do we so often find that our longings are not met? Why is it that unfulfilled desires become the dominant theme of our existence?

Young couples marry and look forward to children and then confront infertility. People doing well in their jobs are suddenly cut off without warning, fired. They try honestly to find other work and it just doesn't come. Single people, many of them, have a real desire to be married. Others who were married become divorced, though they do not want to be. I was told this morning of another divorce in our congregation. It's not what they want; it's just what people are doing to them.

What are we going to do with all these unfulfilled desires? Verse 4 says to us, "Delight yourself in the Lord and he will give you the desires of your heart." We've got a problem here. We know we are supposed to believe verses like this. We have them underlined in our Bibles till those lines come through to the maps. *"Delight yourself in the Lord and he will give you the desires of your heart."* But many of us, if we are honest, would say that behind the smiling exterior is a heart that is frustrated because of unfulfilled desires. We can't figure out why that verse says what it does, and our desires remain unfulfilled.

Well, there are various possibilities we try to examine to find out why. But notice, please, that we should always interpret Scripture in its context, and verse 5 goes on to say: "Commit your way to the Lord. Trust in him and he will do this." Do what? "He will make your righteousness shine like the dawn, the justice of your cause like the noonday sun." In short, what the psalmist is saying is that God will give you the desires of your heart, but that does not mean carte blanche. That doesn't mean you can come before God with any old thing on your mind and say, "Oh, God, you said it; I believe it; that settles it! 'Delight yourself in the Lord and he will give you the desires of your heart.' I desire this...do it!" He says, "No, it has to do with your righteousness shining like the dawn and the justice of your cause like the noonday sun." In other words, the desires of your heart have to be legitimate, they have to be right; they have to be right in accordance with the eternal purposes of God, who wills what is best for you.

I remember the early days of Billy Graham's ministry in England. He was something of a phenomenon over there. When this long, lanky Carolinian came over, wearing flashy ties the likes of which we had never seen before, he began to speak to us in his very appealing Carolinian drawl. On one occasion I heard him say, much to my amazement, "If you ain't seen the moon in Carolina, you ain't seen the moon." To say that he was somewhat different from our normal English clergymen is putting it mildly.

This was at the time that Elizabeth Taylor, the beautiful English actress, was hitting the headlines. (When did she not hit the headlines?) In those days, she was still young and still beautiful, but she was running into all kinds of problems. Billy Graham told a congregation that he had been in touch with her and knew what was going on, and a mutual friend of ours called Dr. Joe Smart saved her life when he operated on her in a critical emergency. Billy Graham said to the congregation, "Don't envy Elizabeth Taylor; pray for her." And a little fellow on the back row stood up and said, "I pray for her every night but I never get her." I wonder if he had underlined that verse: "Delight yourself in the Lord and he will give you the desires of your heart."

There was a young soldier who was desperately injured during the Civil War and was crippled for the rest of his life. This is what he wrote.

I asked for strength that I might achieve.
   I was made weak that I might obey.
I asked for health that I might do greater things.
   I was given infirmity that I might do better things.
I asked for riches that I might be happy.
   I was given poverty that I might be wise.
I asked for power that I might have the praise of men.
   I was given weakness that I might feel the need of God.
I asked for all things that I might enjoy life.
   I was given life that I might enjoy all things.
I have received nothing I asked for
   and in all that I hoped for,
      my prayer is answered.

Joachim Neander, a thirty-year-old German pastor who was dying of tuberculosis, sat down and wrote one of the great hymns of the faith, "Lobe den Herren." He wrote:

Praise to the Lord, who o'er
   all things so wondrously reigneth,
who, as on wings of an eagle,
   uplifteth, sustaineth.
Hast thou not seen
   how thy desires all have been
   granted in what he ordaineth?

That's the problem. If God gave us what we asked for, if God really gave us all the desires of our heart, there would be such an illegitimacy to them that they would be desperately detrimental to us. But one thing we can be convinced of, in the area of unfulfilled desires, if we are bringing them before the Lord according to his righteousness and according to his sovereign purposes, he is committed to granting to us that which is best for his purposes. That which is best for us in the long run. It's hard, isn't it? It can be very frustrating, waiting.

Then there is the frustration of life's injustices. The psalmist seems to be really rankled, really frustrated, with all the injustices of life. Probably one of the biggest injustices that believers discover is that, for some incredible reason, being a believer is so hard, yet unbelievers have it so good. Now if we were God, we would reorganize it. We'd say, "Okay, you believers, you're the good kids on the block, you're the guys wearing the white hats; you can have it real good. These other guys, I'm going to zap them. I'll show them." For some reason it doesn't work that way. The ungodly seem to have it so good. They do the enviable things. But look at verse 1. "Do not fret because of evil men, or be envious of those who do wrong."

Pick up a copy of *People* magazine at the checkout counter sometime. Just leaf through it, and as you do, notice all the stuff the rich and famous are enjoying — all the stuff that just once in a while you think you'd like to do. Then look at the lifestyles and say to yourself, God, how in the world can those folks do all that stuff and get so rich and so famous? It's not fair.

"*Be still before the Lord, and wait patiently for him. Don't fret when men succeed in their ways, when they carry out their wicked schemes.*" God, do you know that these people who are so successful, that so many of them are such rascals? Do you know that the guy who works in the office next to me is cutting all the corners, padding his expense sheets? Do you know what he does when we go away on a trip? We stay in a hotel together, and you know, God, that I am a straight arrow. And, would you believe, he gets the order we were both trying to sell? Honestly, God, they seem to get away with murder so often, the ungodly. "*The wicked plot against the righteous and gnash their teeth at them.*" In my situation, Lord, I try to do what is right. I try to be what I am supposed to be and I just get gnashed on by these people. And they get away with it.

Listen to verses 16 and 17: "*Better the little that the righteous have than the wealth of many wicked; for the power of the wicked will be broken, but the Lord upholds the righteous.*" You say, Right, that's good. But notice, it's the wicked that have the wealth and the wicked that have the power. Why, Lord, is it that so often it seems the people getting the power and the people making a bundle are the ones that don't do it the way you said it should be done? That's not right; it's not fair. It's very frustrating business, Lord, seeing the way the ungodly have it so good. (Verse 21, *"The wicked borrow and don't repay."*) They get away with dishonesty. It's amazing how some folks can go on serenely from one scam to another and never get caught. They get all the breaks. (Verse 35, *"I have seen a wicked and a ruthless man flourishing like a green tree in its native soil."*) Lord, it's rough. Life is unjust. Not only do the ungodly seem to have it so good, but the godly find life so difficult. They are required to trust God when they don't understand. (Verse 3, *"Trust in the Lord and do good; dwell in the land and enjoy safe pasture. Delight yourself in the Lord and he will give you the desires of your heart."*)

Lord, I want to tell you something. I have seen all these ungodly people getting away with it, making a bundle, getting all the power and enjoying all the stuff I'd like to enjoy. I don't have any of these things. Here I am trying to be godly; nothing is working out, and I don't understand what is happening, and then someone from Elmbrook comes up holding a big Bible, smiles at me with that sickly angelic smile, and says, "Just trust in the Lord, just trust in the Lord; that's all you need to do."

Why do I have to trust God when all the other people aren't trusting God, and it seems to work for them and it doesn't work for me? I'd rather just figure it out, just plan the whole thing. I'd rather control the whole thing. I'd rather do the sensible thing. Look, it's what they're doing and it works. I'm supposed to trust and it doesn't work.

I'm frustrated, Lord. You told me I have got to do good. The other folks don't do good. I'm the one that's supposed to have the servant's spirit. The other folks won't even lift a finger. The ones that don't lift a little finger get all the breaks. And the ones that are trying to do the right thing, trying to be servants to others, to make themselves available, who really want to serve you — what happens? It doesn't work. (Verse 7, *"Be still before the Lord and wait patiently for him."*) Sure, I'll be still while everybody is leaving me in their dust. I wait patiently for you and they don't wait patiently for anybody. They just keep going.

Why do I have to wait patiently? Why don't you just do something instead of me having to be patient? It's hard, Lord, trusting you when I don't understand. It's very hard doing good when other people won't. And it's very difficult being patient and waiting when nobody else is.

Verse 8, *"Refrain from anger and turn from wrath."* There you go again, Lord. Now I've got to keep my cool when nobody else does. It would be so nice, Lord, if just once in a while you'd give me a day off. When I'm in an airport and my flight is canceled one more time, and all these other people lose their cool, bang on the desk, demand this and demand that and it's very quickly handled. Then I come up, quiet and gracious, and no one even takes notice of me. Lord, what I would really like to do is just let it rip like everybody else. Why do I have to refrain from anger and turn from wrath? They don't, and I get bumped and they get seen to.

I remember the time when our kids were young teenagers, and we had to go away for two or three nights. We asked a young couple in the church if they would like to watch over our three teenagers. It wasn't a very successful relationship. When we got back this young couple sat us down and said that they were appalled to find out how a pastor's teenagers really behaved. They were very concerned about our teenagers and our ability as parents. They said that they would not really want to look after our teenagers again. So they left, and our teenagers came in. "Don't ever bring them in this house again," they said. "They don't understand teenagers, and they don't even *like* teenagers. Don't ever bring them here again. We will be fine. We don't need anybody babysitting us. We are responsible. The next time you go away let us just look after ourselves."

So the next time we were going away, just for an overnight, I sat the three teenagers down (they were 16, 14, and 12 years old). "Okay, we are going to trust you. We expect you to behave yourselves. You are going to behave yourselves. We are going to be gone overnight. Here's the phone number where you can reach us. You can call the neighbors if you need anything, etc., etc." and off we went.

When we came back the first thing we said to the kids was, "How did it go?" Dave, our eldest, said, "Pretty good." This was his normal response for most things. Judy, however, gave us the scoop, which is normal too.

"Dad, you would not believe it. The phone rang and Dave picked it up and this lady said, 'Can I talk to your father?' and David said, 'He's out of town.' Then the lady said, 'Can I talk with your mother?' And David said, 'She's out of town.' 'They're both out of town!' 'Yes.' 'Then can I speak to the person who is looking after you?' 'We are looking out for ourselves.' 'Your parents have gone out of town and left you on your own?' 'Yes.' 'Well, I think that is absolutely disgusting. I can't believe it! A pastor and his wife who would go away and leave three teenagers home alone. This is absolutely a terrible thing to do,' said the lady.

"Dad, David was so nice to this lady on the phone. I just wanted to say, 'Lady, up your nose with a rubber hose.'" Then Judy looked at me rather tentatively and said, "Dad, would that have been all right?" and I said, "Perfectly." I couldn't say it, but why not let my teenagers say it?

But, Lord, just once in a while, won't you let me say to some of these people, "Up your nose...."? It's hard, Lord, being godly, living by faith. It's hard doing it your way. I've got to trust God when I don't understand it. I've got to be good when other people don't. I've got to be still while other people pass me. I've got to keep my cool while others are losing theirs. Then, Lord, you tell me that the meek will inherit the earth. Sure. This is a rat race down here, Lord. It's no place for meek people.

John Paul Getty, the former oil baron, said, "The meek may inherit the earth, but they sure won't get the mineral rights." Meekness is just being weak. Just being a doormat. Let everybody run all over you wherever they want to go. Rademacher says, "If you think meekness is weakness, try being meek for a week. That will cure you."

Meekness didn't work for me, Lord. Then on top of that, Lord, I'm supposed to be generous. You admit, Lord, in verse 16, "Better the little that the righteous have than the wealth of many wicked." You admit that if I'm righteous — do it your way — then I won't have as much as a lot of wicked people. Then you say, "The wicked borrow and don't repay, but the righteous give generously." And added to that, you go and tell me that the righteous people are the ones that lend generously. Now, Lord, let me get this right. You say that if I'm righteous, I probably won't have as much as the wicked and that the wicked won't share what they've got. But I don't have as much and I've got to share. Now, that's not fair. I'd like to reorganize it, Lord. If you insist on giving the wicked people so much, then make them be the ones that do the giving. Let them do it. And let those of us who don't have as much get off the hook.

God says it doesn't work that way. You are the ones that have to be generous when other people aren't. You're the ones that have to be meek when people rip you off. You are the ones that keep your cool when others lose their temper. You're the ones who still wait while others pass you by. You're the ones that do good when other people don't. You're the ones that trust God when other people just get organized. Lord, I want to tell you something — it's hard and it's frustrating.

The frustration of life's unfulfilled desires and the frustration of life's injustices and the frustrations of life's battles — the psalmist is very straightforward about this in verses 12 and 13. He talks about battles against blatant evil. We just have to hit it head-on so often, Lord. Verses 23 and 24 talk about the struggles that we have against life's stumbling blocks. Verses 31 and 32 remind us that life is full of slippery slopes and hidden pitfalls. Lord, so often it's a case of one step forward and two steps back, of thinking that you are going along fine, and then you fall into a ditch. You find people battling against you all the time and that things are opposed to you. Lord, life is full of battles.

Well, these frustrations are building up. We still can't get around what it says we are to do: "Trust in the Lord and do good. Delight yourself in the Lord, and he will give you the desires of your heart. Commit your way to the Lord and trust in him and he will do this."

What does this all mean? Let's look at the life lessons that we have to learn. There are four that come through loudly and clearly in this psalm — things that you either believe or you don't believe. That's why we call it the life of faith.

1. Good will eventually prevail (vv. 9–15).
2. God will eternally triumph (vv. 18–20).
3. Grace will continually flow (vv. 23–25).
4. Godliness will ultimately satisfy (vv. 37–40).

Let me tell you something. If we are ever going to live with frustrations, we must learn these four fundamental lessons. Do I honestly believe that *good will eventually prevail*? Despite the fact that, as I look around, I see all kinds of people who are not interested in being good, not interested in doing good, apparently succeeding very nicely? Do I believe that eventually this will happen? Over and over again in this psalm I'm told not to get frustrated, not to get worked up because of all these people. Verse 9, "Evil men will be cut off, but those that hope in the Lord will inherit the land. A little while, and the wicked will be no more; though you look for them, they will not be found. But the meek will inherit the land and enjoy great peace. The wicked plot against the righteous and gnash their teeth at them, but the Lord laughs at the wicked for he knows their day is coming." Do I know, deep down in my heart, even though I'm tempted and frustrated by all that is going on around me, that *good will eventually prevail*?

Am I convinced that *God will eternally triumph*? Do I know the end of the story? Do I know that for reasons known only to himself, the Lord is at work, even in circumstances like this? Verses 18–20: "The days of the blameless are known to the Lord, and their inheritance will endure forever. In times of disaster they will not wither; in days of famine they will enjoy plenty. But the wicked will perish: The Lord's enemies will be like the beauty of the fields, they will vanish — vanish like smoke." Do I believe that good will eventually prevail? Do I believe that God will eternally triumph?

In the midst of these situations do I believe that God will give me the ability to live wisely and well in circumstances that I cannot change? We are in such a "fix-it" frame of mind in our culture. We assume that we have the right to a cure for everything. And it should be as quick and painless and as inexpensive as possible. When, in fact, reality would tell us that there are some things for which there are no solutions; some things that are not going to get fixed. And there are some things that will only be fixed slowly and, often, very expensively. Instead of always assuming a fix and a cure, is it not better to ask, Is there grace for me to live well in my situation?

"If the Lord delights in a man's way, he makes his steps firm; though he stumbles, he will not fall, for the Lord upholds his hand." "I was young and now I am old, yet I have never seen the righteous forsaken or their children begging bread." Do you believe that? Do you believe that in the midst of these circumstances, *grace will continually flow*? And do you believe that godliness, ultimately, will be more satisfactory than the alternative lifestyle? Verses 37–40, "Consider the blameless, observe the upright; there is a future for the man of peace. But all sinners will be destroyed; the future of the wicked will be cut off. The salvation of the righteous comes from the Lord; he is their stronghold in time of trouble. The Lord helps them and delivers them; he delivers them from the wicked and saves them, because they take refuge in him." Yes, godliness ultimately is the way to go. *Godliness will ultimately satisfy.*

The question that I have to ask myself is this: Do I allow the frustrations of life to govern my heart or do I allow these four fundamental principles to be the bedrock of my life and the cause of my attitudes?

This leads to the third and final part of this sermon. If it is true that the four principles we have just examined adhere and apply in these frustrating circumstances, then three simple disciplines are necessary. Let us look again at the famous verses at the beginning of the psalm.

*Discipline #1.* "Trust in the Lord and do good." Oh, you say, "I'm tired of this platitude of trusting in the Lord and doing good. I'm so tired of it...." Then let me ask you a couple of questions. Are you trusting God to deal with all of your past? All the past, with all its shame? With all the stuff you don't want written up about you? All the past you can't forgive yourself for? Are you trusting God, for Christ's sake, to forgive that? You say, "Yes"? When you die, where do you think you're going? Well, you say, "I think I'm going to go to heaven. 'Goodness and mercy shall follow me all the days of my life and I will dwell in the house of the Lord forever.'" So, what makes you think that? "Well, I'm trusting that the shed blood of Christ will be the basis upon which God, for Christ's sake, forgives me." So, in other words, you are trusting God with your past and trusting God with your future? "That's right."

Well, here is a very simple question. If God is trustworthy enough to deal with your past and God is trustworthy enough to deal with your future, what suddenly went wrong with God that you can't trust him today? Or put it another way. If God is capable of handling all your past and dealing with it, and he is capable of securing your future and eternal destiny — if he can handle all of this and all of that, why can't he handle the now?

So, the discipline is to begin to be consistent in applying to the *now* that which applies to the *then* and *thereafter*.

"*Trust in the Lord and do good.*" So do what is right. I don't know how many times in the course of one week I sit down with people and in the end tell them, I don't know an answer to your problem. I don't know how you can change what your husband is doing. I don't know how you can stop that divorce going through. I don't know what you can do about those teenagers who are going wild. I don't know what you can do about all these things that are happening, but I do know that they are not your primary concern. Your primary concern in the midst of situations you cannot change, is that you do what's right. You can do that. Nobody can take that away from you.

Viktor Frankl observed in his imprisonment in the Nazi concentration camps that when people were starving because there wasn't enough bread to go around, there actually were some people in those camps who would share their meager rations of bread with more needy people. And he said that he learned something terribly important there: "Even in the most horrid situations, where people are totally controlled, there is one thing that can't be controlled. They cannot control your ability to do what is right. They can't do it. Nobody has that power over anybody."

So, the first discipline that I build in is trust. On the basis of my trust in the past and my trust in the future, I trust God in the now and will exert all my God-given energies and the power of the Holy Spirit to do what is right.

*Discipline #2.* I will delight myself in the Lord on the understanding that he will begin to work on my desires — that it won't be so much that I can desire anything I like and he will give it, but that I will delight myself so much in the Lord that he will give me a new set of desires. Did you notice that? It's not that I have carte blanche to go ahead with a set of my desires; it's that I so much delight myself in the Lord that he implants in me the desires he wants me to have. Oh, that would be interesting, wouldn't it?

*Discipline #3.* I commit my way to the Lord on the basis of the trust I have in him. Notice that it is necessary for me to do the initial committing and to keep continuing the trusting. On one of my earliest visits to America, I remember doing a series of meetings every morning and evening. My hosts had made arrangements for me to be picked up for the morning women's meetings. One of the ladies who came for me was very large, and she had four very large friends. Fortunately, she also had a very large car, a Lincoln Continental which resembled a Sherman tank. I would be squeezed into the back seat on the right, catercorner from where she was in the left front seat. She had the most disconcerting habit of talking to me while she was driving along. One morning, as she went barreling through a red light, she said, "Mr. Briscoe, I get the impression that you're not listening to me." I said, "I wasn't. I was watching the road for you."

The reason I tell you this story is that it is one thing to get into a car and trust somebody, and it's an entirely different thing to go on committing your way to them if they don't warrant your trust. I want you to know that on several occasions I was leaning over to get hold of that steering wheel. There are some people who will get into a situation where they commit themselves to the Lord, but then don't go on trusting him.

The disciplines are very straightforward. It's a case of accepting the principle that it's necessary to trust the Lord, delight yourself in him, commit to him. Then, through that intimacy of relationship, he is going to be working on your desires. Be assured that he will touch you in such a way that you are no longer a frustrated victim of your circumstances but a person who has begun to discover the peace that passes understanding. Deep down in your heart.

# COMMENT

"It's not fair," cries the child at play when denied his turn in the game. "It's not fair," cries the young woman whose husband dies of cancer. "It's not fair," cries the older executive who loses his job to a rising star. "It's not fair," says the person of faith when a business associate dishonestly turns a huge profit and gets by with it. "It's just not fair," cries a culture of affluence and entitlement when success and the American dream go unrealized.

The psalmists in ancient Israel were neither naive optimists nor philosophical pessimists. They knew about the "real world." They knew that the wicked often appear to do well, while the righteous suffer. They knew about pain and injustice. But they also knew about God. They believed in the faithfulness of God and the ultimate vindication of the righteous. They could live with hope in a world of despair. They could perceive the mystery of life where others might see only misery. They believed that relationship with God alone enables one to live with purpose and integrity in a world of confusion.

Stuart Briscoe's sermon, "Secrets of the Heart," addresses the anguished cry "It's not fair!" with the wisdom of the psalmist who answers, "Trust in the Lord, and do good. Commit your way to the Lord...and he will act." The good news of this sermon is that when we trust God, God will touch us in such a way that we are no longer frustrated victims of circumstance, but people who begin to discover a peace that passes all human understanding.

Briscoe's sermon is distinctive for three reasons. First, it addresses in a practical way the difficult issue of life's perceived injustices as faith encounters the real world. Second, the sermon allows the biblical text itself to define the problem, to proclaim the truths of faith, and to invite a response. The text predominates throughout this sermon. Third, although the sermon has a basic expository style, the preacher avoids a monologue. He does not talk "at us." He speaks "with us," entering into active dialogue with us. The text, the preacher, and the congregation are all in conversation with each other. When that happens, active listening can occur and a true hearing of the Word of God can transform lives.

## TYPE OF TEXT

Before reviewing the sermon, let's think about the importance of knowing the background of a biblical text. The literary form or genre of any passage of Scripture is important to know as part of its accurate interpretation. It is important to ask how a specific passage fits into larger patterns of literary expression within the Bible. The text for this sermon, Psalm 37, is classified by scholars as a "Wisdom psalm." It expresses the teaching of Israel's Wisdom tradition represented elsewhere in the Old Testament by books like Proverbs, Ecclesiastes, and Job. Psalm 37 is didactic in tone, a collection of sayings that might easily be found in the book of Proverbs.

Wisdom psalms characteristically speak of the sharp contrast between the righteous and the wicked. They give advice about conduct that results in either welfare or misfortune. The premise of Israel's Wisdom teaching is that "the fear [reverence] of Yahweh" is the starting point of all wisdom (Proverbs 9:10). The Wisdom of God teaches people to walk in "right paths" by faithfully following God's *torah* ("teaching, instruction"). We can see many of these Wisdom themes in Psalm 37.

Awareness of the background and literary form of a text is essential in good preaching. This is especially true when preaching from the psalms. In addition to Wisdom psalms, there are many other types of psalms, including hymns, laments, songs of thanksgiving, and royal psalms. Each type bears distinctive characteristics and content. The knowledge of these types is important in interpreting the text. Good commentaries can provide this background information which will inform and enrich your preaching of the text.

## USE OF TEXT

After opening the sermon with the reminder that God is more concerned with our hearts than with the external images in our lives, Briscoe introduces the text, and along with it, the problem this sermon addresses. Reading Psalm 37:1–11, he calls attention to the recurring phrase "Do not fret," which points to the problem of frustration over life's injustices and unfulfilled longings. The repetition of the phrase "Do not fret" suggests the psalm is addressed to anyone who experiences unfulfilled desires in life or thinks that God's rule is unfair or ineffective.

Notice how the text and description of the problem are the burden of fully two-thirds of this sermon. It is not until the last portion of the sermon that Briscoe finally asks "What does all this mean?" and proceeds to the Proclamation section. By giving this much time to the problem of the frustrations of life, the preacher is true to the text as it acknowledges difficult issues such as the wicked who oppress and seek to kill the righteous (vv. 12, 32, 35).

These weighty life-and-death issues in the text are true to life in the real world as we all experience it. Evil all too often dominates and seems to triumph. The wicked prosper. Bad things happen to good people. Suffering and loss come to people of faith. It is important that the preacher take the time to explore these issues and help people wrestle with them. This is where the ancient biblical text intersects our own lives and speaks to our questions and concerns. The fears and frustrations of life voiced in the text prepare us to receive the good news of the gospel found later in the sermon.

In preaching it is important to develop fully the need or problem which the text addresses. As listeners are able to identify with issues of sin and brokenness or questions about faith and God, they are prepared more fully to hear the proclamation of the gospel. Take the time to develop the need for the gospel, as Briscoe has done in this sermon.

### PROBLEM

Briscoe identifies three aspects of the problem of life's frustrations and in each case points to the psalm: 1) unfulfilled dreams (vv. 4–6); 2) life's injustices (vv. 1, 16–17, 21, 35); and 3) life's battles (vv. 12–13, 23–24, 31–32). In each of these areas the preacher quotes the text, illustrates the problem with contemporary examples from people's lives, and wrestles with the faith issues surrounding these struggles.

In the case of unfulfilled desires (vv. 4–6), Briscoe points to modern examples such as infertility, job loss, divorce, and singles who long to be married. Notice how he places alongside these painful situations the promise of the text: "Delight yourself in the Lord, and he will give you the desires of your heart" (v. 4). Then he says: "We've got a problem here. We know we are supposed to believe verses like this. We have them underlined in our Bibles.... But many of us, if we are honest, would say that behind the smiling exterior is a heart that is frustrated because of unfulfilled desires. We can't figure out why that verse says what it does and our desires remain unfulfilled."

The key word here is *honest*. Briscoe wants us to be honest about those places where our faith doesn't seem to match up to reality. We pray but there seems to be no answer. We trust God, but life doesn't seem to work out as we hoped or imagined. What then? How are we to understand the promise "and he will give you the desires of your heart"? Briscoe goes on to relate this issue to the phrase "Commit your way to the Lord..." (v. 5), and says that our heart's desires must be right and in accord with God's eternal purposes. The stories about Billy Graham, the Civil War soldier, and Joachim Neander all illustrate the point in different ways. God grants to us what is within God's purposes and best for us in the long run. But notice Briscoe's empathetic conversational tone as he concludes the point: "It's hard, isn't it? It can be very frustrating, waiting."

The sermon then takes up the frustration of life's injustices (vv. 1, 16–17, 21, 35). Here the preacher focuses on how those who do not believe in God seem to prosper and have it so good, while the godly often find life so difficult. The ungodly get away with all kinds of dishonest acts. Life seems to work for them: "I have seen the wicked oppressing, and towering like a cedar of Lebanon" (v. 35, NRSV). On the other hand, the godly, who try to trust God and do the right thing, seem to face one moral dilemma after another and often meet failure and rejection.

Notice in this section how Briscoe puts the issues in first-person speech: "Lord, it's rough. Life is unjust." "Why do I have to trust God when all the other people aren't trusting God, and it seems to work for them and it doesn't work for me?" "I'm frustrated, Lord. You told me I have got to do good. The other folks don't do good." "I wait patiently for you [v. 7] and they don't wait patiently for anybody.... Why do I have to wait patiently?" "It's hard, Lord, being godly, living by faith. It's hard doing it your way."

Throughout this portion of the sermon Briscoe has created a dialogue between the people and God. Look back at the sermon and note the pre-dominance of the first-person pronouns "I," "we," and "us" throughout most of the sermon. By this technique Briscoe includes himself with the listener. The preacher is not speaking "at" or "down to" the audience. Rather, preacher and listener are all hearing the text as Word of God together. The "I" and "we" speeches address God directly, responding to the text and voicing how difficult life and faith are.

This first-person style makes the sermon more personal and enables us to identify with the issues. As listeners, we are given permission to express our complaints before God over life's felt injustices. Here Briscoe is helping us wrestle with some of the hard realities of faith in a direct and honest way. In preaching it is good to consider occasionally using this first-person technique as a way of interacting with the text and with our listeners. Only toward the end of the sermon does Briscoe more frequently use the pronoun "you" to address his hearers when in the Response section of the sermon he invites his hearers to believe and to act.

The final problem Briscoe touches on is the frustration of life's battles, referring to battles against evil (vv. 12–13), against life's stumbling blocks (vv. 23–24), and against life's hidden pitfalls (vv. 31–32). As his discussion of the problem concludes, the preacher is ready to proclaim the truths of Psalm 37 which answer the questions raised. He will challenge us to trust ever more deeply in the goodness of God.

## PROCLAMATION

In the face of all the issues outlined, Briscoe identifies four truths which "come through loudly and clearly in this psalm." These, he says, are the lessons we need to learn if we are going to live with the frustrations of life. They are faith affirmations. Our choice is whether we will believe them:

1. Good will eventually prevail (vv. 9–15).
2. God will eternally triumph (vv. 18–20).
3. Grace will continually flow (vv. 23–25).
4. Godliness will ultimately satisfy (vv. 37–40).

These truths are the good news proclaimed in this sermon. As a Wisdom psalm, Psalm 37 instructs us regarding God's protection of the righteous and the inevitable judgment which comes upon the wicked. In the face of so much evil, the psalm exhorts us to trust the Lord, who will vindicate the righteous. We are not to be disturbed by the wicked who will soon pass away (vv. 1–2). The wicked perish, but the good will inherit the land (vv. 9–11). Good will prevail. God is at work even now, and he will eternally triumph (vv. 18–20). God's grace will enable us to live through any circumstances in life (vv. 23–24). Godliness is ultimately more satisfying than ungodliness (vv. 37–40).

The preacher then asks, "Can we believe each of these truths? The question that I have to ask myself is this: Do I allow the frustrations of life to govern my heart, or do I allow these four fundamental principles to be the bedrock of my life and the cause of my attitudes?" In other words, will we accept and believe the good news of this psalm? That is the challenge of faith.

## RESPONSE

Briscoe concludes by returning to the opening verses of the psalm and inviting us to adopt three simple disciplines in response to the problem and proclamation of the text:

1. "Trust in the Lord, and do good" (v. 3). Here, in a series of questions, the preacher asks if we are trusting God with our past and future; and if so, why not trust God with the present, with today? "Trust God in the now… and do what is right!"

2. "Delight in the Lord, and he will give you the desires of your heart" (v. 4). Take delight in God in such a way that God gives you a new set of desires.

3. "Commit your way to the Lord; trust in him, and he will act" (v. 5). Make a commitment to God, continue to trust him day by day, and the promise is that God will act in your life. God will bring healing, deliverance, and freedom from the frustrating circumstances, unfulfilled desires, and injustices of life.

Throughout this sermon Briscoe has let the text point to the needs and issues of life. The text has also proclaimed God's goodness and grace which will ultimately prevail. The response to all of this is simple: Trust, Delight, Commit! The good news is that as we do this, we can begin to discover the peace that passes all human understanding, even in the midst of a world that seems confusing, unfair, and unfulfilling. Psalm 37 proclaims that the way of Wisdom is to trust God. All other appearances to the contrary, faith works! So, "Wait for the Lord, and keep to his way, and he will exalt you" (v. 34).

## SUGGESTIONS

- Consider how you can increase the level of "dialogue" in your preaching as Briscoe has done in this sermon. How can you create greater dialogue between the biblical text and your listeners by your choice of tone and techniques such as first-person speeches which interact with the text and with God?
- Study other Wisdom psalms and compare them with Psalm 37. Do some reading in commentaries on the distinctive themes and characteristics scholars have identified in this type of psalm. Develop one or more sermons based on the following Wisdom psalms: Psalm 1, 14, 36:1–4, 49, 73, 78, 112, 127, 128, 133.
- How do the themes in Psalm 37 and Briscoe's sermon relate to Jesus' teaching in the Gospels? Make a list of Gospel passages which deal with the frustrations of life and the contrast between following Jesus' teaching with following evil and foolish ways. Begin with passages such as Matthew 5:1–12; 6:19–34; 7:13–14; 7:24–27. Develop a sermon series on "The Two Ways: Choosing the Right Path."
- Develop your own sermon on the phrase "Do not fret" (Psalm 37:1, 7, 8), perhaps pairing this text with Matthew 6:25–34.

- For additional reading, see Elizabeth Achtemeier, *Preaching the Old Testament* (Westminster/John Knox Press, 1989). Achtemeier has a good discussion on the importance of the Old Testament for the church and gives some valuable how-to's on preaching from the Old Testament.

*Gary W. Klingsporn*

# WHEN BOOTSTRAPS CAN'T HELP

EPHESIANS 2:8–9

REV. DR. JOHN EAGEN
GRACE CHURCH EDINA
EDINA, MINNESOTA

# WHEN BOOTSTRAPS CAN'T HELP

EPHESIANS 2:8–9

W hen I was five years old, growing up in South Minneapolis, every Saturday morning my life was indelibly enriched by faithfully watching the adventures of Superman. After the program was over, it was my practice to head outside with the largest bath towel I could find. I tied the ends of it around my neck and reenacted the episode I had just watched. Even in those days, I had a hunger for quality, so as I reenacted the episode I made a few changes which I felt would improve the drama! I took the trouble to memorize the standard introduction to every episode: "Faster than a speeding bullet; more powerful than a locomotive; able to leap tall buildings with a single bound. Look up in the sky! It's a bird. It's a plane. No, it's Superman!" I even remembered his mission in that standard opening: "to defend truth, justice and the American way."

At age five, that last part was a little fuzzy to me. Exactly what was "the American way"? As I grew older, that question became clearly answered. The American way was identified by the phrase "bootstraps." It meant working hard to capitalize on, and even create, opportunity — doing for yourself what needed to be done rather than asking or expecting someone else to do it for you. Becoming self-reliant, independent, self-sufficient.

Literally, pulling yourself up by your own bootstraps rather than by accepting a helping hand from someone else.

This ideal is as American as apple pie. And it is given a number of names — among them the "Protestant work ethic." I have found its equivalent in very few nations of the world that I have visited. It has been the foundation for an energetic, industrious, innovative, and ambitious nation of people. Many today believe this aspect of our national life is seriously threatened and in decline. They worry that it is being replaced by a debilitating dependency upon government and by a philosophy of victimization.  The current debate across America about welfare reform, for example, is largely attributable to this philosophy of bootstraps.

Nevertheless, bootstraps remains a powerful aspect of the American psychological and philosophical landscape. This belief spills over into the way people understand God and their relationship to him. For example, it is not at all unusual to find people in our country who will say the way to go to heaven and to spend eternity with God is to live a life sufficiently meritorious so that our good deeds, at least a bit, exceed our bad deeds. And on that basis, we earn or achieve eternal life.

Not long ago, I was talking with a man concerning his understanding about how to go to heaven. He gave me a response which was a typical bootstraps philosophical approach. I asked him how he was doing in this quest of his. His reply was, "I'm doing the best I can." This is the way he would talk about his job or his marriage or his parenting skills: "Just trying to do the very best I can."

World religions are all predicated upon a bootstraps philosophy. Whether we are describing Hinduism or Buddhism or Shintoism or Islam or other world religions, they are all based on the idea that if you live in a certain way and do it well enough, then maybe you can achieve heaven (or whatever it is called). For example, the idea of reincarnation, so hostile to biblical Christianity, is rooted in a bootstraps religious philosophy. In Hinduism, according to whether you have performed well or poorly in your present life, you acquire either good or bad "karma." That karma in a subsequent reincarnated life brings you farther along the path to heaven or takes you farther away. And in the course of subsequent lives, if you live perfectly enough, eventually you become a god yourself and achieve heaven.

Incredibly enough, though it is totally foreign to biblical teaching, this idea of bootstraps religion has even found its way into some expressions of Christianity. Historically there is a tendency for various groups to create bureaucracies that announce the rules and regulations and hoops and trials and tests whereby an individual, through compliance with those rules and regulations, can achieve an opportunity to go to heaven. Such groups may say if you are baptized (especially in their church) or receive communion (especially in their church) or if you go through some set of religious classes (especially in their church), or whatever else the rules and regulations are, then you have earned the right to go to heaven. It is not at all uncommon for various expressions of Christian faith to be predicated upon a bootstraps approach to our relationship with God.

As a result of this, if any of you were to say with absolute confidence to people with whom you live in your neighborhoods or see at work, "I know I am going to heaven," most of the people hearing you say that would accuse you of arrogance and pride. Why? Anyone who accuses you of arrogance about the statement that you are going to heaven is a person who is revealing that he or she embraces a bootstraps philosophy of faith. In their view, by saying you know that you are going to heaven it is as though you are boasting that your merit is so great you are confident of eternal life.

Into this spiritual, psychological, and philosophical milieu comes the radical message of the Bible. Ephesians 2:8-9 (NIV) reads as follows: "For it is by grace you have been saved, through faith — and *this* [italics mine] not from yourselves, it is the gift of God — not by works, so that no one can boast." Let's take a careful look at this text. There are three primary ideas to be considered.

The first consideration is a grammatical one. The pronoun *this* refers to what antecedent? Does it refer to grace? Is it grace that is not of our own? Is it salvation that is not of our own? Or is it the faith that is not of our own? What is not from ourselves? The answer is that all three are not from ourselves! God's grace is not from ourselves. Salvation in Christ is not from ourselves. And — if you can swallow this — even faith does not originate from ourselves.

Jesus said in John 6:44, "No one can come to me unless the Father who sent me draws him." God births in our hearts the desire to believe him and to trust him for our lives. And the radical message here is that this process of salvation is a gift God grants which we act to receive. It is not the result of works, so that "no one can boast."

Let's make sure we understand our terms. *Grace* is used in the Scripture to describe "undeserved favor." It refers to God's disposition toward us without regard to who we are or what we have done or haven't done. It is related only to God's own nature, which is loving and gracious.

By grace we have been *saved.* Salvation refers to the truth that all of us were born with a sin condition — every one of us. As a result, we are separated from the life of God. While we may try to bridge that gap by good works, the Scripture says it cannot be done. So Jesus came into the world and offered the gift of that bridge. Our role is to receive it by faith, believing Christ to be God's Son and receiving him into our lives. Salvation refers to reunion with God and both fellowship with him now (knowing him now) as well as in his timeless eternity.

What is *faith?* Every person in the state of Minnesota is a person of faith. Now I didn't say what they have faith in, but simply that every person is a person of faith. When you are seated, you believe that the chair is going to hold you. If you sit under a roof, you believe that it will not collapse on you. When you get into a car, you express faith in that vehicle and the roads and in other drivers' behavior.

Faith is common and universal. Religious faith is common and almost universal. Buddhists believe things. Hindus believe things. Muslims believe things. And some people say Christian faith is to believe that God will do a certain thing for you. Many people are disappointed with God because they trusted him for something that he failed to perform for them, and as a result they become bitter and resentful.

That is not what the Bible teaches about faith. The Bible says faith begins with information from God's Word. It is no leap in the dark, no blind step, nothing done in ignorance. Faith starts with what God has specifically said. The next step is to come to a conclusion about whether what God has said is true or not. That is an act of your will. Faith starts with your mind in acquiring information about the Scriptures, moves to your will as to whether it is true, and finally leads you to act upon what the Word says. So biblical faith starts with the Bible, moves to belief, and ends up with action or response. This sequence is beautifully portrayed in Romans 10:13–17.

What does the word *works* refer to in the phrase "not by works, so that no one can boast"? The Bible uses the term *works* to describe behaviors that are generally deemed by society to be positive, salutary, and favorable actions; that is, doing good deeds, doing things particularly for other people. As Romans 3:20 clearly and unequivocally states, absolutely no one can ameliorate their sin problem and find their way to heaven on the basis of their good works. So the radical message of the Scripture in this bootstraps nation of ours is that we cannot build that bridge to God. Only God can do that for us, and it is done not because we deserve it but on the basis of his mercy and his grace and as a gift offered. Our response is to receive the gift.

This past week I read a poem entitled "The Pit" by Kenneth Philkens. It reminded me of this truth. Here is how it goes:

A man fell into a pit and he couldn't get out.
A Subjective Person came along and said: "I feel for you down there."
An Objective Person came along and said: "It's logical that someone would fall down there."
A Christian Scientist came along and said: "You only think that you are in the pit."
A Charismatic Triumphalist came along and said: "Just confess you are not in the pit."
A Pharisee said: "Only a bad person would fall in a pit."
A Fundamentalist said: "You deserve your pit."

Buddha said: "Your pit is only a state of mind."

A Hindu said: "Your pit is for purging you and making you more perfect."

Confucius said: "If you would have listened to me, you would never have fallen into that pit."

A New Ager said: "Maybe you should network with some other pit dwellers."

An Evolutionist said: "You are a rejected mutant destined to be removed from the evolutionary cycle. You are going to die in the pit so you do not produce inferior pit-falling offspring."

A Self-Pitying Person said: "You haven't seen anything until you've seen my pit."

A News Reporter said: "Could I have the exclusive story on your pit?"

An I.R.S. Man said: "Have you paid your taxes on the pit?"

A County Inspector said: "Do you have a permit for that pit?"

A Realist said: "That's a pit."

An Idealist said: "The world shouldn't have pits."

An Optimist said: "Things could be worse."

A Pessimist said: "Things will get worse."

Jesus, seeing the man, took him by the hand and lifted him out of the pit.[1]

There are some who have a problem in accepting God's grace because of the way they tenaciously embrace bootstraps. Let me describe them in two categories. First are those in religious authority who run the religious bureaucracies and are very threatened by the idea that salvation is based upon God's grace and is a gift to all people. That kind of thinking disempowers them from the loyalty and allegiance they seek to engender from their followers through the rules and regulations of the bureaucracies. Many of you have come out of these religious systems.

Yet, some who escape such systems experience an irony. You would think there would be a sense of exhilaration at being out from under the yoke of such a system. But, in fact, I have met some of these people who find it hard to accept God's grace because they rather like the idea of boot-straps. They have pulled themselves up by their bootstraps from the time when they were very young and have accomplished "this and that" in life. This is *their* education, this is *their* knowledge, this is *their* job accomplish-ment, this is *their* family, and this is *their* health, etc. And all of the stuff with which they surround themselves as a basis of feeling okay about themselves is based on the idea of pride and arrogance.

Some think, "I can get my way to heaven." The message of the Bible is: it cannot be done. Let me illustrate the point. Now it may be true that some are better swimmers than others, but everyone trying to swim the Atlantic Ocean will drown. Whether you drown at the first mile mark or the twen-tieth mile mark is a small consolation as you head to the bottom of the Atlantic.

Into this understanding of grace comes humility. God did something for us which we could not do for ourselves. Jesus is the only one who can lift us out of that pit. The Bible says in John 1:12: "Yet to all who received him, to those who believed in his name, he gave the right to become chil-dren of God." Notice that the right to become a child of God is not a func-tion of a set of perfect behaviors or hoops or rules and regulations. It is receiving Christ.

What does that mean? Romans 10 tells us that the way a person comes into a personal, forgiven relationship with Christ is to believe that Jesus is precisely who he claimed himself to be: God's Son who came to earth, who died for our sins to pay the penalty our sins deserve, who was buried, rose again from the dead, ascended into heaven, and now is preparing to return to earth. The Scripture says that we must believe those things. But more than that, we have to receive Christ as the gift of eternal life. A gift offered is possessed only when it has been received.

So the Scripture tells us that the next step is to ask Christ to come into our life, to become our personal Lord and Savior. It does not happen by osmosis or by growing up in a home with others who have received Christ, or by good intentions, or by goodwill. It happens when we act upon the gift presented to us and ask Christ to come into our life to forgive us and to wash us clean from our sin and make us his man or his woman.

The Scripture raises the question: "When is a good day for someone to experience this gift of salvation?" 2 Corinthians 6 answers it by saying: "Today!"

Has God brought you to a place today where you are ready to trust him for your eternal life? Are you ready to surrender the bootstraps and all the human efforts to "earn" heaven, to surrender the idea that you don't "need" salvation? You know you do. No one is perfect. Are you ready to surrender the unbiblical notion that because you are better than some other people, you are likely to go to heaven? Are you ready to accept God's free gift of eternal life?

If you are, you can pray a prayer something like this:

*"Gracious heavenly Father: I admit to you today that I am a sinner and that I have fallen short of your perfect moral standard. I know that Christ is your Son and that Jesus died for me. I know he rose again from the dead. Right now, I ask you to come into my life and to forgive me. I want to receive the gift of eternal life. I want to turn away from sin and I want to follow Christ and be the person in Christ he wants me to be. Because I believe you have done this, right now, Lord, I want to thank you. In Jesus' Name. Amen."*

Notes
1. Kenneth Philkens, "The Pit," Source unknown.

## COMMENT

John Eagen's sermon "When Bootstraps Can't Help" is a fine example of a
doctrinal sermon with a solid evangelical thrust. In a clear, straightforward
manner the sermon presents the biblical doctrine of salvation by grace
alone through faith in Jesus Christ. *Sola gratia:* "by grace alone," the cry of
the Protestant Reformation, resounds throughout this sermon. The sermon
challenges the widespread popular "bootstraps" philosophy of modern culture that we are self-made, self-sufficient human beings who by working
hard enough can make it on our own and somehow even earn heaven.
Here in classical Protestant theological expression, the preacher asserts the
supremacy and all-sufficiency of Christ as the only means of salvation over
against every notion of human merit or works righteousness as a means of
becoming right with God.

### PROBLEM

This sermon effectively brings the doctrine of salvation by grace into dialogue with modern culture and with popular notions of achievement familiar to all of us. By building the sermon around the image of "bootstraps" as
an expression of the American ideal of opportunity and hard work, Eagen
has brought the biblical concept of grace directly into conversation with
our well-known and cherished American ideal of self-reliance. This creates
not simply a nice comparison between "bootstraps" and "grace," but a compelling contrast in which the biblical notion of grace radically challenges
some of our most deeply held assumptions about meaning, purpose, and
success.

To state the problem, Eagen begins the sermon with the vivid childhood memory of reenacting scenes from the adventures of "Superman."
From there he focuses on the memorable phrase "the American way" from
the Superman episodes. "What is the American way?" he asks. Part of it,
Eagen has come to realize, is working hard to create opportunity and to

capitalize on it. It means doing for yourself what needs to be done rather than expecting help from anyone else. It means pulling yourself up by your own bootstraps rather than accepting a helping hand from someone else. The bootstraps philosophy "is as American as apple pie" and constitutes a powerful aspect of the American psychological and philosophical landscape.

Eagen quickly connects the bootstraps philosophy with popular spirituality by saying that the notion "spills over into the way people understand God and their relationship to him" (para. 4). The popular belief widespread among people is that salvation is somehow ultimately achieved by living a life of good deeds and doing the best we can to please God. Indeed, Eagen asserts, even some expressions of Christianity set down rules and rituals through which people seem to "earn" the right to go to heaven (para. 7). Later, he suggests that there are some in religious authority who subtly promote a bootstraps view of faith in order to maintain power structures in their religious systems. Even those who reject such systems often find it hard to accept God's grace because they rather like the idea of bootstraps faith and because they live by that philosophy in every other area of their lives.

The problem this sermon addresses, then, is the subtle or not-so-subtle illusion that we can somehow earn, merit, or achieve eternal life with God. The idea that we can earn the right to go to heaven, or somehow make our way to heaven on our own, is a profound contradiction of biblical faith and of the Christian gospel. "The message of the Bible is that it cannot be done," says Eagen. And yet, a bootstraps view of faith widely persists in the popular mind, fed by American cultural beliefs and by biblical illiteracy.

By choosing the "bootstraps" image for this sermon, Eagen has tapped into something deeply ingrained in much of our American history and culture. The "bootstraps" philosophy he describes is so much a part of "the American way" and "the American dream" that it is commonly accepted at material and economic levels by most people in North America. It is a common social and economic philosophy, especially among affluent middle-

and upper-class Americans who have benefited from the privilege of economic opportunity in our society. As a material and economic philosophy, it easily influences our spiritual and theological beliefs.

As we have noted, this is a doctrinal sermon on the role of grace in salvation. When we preach on such a biblical or doctrinal theme, it is possible to focus so much on the presentation of the theme or doctrine itself that we fail to relate it effectively to the contemporary needs or life situations of our listeners. We can become so involved in presenting the biblical knowledge and insights that we easily forget every good sermon must speak to people where they are.

Some of our best biblical exegesis and theological reflection can fall short of effective proclamation if it does not connect with the day-to-day needs and issues in the lives of our listeners. Good preaching must not only be faithful to the biblical tradition, but it must be relevant. It must speak home to the hearts of our people and gain meaning and application in their lives.

By discussing the biblical concept of grace in relation to popular "bootstraps" thinking, Eagen connected with his original listeners in a congregation in an affluent suburban context. At the same time, the sermon speaks to large segments of privileged North American society and proclaims that at the very center of life, in the place of ultimate meaning and purpose, "bootstraps can't help." We cannot earn or achieve life and salvation. Only the God of grace can give us true life.

COMMENT

## TEXT

After he has described the problem he is addressing in the sermon, Eagen introduces the text in three short sentences: "Into this spiritual, psychological, and philosophical milieu comes the radical message of the Bible. Ephesians 2:8–9 reads as follows: 'For it is by grace you have been saved, through faith — and this not from yourselves, it is the gift of God — not by works, so that no one can boast.' Let's take a careful look at this text" (para. 9).

Here the preacher introduces the text in a very simple way and places it alongside the description of the problem (bootstraps religion). The words of the text counter all notions of bootstrap faith: "It is by grace,…this [is] not from yourselves, it is the gift of God — not by works.…" Here the text speaks for itself and challenges all popular distortions of the gospel. Note how the preacher connects the text to the problem: "Into this…milieu comes the radical message of the Bible." He then lets the text speak in the remainder of the sermon.

## PROCLAMATION

All that remains is for the preacher to interpret three key words in the text: *grace, saved, faith.* In the proclamation section of the sermon Eagen declares that grace, salvation, and faith all come from God, not from our-selves. *Grace* is God's undeserved favor for us, coming from the very nature of God's own character of love. *Salvation* is being restored by God from sinful separation to reunion and fellowship with God. *Faith* is a believing acceptance of what the Scripture says about God. Even faith originates from God, not from ourselves! The Ephesians text says none of this is by "works," or good deeds we as humans do. All of this is from God alone as a gift to us.

Notice how carefully the preacher here stays right on task in the proclamation. Grace, salvation, and faith are rich and complex biblical themes extending throughout the Scriptures with endless variations of story and nuance. So much could be said about each of them. Three more sermons could be preached within this sermon. But it is important that the preacher stay focused and disciplined. Eagen does that. He defines grace, salvation, and faith minimally but adequately, then returns to the primary focus of the sermon: the problem of bootstraps theology.

One of the great temptations in preaching is to say too much and to develop too many ideas in one sermon. This sermon is not designed to explore all the depth and meaning of the concepts of grace, faith, or salva-tion. Its singular focus is that a bootstraps philosophy cannot save us. Every good sermon should have one primary point or thesis throughout. There may be subpoints or secondary points, but they should serve the main point. Listeners should be able to hear clearly that one primary point in the sermon.

In sermon preparation it is important then to ask ourselves, "What is the primary point of my sermon?" Early in the process of preparation it is helpful to write out the sermon's thesis statement and to use that statement as a guide in writing, shaping, editing and revising the sermon.

When your sermon notes or manuscript are completed, ask yourself again if everything in the sermon is necessary to make that one point. If it's not necessary, then omit it! Effective preaching requires discipline and focus. We may have a great story or illustration we want to share, but if it finally doesn't fit the sermon's thesis, or if it lengthens the sermon beyond toleration, it's best to save it for another day and another sermon.

Eagen summarizes the proclamation of the text by saying: "The radical message of the Scripture in this bootstraps nation of ours is that we cannot build that bridge to God. Only God can do that for us, and it is done not because we deserve it but on the basis of his mercy and his grace and as a gift offered." This is a good example of the thesis statement of a sermon. Here in two sentences is the essence of the sermon. Notice again how the bootstraps image is carried consistently through the sermon and appears in this summarizing statement near the sermon's end. The preacher has taken us from problem to text to proclamation of the text. The invitation to respond will be the final step in the preaching process.

RESPONSE

The invitation to believe and to act in this sermon is simply stated: "Our response is to receive the gift." This means believing that Jesus is who he claimed to be—the Son of God incarnate in human flesh (Romans 10). It means asking Christ to come into our lives, to become our personal Lord and Savior. "Today" is the day to receive Christ and accept this free gift of eternal life.

The preacher concludes the sermon by returning to the problem addressed from the beginning: "Are you ready to surrender the bootstraps and all the human efforts to 'earn' heaven?" The sermon then closes with an invitation to receive Christ, to accept God's grace.

The invitation and the closing prayer of salvation stand within the great tradition of American evangelical Christianity. It is appropriate that this sermon on the biblical doctrine of salvation not simply end with a nice closing story, poem, or thought. Rather, the sermon ends with a clear and direct invitation to act, and to receive this free gift of eternal life from God. From start to finish, the sermon has been clear and consistent with the biblical text: By grace alone we are saved through faith and this is the gift of God! Luther and Calvin would be proud, along with centuries of saints and martyrs. *Sola gratia!*

## SUGGESTIONS

- If you haven't preached recently on this biblical text, develop a sermon around Ephesians 2:1–10 focusing on verses 8–9. What "problem" or need would you see your sermon addressing in your ministry context?
- The notion of needing to gain or earn acceptance with God is commonplace in every age. How have you personally experienced this tendency in your own life? How can you address this issue in one of your sermons? Can you begin the sermon by telling your own story?
- The "bootstraps" image gives this sermon coherence and focus. In your next five sermons, try to choose one image or metaphor which becomes the controlling image for each sermon.
- Have you preached any "doctrinal" sermons lately? If so, how do you feel about them? If not, what doctrinal themes might you address? Make a list of them and why you feel each is important. How can you address them from the pulpit? How can you make each one relevant to your listeners?

*Gary W. Klingsporn*

# THE
# ECOLOGY OF
# THE SOUL

LUKE 12:13–21

REV. DR. RUSSELL FRIEND-JONES
MAYFLOWER CHURCH
MINNEAPOLIS, MINNESOTA

REV. DR. RUSSELL FRIEND-JONES

# THE ECOLOGY OF THE SOUL

## A SERMON FOR TWO VOICES

### LUKE 12:13–21

I worshiped with an overflowing Siberian congregation on Easter Sunday three years ago. The Scripture was from Matthew. Before the minister read the text, he gravely said to the congregation: "Some of you are hearing this text for the first time. Some of you are hearing it for the last. Have you attended to the needs of your soul?"

This is the central question of our text this morning. In Luke 12:13–21, two children argue over the division of a family inheritance. An entrepreneur engages in self-congratulation for a year of outstanding growth and expansion. With a sizable portfolio of investments, with the future financially secure, a person of considerable wealth thinks that all of life's needs have been met, and decides to retire — to eat, drink, and be merry.

Alarmed at this thinking, Jesus appears to become the wet blanket at the celebration. Against human achievement he sets human mortality. Into this mix of human activity, he sets a different measure altogether.

"What does it profit anyone," Jesus asks, "if that person gains the whole world and loses his or her own soul?" (Mark 8:36). But if life does not consist in the abundance of our possessions, in what does it consist? What if, as Alexander Solzhenitsyn once pondered, "the meaning of earthly existence lay not, as we have grown accustomed to thinking, in prosperity but...in the development of the soul?"

*The year was 1974. It was one of those breezy, cool, spring mornings in South Paris, Maine. After stopping at the church on Main Street, I drove around Market Square to the post office to drop off some mail. I could see Marvin Beebe talking to customers in the paint and wallpaper store, but I didn't recognize them. Wilbur Viles, Tally DeCato's father, and president of the South Paris Savings Bank, was entering Roland French's barber shop to get a trim. "Pokie" French was a silver-haired gentleman who lived on Pine Street, across from us. I waved at them both. They waved back, smiling. Claire Matolcsy was just entering the town Selectmen's office on some business. I always thought it looked more like a store-front church than the deliberating chambers for local government, but Claire would not have been caught in any church, much less a store-front.*

*Dick the barber yelled from his shop across the street to Chandler Bean. Chandler changed his direction and headed toward Dick's. I turned off Main and onto Western Avenue, and then again onto a narrower street lined with tall, swaying pine trees. I drove up a steep hill and parked my car in front of a modest shingled home. It belonged to Helen and Don Preble and their two sons, Jeffrey and David. Don was an accountant and treasurer of my church. The boys were in junior high and elementary school. Helen had always been very quiet, and it was through her illness of the last year that we became close.*

*I approached the side door. I hadn't called ahead; it wasn't necessary in those days. I knew she would be glad to see me, but I carried a heavy heart that morning. I came bearing a message that would be difficult for both of us, but I also knew it couldn't be delayed. I knocked.*

I've always thought that a primary indicator of the condition of the soul can be seen in a person's sense of humor. If a part of you inhabits the larger universe of the spirit, then you will see reasons for mirth in the muddles of the situations we create. Some of our most serious efforts will cause you to smile. Even in the midst of great tragedies, a well developed soul may laugh. Humor may be wry and ironical, or adolescent or silly. It may be slapstick or subtle. But a lack of humor reveals a seriously neglected soul.

*Once I gave what I thought was a particularly brilliant sermon. I had traveled somewhere by airplane. I had plugged those little headphones into my ears and listened to a Mozart sonata at 30,000 feet. My remarks that Sunday were about mystery, and I expounded at length on the marvel of music in the air. The composer had been dead for centuries; the musicians had gone their separate ways years ago; the studio technicians were sleeping soundly somewhere below. Yet here I was, enthralled and excited by the beauty and mystery of the same music that had enthralled and excited so many others.*

*After the service we shook hands at the door of the sanctuary. "Reverend Jones," Helen commented in her dry down-easterly manner, "I don't think I've ever met anyone who could make so much out of so little."*

Souls require a special kind of care — a care which our culture neglects. Most therapy is oriented toward solving problems and helping us adjust to life's situations. But care for the soul sometimes takes us into those situations, however ominous they may appear. There we may wrest knowledge to be gained nowhere else. Curators of the soul will not keep us from the valleys of death's shadow; they will accompany us on our journeys through threatening places.

*After a few minutes Helen responded to my knock. A person could tell that the cancer and the chemotherapy were using her body for a battlefield, but when she greeted me that morning she was alert, chipper, and bubbly. I sat at the kitchen table. She put on a fresh pot of coffee. She set out a plate of freshly baked peanut butter cookies. We chatted about the boys, the church, the weather. She told me how Don was so strong for her, even though he knew that her condition was terminal.*

*She worried about how he would do when she was gone, but she was sure he would manage fine. We talked about the last chemotherapy treatment and the progressing weakness that was overtaking her. Still, she intended to see both boys attain the rank of Eagle Scout and graduate from high school. Jeffrey had six or seven years to go. So she was planning to stick around for a while, whatever it took.*

*More than a year before, Helen had received the fateful diagnosis of an aggressive cancer that was, essentially, untreatable.*

*Chemotherapy offered the hope of additional weeks — at best, months, but nothing more. The doctors at that time had been unanimous and grim as they pronounced a verdict: she had, at most, a matter of weeks to live. She and Don decided she would begin the chemotherapy at once. They decided to be open with everyone abut the nature of the illness and the prognosis. And they decided not to give in.*

*The news got back to South Paris almost before the Prebles did. That first evening friends called and stopped by with casseroles. Most people were not comfortable actually talking about the disease or prognosis in Helen's presence. They said simply, "Hope you're feeling better soon," or, "Take care of yourself, you hear?" Helen smiled at their reticence. Understanding their reluctance, she sensed behind their awkwardness an ocean of goodwill and concern. She graciously accepted their presents as evidence of their love, and their reticence as evidence of their helplessness before the mystery that was invading their community.*

What is your soul? Your body can be photographed. Your lungs can be X-rayed. CAT scans can give tangible evidence of the electrical activity of your brain. Psychological instruments have been developed to give an objective look at your personality. Molecular geneticists can even examine your DNA and discover all sorts of things. Sociologists and market researchers can look at the patterns of your life based on your place in this or that demographic category. While all of these may touch on the soul, they are not your soul, and the sum total of these does not define it.

What is this thing which is "more than food" but less weighty than a pixie's sneeze? Where is this elusive and ephemeral quality of our selves which Jesus regarded as more important than the accumulation of wealth, power, accomplishment, and prestige? Psychotherapist Thomas Moore thinks that this question, taken seriously, will revolutionize our practices in psychology, religion, politics, and economics. Answering will contribute to the healing of our cities and our world as well as of ourselves.

Dr. Moore recently published a book on this subject, *Care of the Soul*, which has been on the *New York Times* best-seller list since last December.[1] No doubt many of you have read it. He says it as well as anyone: "…Soul lies midway between understanding and [the] unconscious: its instrument is neither the mind nor the body, but imagination.… Soul is in the middle, holding together mind and body, ideas and life, spirituality and the world. Fulfilling work, rewarding relationships, personal power, and relief from symptoms — [these] are gifts of the soul." The soul is the seat of the imagination. Love is its language. The soul requires attention, cultivation, and care. The aim of what he calls "soul-work" is not adjustment to accepted norms, but the fostering of "a richly elaborated life, connected to society and nature and woven into the culture of family, nation and globe." Care of the soul is an "application of poetics to life."

> *Sometimes when people did try to speak to Helen and Don, they said the opposite of what they intended. I was with Helen when a neighbor came by. As she handed the foil-wrapped casserole to Helen she said to her, "I hope this doesn't kill you." Helen burst out laughing, but the young woman's face turned as red as a sugar maple in autumn. The more she tried to extract her foot from her mouth the worse it got, but Helen laughed until the neighbor was laughing too. That's the kind of woman she was.*

One's soul never exists or develops apart from its context. Its context includes its community, its vocation, and its heritage. Dr. Moore believes it especially includes family. Indeed, he calls the family "the nest of soul."

> *Although her "sentence" had been delivered in the depths of winter, and not many of us thought she would live through spring, Helen and Don and the boys planned a summer trip. Helen had always wanted to visit Washington, D.C., so the whole family drove south. Helen and Hurricane Agnes arrived at roughly the same time, so you might say she*

*took the capital by storm. The Prebles saw the hallowed halls of Congress, visited the White House, the monuments, and spent days in the Smithsonian. Like many another tourist, Helen complained of the humidity, the crowds, the rudeness of the people, but she loved the city. Her one disappointment came when she went to visit the Pentagon. The Prebles arrived just after a large group of demonstrators. These long-haired "hippies" had formed a ring around the Pentagon and were trying to levitate it or make it disappear. Rock-ribbed Republican and practical mother that she was, this was all nonsense to her, and their rowdy behavior spoiled the moment.*

*They actually took several trips. The next summer, they made arrangements to hire a caravan, as they called it, and they planned an itinerary that would take them from the seacoast of Maine to the Grand Canyon and points beyond. Helen carefully calculated the distances, and made arrangements to receive chemotherapy treatments in local hospitals at strategic points along the way. She ordered a supply of chemicals, needles, and tubes, and intended to pack them with the other gear they were going to stow on board.*

There was a time when I thought souls, if they existed at all, were autonomous, isolated, individual entities on their journeys to heaven or hell. This radical individualism permeates Western thinking. This is certainly what the Siberian pastor had in mind. John Bunyan's classic, *Pilgrim's Progress*, describes the journey of an individual soul through hardships and temptation until it finds its way to God. In my own evangelical upbringing, I was taught that my soul ultimately stands alone before God Almighty's awful judgment. Is it any wonder that I was lonely? This is a veritable prescription for isolation and alienation. In the church of my childhood, "attending to my soul" involved strangling my imagination and creativity, and subjecting myself to the rigid dogmas of my elders. This is hardly what Dr. Moore has in mind.

But the boundaries of the soul need not be rigid, fixed, or immutable. They can be soft and permeable. The soul exists in and for community, in and for the world. When the Old Testament writer wanted to describe the depth of love between two men, he wrote, "The *soul* of Jonathan was bound to the *soul* of David…or he loved him as he loved his own life." Tolstoy describes two of his characters as "sharing the same soul." These are examples of what feminist ethicist Diana Fritz Cates calls "character friends."[2] Character friends live their lives in mutual awareness of their love for each other and in their mutual commitment to deepening that love. Over time, she observes, they come to share a self; they come to share a soul.

> The treatments, of course, made Helen nauseated and weak. She lost her hair but acquired a rather attractive hairpiece with a good fit. She continued to lose weight, but she must have altered her clothing, for it always looked neatly tailored. All that winter and spring, she continued to show up for Sunday worship. She attended the coffee hours in the large vestry downstairs, but I noticed a difference. She enjoyed herself more now. She entered into the conversations; she took the initiative. She didn't hold back as she had in the past. She was determined to live. The love she shared with Don blossomed; sometimes they looked and acted like giddy young lovers whose intimacies embarrassed the rest of us. If anything, Helen was more alive now than at any time I had known her.

I never thought about souls having size, since they were considered immaterial. But in the same year that Helen was planning her family's great North American tour, a professor of philosophical theology in Berkeley, California, was developing a new idea about size — the size of God, the size of the soul, size as a measure of value. Dr. Bernard M. Loomer was beginning to write not about physical size, but about the stature of the soul, the largeness of the spirit. "By size," he wrote, "I mean the range and depth of your love, your capacity for relationships, the volume of life you can take into your being and still maintain your integrity. I mean the strength of your spirit to encourage others to become freer in the development of their diversity and uniqueness."[3]

When souls are cultivated and cared for, they will grow and expand.

They will become more inclusive. Their boundaries will become more permeable; they will be increasingly more godlike and worldly, as they allow the energies of God and the world to flow through them.

*The day came when Helen, Don, David, and Jeff climbed into the caravan, drove out their driveway, down the tree-lined hill of a street, and made a right turn across America. I don't remember their exact itinerary, but it took her to places I often dream of going. I know they saw the Grand Canyon, Little Big Horn, and the great stone presidents. They visited Yellowstone, Yosemite, Lake Tahoe, and Disneyland. They drove through the Rockies.*

*They came to Minneapolis on their journey, not knowing that their pastor would be invited to a church here the following summer. Actually, they came to Bloomington. It wasn't the Guthrie Theatre or the lakes that attracted them. It wasn't that they had friends or family here. It was the Minnesota Twins. Helen had been a Twins fan for years, and she planned the trip so they would arrive when the Twins were playing at Metropolitan Stadium. To see the mighty Harmon Killebrew and Rod Carew on their own turf was another dream come true. I hope they each hit one for Helen.*

*They returned to Maine. Although it had been difficult, Helen survived another winter and was there to greet me with coffee and cookies that morning as I sat at her kitchen table. After we chatted a bit more, I told her what I had come to say. I had accepted the invitation of a large downtown church in Minneapolis to join the staff. I wouldn't be leaving immediately, and we'd have more opportunities to talk. But I would be gone by the time the school year began. She was among the very first to know, and I asked her not to discuss the matter outside the family. I told her how much she meant to me, how much she had given me, and how much I would miss these visits.*

*She was quiet for a while. Then she asked how Gretchen felt about the move, and the new church and community. She said she had come to depend on me and would have to find another way now, but it was for the best and she knew she would be okay. She said she was happy for me and wanted only the best. After a few more pleasantries, I took my leave, feeling the guilt of being about to abandon a good friend in her hour of need.*

*We had a number of visits before I left in July. Through a particular dream she shared, I am confident that she accepted my departure, and even blessed it. She, Don, and I cried together through the reception following my last Sunday with them.*

*Helen passed away more than a year later, on December 6, 1975 — not before, however, her eldest son graduated from high school.*

Are souls eternal? Our Siberian preacher certainly thought so. That's the point, after all, of so much religious practice: to guarantee the afterlife. "Fire insurance" it's been called—"pie in the sky when we die by and by." But unless she changed her views after I left, Helen wasn't at all sure about the afterlife. Oh, she accepted it as a remote possibility, but she didn't pin any hopes on it. Perhaps that's why she lived so expansively and fully in the present moment. She believed that this life might be all that she would have.

There is some dispute, of course, about the meaning of the word *eternal* in Scripture. Literally it means "life of the age." Some suggest it is the age to come, the age of God's *basileia*, the age of God's unchallenged reign over all creation, the age when wars cease, and all tears are wiped away. Others translate "eternal life" as "authentic life"—life that is genuine, congruent, and grounded in divine reality. Mere duration into infinity has nothing to do with any serious definition. Always there is an element of the soul's transformation involved. In Christian teaching there is an element of giftedness about it, of God's gracious and loving embrace.

I asked a good friend of mine, Casey Alexander, what she believed about the soul. Casey said it this way: "The soul is the seat of the precious love and life that God gives us. It is something so exquisite and lovely that God insists it will be eternal."

*John Coleman once wrote that saints are those who "invite us to conceptualize our lives in ways other than mastery, usefulness, autonomy, and control." They invite us into a world where virtue has meaning.*

*They invite us into the world of the soul's development. Those of us who were privileged to share her last years regarded Helen Preble's life as just such an invitation. She never would have accepted being called a saint. She was too rascally and straightforward for that. She suspended no laws of nature. She worked no obvious miracles. Yet when cancer clasped her tightly in its grasp, never to free her again in this life, Helen rose up against it. She grew big in stature even as her body wasted away from the combined ravages of the cancer and its treatment. Although she would laugh to hear me say it, she was a big soul, and a big saint in the temple of my spirit. She taught me much about the care and feeding of the soul.*

## Notes

1. Thomas Moore, *Care of the Soul* (New York: Harper Collins Publishers, Inc., 1992), p. xiii.
2. Diana Fritz Cates, "Toward An Ethic of Shared Selfhood", *The Annual Society of Christian Ethics,* 1991, pp. 249-57.
3. Bernard M. Loomer, "S-I-Z-E", *Criterion,* Spring, 1974, p.6.

# COMMENT

"Helen Preble's life taught me much about the care and feeding of the soul." This is the point of the sermon by Russell Friend-Jones, "The Ecology of the Soul." This sermon is a study in complexity. It takes a difficult subject, "the care of the soul," and explores it in some depth from multiple perspectives.

In this sermon we hear from Scripture, a Siberian preacher, psychologists like Thomas Moore, writers like Bunyan and Tolstoy, an ethicist, and a philosophical theologian. But most of all, we hear from Helen Preble, a woman dying of cancer. The writers and thinkers have profound things to say about the soul. But Helen Preble, a real person like you and me, is finally the heart of this sermon. Her story "proclaims" truth in a powerful way, and it is Helen who finally teaches us much about the care and feeding of the soul.

This sermon was chosen for *The Library of Distinctive Sermons* for two reasons. First, it is a beautiful reflection on an important subject, the tending of the soul. Much North American religion has focused on "the soul" almost exclusively as a matter of individual salvational concern. Care of the soul has often meant no more than "Are you saved?" The focus is on radical individualism. As Friend-Jones says of his own childhood experience, "Attending to my soul involved strangling my imagination and creativity and subjecting myself to the rigid dogmas of my elders."

But Friend-Jones seeks to expand our understanding. Caring for the soul is about growing as a person, and it requires "soul-work." It is about humor and creativity and imagination. Souls exist in and for community and the world, not just for ourselves or the afterlife. The soul is about the way we respond to this life, as Helen Preble responded to her life-threatening struggle with cancer. "The Ecology of the Soul" may challenge some of our theological assumptions and cause us to wonder about our definitions. That's a distinctive point of the sermon: true caring for the soul will always challenge us to grow.

Second, the sermon is included in this volume because of its unique form as a "sermon for two voices." When originally presented, Friend-Jones and a member of his congregation preached this sermon in dialogue form, one preacher speaking the Helen Preble passages and the other the alternating sections. The form is ideal for this particular sermon. On a practical level, the use of two very different voices relieves the listener of the problem of having to focus attention on one person's voice throughout a fairly lengthy and complex sermon. On an intellectual level it creates an interesting interplay between two speakers and among the speakers and congregation. But most important, the dialogue form allows Helen Preble's story, her "voice," to unfold first as illustration for the subject of the sermon, and eventually as the sermon itself. Woven throughout the sermon, Helen's story powerfully addresses the question of soul-care, proclaims the gospel, and invites us to care for our own souls.

## TEXT

Notice that Friend-Jones has chosen to focus on the biblical text (Luke 12:13–21) in the opening paragraphs of the sermon. This Gospel lesson will have been read earlier in worship or just prior to the sermon. As he begins, Friend-Jones simply recalls the passage for his listeners: "Two children argue over the division of a family inheritance. An entrepreneur engages in self-congratulation for a year of outstanding growth and expansion" and decides simply to "eat, drink, and be merry." Over against this thinking, Friend-Jones contrasts Jesus' point of view — that life does not consist in the abundance of possessions — by quoting Mark 8:36 (appropriate to the Luke 12 passage): "What does it profit anyone if a person gains the whole world and loses his or her own soul?"

Placing the biblical text in the opening lines of the introduction, Friend-Jones allows the rest of the sermon to interpret and proclaim Jesus' point. The true meaning of life is not in arguing over family inheritances or building bigger barns to store more possessions. Rather, taking care of the soul is what life is finally all about.

In the remainder of the sermon, Friend-Jones lets psychologists, writ-crs, theologians, and Helen Preble explore the meaning of Jesus' parable of the Rich Fool. But Jesus' words, heard before the sermon and in the opening lines of the sermon, are always there, playing between the lines of the dialogue, mysteriously and unavoidably lurking around the edges of the sermon: "What does it profit anyone...?"

Some readers or preachers schooled in certain traditions of homiletics may miss in this sermon the kind of detailed exposition of the biblical text to which they are accustomed in preaching. Phrase-by-phrase exposition is certainly a valuable and effective preaching tool, but it is not the only form of preaching offering a valid proclamation of the Word. It is important to vary one's styles and preaching forms. A steady diet of expository sermons can be too much of a good thing. Try a story sermon or a dialogue sermon now and then. Look back over "The Ecology of the Soul" and ask yourself if there are not other creative ways of proclaiming a text. Think about how you can do this kind of sermon if you haven't used this form.

Friend-Jones briefly places the text at the very beginning of the sermon. He trusts the hearer with the text. He chooses not to drum the lines and phrases of the text into the listener with detailed citations of Greek or Hebrew word meanings or esoteric grammar. He treats the text sparingly but effectively. He allows the biblical story to speak for itself in and through the lives of real human beings like Helen Preble.

It's a good point: Let the "story," the incredible good news of the gospel of Jesus Christ, speak for itself whenever you can! Simply offer it to yourself and to your hungry listeners, and through the power of the Holy Spirit, the Word itself will feed the soul.

## QUESTION

The question which Friend-Jones's sermon addresses is clear in the opening lines. It is raised by the Siberian minister: "Have you attended to the needs of your soul?" Friend-Jones then immediately says, "This is the central question of our text (Luke 12:13–21) this morning." That is clear and to the point. We know very early exactly what issue this sermon addresses in our lives. Jesus' word about materialism and "losing the soul," and

Solzhenitsyn's phrase "development of the soul" carry us immediately into Helen's story. The rest of the sermon asks: "What is the soul? How do we care for the soul?"

## PROCLAMATION

As we observed earlier, this sermon proclaims the importance of caring for the soul by feeding and nurturing it spiritually and aesthetically. The meaning of life is not found in material possessions (as Jesus so clearly illustrates in the parable of the Rich Fool). The true meaning of life is found in developing one's soul in relationship to God, to other people, and to the larger world.

Great writers, psychologists, and theologians help proclaim this truth and explore its depth and complexity as a spiritual and psychological question. But most of all, as we have noted, Helen's story proclaims what it means to grow a soul.

Notice how carefully Friend-Jones introduces Helen and allows her to speak. He presents Helen as a real person in a small town in Maine where life is simple and ordinary. It's a town with a paint store, bank, and barber shop, where everyone knows everyone else. Friend-Jones takes us with him to the home of Helen Preble. We know she is ill. And we know that Friend-Jones carries a heavy heart that morning. "I came bearing a message that would be difficult for both of us, but I also knew it couldn't be delayed. I knocked...." But for now, he tells us nothing more.

As listeners, we wonder what message he brings to Helen and why his heart is heavy. This is good storytelling. He keeps us guessing until the end of the sermon, when he finally tells us he has come to Helen's house as her pastor to tell her good-bye because he is leaving South Paris while she is nearing the end of her life. Helen's story piques our curiosity throughout the sermon. And only at the end do we fully come to understand how her story proclaims the message of the sermon. Helen shows us, teaches us much about the care and feeding of the soul.

But what sorts of things do Helen and these psychologists and writers have to say about the soul? The body of the sermon touches on a number of things. A sense of humor is a primary indicator of the condition of the soul. Friend-Jones uses a vignette about Helen early in the sermon to illustrate her sense of humor. She once said to him at the church door, "Reverend Jones, I don't think I've ever met anyone who could make so much out of so little."

Caring for the soul takes us into the pain and darkness of life, and there we may "wrest knowledge to be gained nowhere else." Tending the soul does not mean avoidance of pain. It means journeying into the threatening places, just as Helen did.

What is the soul? Thomas Moore (*Care of the Soul*) says it lies midway between the understanding and the unconscious. The soul is the seat of imagination. The soul exists as part of its context. It exists not for itself in radical isolation, but for community and the world. And the soul can "grow in size," in "range and depth of love," in capacity for relationships, in strength of spirit to encourage others to become free and to grow. "When souls are cultivated and cared for," says Friend-Jones, "they will grow and expand. They will become more inclusive...more godlike and worldly, as they allow the energies of God and the world to flow through them."

In making these points about the soul, Friend-Jones continually illustrates them from Helen's life. Helen not only illustrates the points; in an important sense, she finally interprets the points and the biblical text. That is why the preacher weaves her story throughout the sermon. Here "theory" and "practice" are one. By living her life "so expansively and fully in the present moment," Helen shows us what a well-tended soul is all about. She proclaims the truth in this sermon.

RESPONSE

In the closing paragraph the preacher uses the word *invite* three times, extending to us a powerful invitation to act in response to the sermon. "Saints" invite us to understand and live out our lives in a different world. It's not a world of prosperity, materialism, mastery and control (the Rich Fool). It's the world of virtue, imagination, and spiritual values (Jesus and

Helen). The invitation is to enter into the world of the soul's development as the sermon has explored this.

Helen Preble's life is just such an invitation, Friend-Jones says. When cancer came, she rose up against it. She grew big in stature even as her body wasted away from the ravages of the disease. "She was a big soul," a "big saint in the temple of my spirit. She taught me much about the care and feeding of the soul." She can teach us all. More important, Helen and Jesus and all the other saints invite us to act. They call to us: "Attend to the needs of your soul! Care for it! Develop it! That is finally what life is all about."

"The Ecology of the Soul" is a study in complexity of form and content. There is great depth, imagination, and mystery here. But finally, there is, as there should be in all sermons, an utter simplicity about it: "Care for your soul!"

## SUGGESTIONS

- Try letting someone's story "preach" the text by interweaving the story and text as this sermon does.
- If you haven't done so recently, experiment with a dialogue sermon and ask a member of your congregation to develop it and present it with you.
- What is the "soul" and how do we care for it? Develop your own sermon on this or a similar text and subject.

*Gary W. Klingsporn*

# "WHO GIVES A RIP?"

LUKE 15:1–7

REV. DR. GARY W. DOWNING
FAITH COVENANT CHURCH
BURNSVILLE, MINNESOTA

# "WHO GIVES A RIP?"

## LUKE 15:1–7

I want to ask you a question this morning. I wonder if you can think back to a time in your life when you were really lost. Now, I don't mean a time when you were too stubborn to stop to ask directions. I mean a time when you didn't know where to turn. You didn't know which way to go. You were just absolutely and utterly lost.

I do remember such a time. It was in July, many years ago. I was working for the county in Youth Corrections and we had taken a group of thirteen junior high guys for a month-long raft trip on a pontoon boat down the Mississippi from Minneapolis to St. Louis. We would stop at a sandbar where we would pull the boat up and cook our meals and camp out, that sort of thing. Some of the guys didn't want to be there. Lonnie took off. We figured that we could catch him, so they dropped me off about three miles down river at the next lock and dam. All I had to do was walk up the levee back to where the boat would be moored again and I would probably cross paths with Lonnie on the way down the levee. What I didn't know at the time was that they had had some flooding along the river and part of the levee was washed out. Since this was early evening when I started walking back, I was feeling okay about things. I figured it wouldn't be too tough to keep the river on my right and follow the levee.

The underbrush got heavier and heavier and then I was walking through swamp water and then the mosquitoes descended and it got real dark. It was one of those cloudy nights — not even any stars. I kept on walking and it got worse and worse and I realized that I was lost. I didn't know if I should turn to the left or turn to the right. I wasn't sure that I hadn't been walking around in a circle. I stopped there. I wasn't afraid of lions and tigers and bears. I was scared of poisonous snakes, bugs, and just being completely lost.

You know what that feels like? It starts way down low inside, that knot, then kind of spreads up inside. It's a frantic feeling of "I'm going to spend the night in this swamp. I might be lost forever." I honestly did not know what to do and I was beginning to panic.

Have you ever felt like that? My friend back at the boat began to figure out that I was taking a little longer than I should have. (As a matter of fact, the kid who ran away had already come back to the boat. It was too scary out there for him.)

My friend decided that maybe I might need some help, so he began to blow the boat's horn. Then he made the kids get out there and blow the horn. And they were irritated by it because it was so loud. But he made them blow the horn anyway because he figured maybe, just maybe, I might be able to hear it. And I did. At first I couldn't tell what it was. But then I made it out. That was the boat's horn. If I could just follow the sound of the horn, I could make it back to the boat. I'd be home free.

It was amazing what a difference I experienced from one moment of being panicky to the next moment of big relief. And when I finally made my way back through the swamp water and through all that mud and all the mosquitoes and brush and stuff and broke out into the clearing, I know I smelled like swamp, but I hugged every one of those guys. What a feeling.

That is a picture of what our Scripture is about today. The focus of Luke 15 is on being lost and being found. The context for this particular passage is that Jesus has been doing some teaching about the cost of discipleship and as he is doing this teaching, he is confronted by some religious reformers who are very critical of him. Later, if you read on, you find out that Jesus begins to talk about the hypocrisy of religious reformers who are so concerned about religious law and ritual, but don't give a rip about the people they are called to lead. And they are challenging Jesus.

It says here, "Now the tax collectors and sinners were all gathering around to hear him. But the Pharisees and the teachers of the law muttered, 'This man welcomes sinners and eats with them.'"

Now, if you were being challenged in your career, how would you deal with that? Maybe if I were in Jesus' shoes, I might want to try to trot out my credentials, or point to my experience or maybe even have a demonstration of divine power. I'd show those turkeys. But Jesus didn't defend himself. Instead, he described his ministry by telling a story. It's a well-known story and a great story — a beautiful story:

"Suppose one of you has a hundred sheep and loses one of them. Does he not leave the ninety-nine in the open country and go after the lost sheep until he finds it? And when he finds it, he joyfully puts it on his shoulders and goes home. Then he calls his friends and neighbors together and says, 'Rejoice with me; I have found my lost sheep.' I tell you that in the same way there will be more rejoicing in heaven over one sinner who repents than over ninety-nine righteous persons who do not need to repent."

What a tremendous story! A real picture of a God who takes the initiative to seek the lost. The focus is not on the lost as much as it is on the Great Seeker. Even in the 19th century, a great Jewish theologian named C. G. Montefiore looked at this parable and said, "There is something revolutionary and distinctive about this story because unlike all other world religions, it shows that God searches out the sinner."

Isn't that a great concept, that it's not how good we are or what we do — that even while we're lost, God comes after us and looks for us? What a concept, what a beautiful truth.

But as I looked at this story, I had a more mundane question. I thought, how did that shepherd know that one sheep was missing? I mean, can you imagine a hundred sheep running around? Remember, these are not the fat-tailed, short-haired, woolly, lazy sheep that we have in North America. These are short-tailed, long-haired, very active sheep, who can pick their way on a rock hillside or on a mountain. And they move. They look more like goats than sheep. How would that shepherd know out of a flock of a hundred that one was missing?

I think this is another picture of how God operates with us. God does not have to keep count because God knows each one of us so personally, so uniquely, that the very hairs on our head are numbered. That God knows when we're lost. And that God searches us out. The Greek term for this characteristic is one that connotes the idea of desperate seeking. It's like the feelings of parents who lose a kid at the shopping mall. They don't just kind of casually search; they are desperately seeking their lost kid.

That's the way God comes for us. Desperately seeking. God actually yearns for us until he finds us. What a tremendous picture!

However, in this day and age as we think about cost-effectiveness, and cost-cutting, don't you think it's rather inefficient for the shepherd to take time away from the ninety-nine sheep he's got in the flock to go pursue that one lost sheep? I mean, wouldn't he do better to spend his time and resources with the flock that are together and not waste it on that one? Why would God care about one person out there who is lost, who can't find his way home? Why would God care?

I don't have an answer to that question. I don't know why. But I do know in this parable that it was very important to that one sheep. I do know that when I was lost on that levee, it was very important to me that my friends should find me. It's important to the lost one. You see, the only solution for being lost is getting found.

It's great to know that God cares, that God does give a rip about our being lost. But why should we care? I mean, we're all here. Isn't this great? Maybe it's a little bit like what happens in our family. Kathy and I have four kids. We go out to the van after church and we get in the van and we look back and there are only two kids there. Two out of four is not bad. Why should we care? The answer is real simple, isn't it? It's because they are not there.

This is the situation we find ourselves in as a congregation. Last January in a massive telephone poll in Burnsville, a representative 400 families were interviewed for an average time of thirty-five minutes. They responded to all kinds of questions about life in Burnsville. One was, "Did you go to church or synagogue last Sunday?" In Burnsville, 47 percent of the people said they had. That's less than two out of four. Is that bad? Why should we care? Who gives a rip?

Or think about our mission as a congregation. We want to be a caring church for the Minnesota Valley. And as you look across the valley, it's obvious that it's growing like crazy. Do you realize that just in Lakeville alone, one of the fastest-growing suburbs in Minnesota, in ten years' time, if all the churches that currently exist in Lakeville were to double their capacity, two-thirds of the people in Lakeville wouldn't have a place to sit in church even if they cared to go?

But who gives a rip? In this country, according to one of the April issues of *U.S. News and World Report*, 70 percent of Americans say that people have to find their own way. Forty-eight percent said that there is no set standard for truth. That can be interpreted to mean that in America we believe that as long as you are decent and sincere, all roads lead to Rome. But for the majority of people, they don't know how to help somebody find the way home. You're on your own if you're lost. Sorry.

Or pull back even farther and consider that in the world as we know it, eight out of nine people today do not personally know that God loves them. But who gives a rip? Why should we care? Why should we be horn blowers, helping people find their way home?

If you're like me, you can think of a lot of good excuses. I come home after work and I'm tired. It's been a busy day. And I don't feel like I have the energy to try to reach out to anybody else. Or I am so busy — can you imagine trying to get four kids to sports and music and school events and to their friends and church and stuff? I mean, we go crazy. Life is just too busy to have time to reach out to anybody else. There are times, frankly, that I'm just emotionally exhausted. I'm too broken up to worry about somebody else who is in pain.

But some of you know there is a secret. And the secret is that when you reach out to a lost person, you don't lose energy. You gain energy.

Somewhere from outside yourself comes the energy, even when you're too tired to reach out. And you discover that in the middle of a hectic schedule you can find real meaning to life by reaching out and that maybe in the process of reaching out to somebody else who is in pain, you experience healing in your own life as well.

And furthermore, when you reach out to somebody who is lost, you experience joy. It's the experience the shepherd had when he found the sheep. He didn't grab that sheep by the back of its neck and say, "Bad sheep!" No, the shepherd picked that sheep up, put him on his shoulders, and carried him home. He was so filled with joy that he invited all his neighbors to come and celebrate with him. You think he served lamb chops?

I need to stop, because I wonder this morning if maybe there are some of you here who can identify very closely with the lost sheep in this story. Perhaps you have come this morning and you don't know where to turn. You've run out of gas. You're broken up. You feel like you've lost your way. You feel like you've wandered away from all the things that you hold near and dear. All the security of the familiar sights and sounds and smells is no longer there. It's real scary to be all alone, to be lost. And you're sitting here this morning knowing deep down inside that you've wandered way from God and you don't know what to do.

Friend, you have come to the right place. I would encourage you, if you feel lost this morning, just to stop where you are and open your minds and your hearts to the possibility that God is looking for you, that God is seeking you, that God yearns for you, that God wants you to be found, and that you can be found right here this morning. And if you do feel that you are lost this morning, I'd like you to just ignore the rest of what I am going to say. I'd like you maybe just to look in your worship folder and read for yourself the devotional paraphrase from Psalm 23, and make that a part of a prayer back to God.

For the rest of us, I want to suggest three simple things:

The first is to remember what it feels like to be lost. We so easily forget. We so quickly turn into Pharisees. Think back in your life to a time when you didn't know where to turn. When you knew that you were lost, that you had wandered away and lost your way and didn't know how to find your way home. Remember what it feels like to be lost.

Second, as you think about the people in your relationship mix — your family, people in your neighborhood, at work, at school, where you go to play — as you think of people you know, can you identify one person you know who has lost his or her way, who has wandered away from God?

And third, think about that one person and make an agreement with Jesus. Consider the possibility of first of all doing nothing until you pray. Pray that God will help you become a horn blower for that person, to help him or her find the way home. And maybe you will have a chance to initiate a conversation, a heart-to-heart talk.

Perhaps, by God's insight, you'll know how to offer a helping hand to that friend who is lost. In an appropriate way, you may have a chance to share you own faith journey with that person — what it felt like to be lost and how God found you. And once again, to pray — to pray that God might use your experience and your relationship to bring divine love from the Good Shepherd into that person's life.

Wouldn't it be something if, instead of being a Pharisee who is really too religious to give a rip about the outsider, instead of being a Pharisee who is too selfish to share the Good News with an outsider, who doesn't care enough to reach out to carry somebody else's burden, that instead you and I can be horn blowers for God, that we can experience the joy of helping a lost person to find the way home. To give a rip through the power of God's love. To experience the joy of coming home.

*The Lord is my constant companion.*
*There is no need that He cannot fulfill.*
*Whether His course for me points*
*to the mountaintops of glorious ecstasy*
*or to the valleys of human suffering,*
*He is by my side,*
*He is ever present with me.*
*He is close beside me*
*when I tread the dark streets of danger,*
*and even when I flirt with death itself,*
*He will not leave me.*
*When the pain is severe,*
*He is near to comfort.*
*When the burden is heavy,*
*He is there to lean upon.*
*When depression darkens my soul,*
*He touches me with eternal joy.*
*When I feel empty and alone,*
*He fills the aching vacuum with His power.*
*My security is in His promise*
*to be near to me always,*
*and in the knowledge*
*that He will never let me go.*

PSALM 23, PSALMS NOW[1]

## Notes

1. Leslie Brandt, *Psalms Now* (St. Louis: Concordia Publishing House, 1973), p. 38.

# COMMENT

"Who Gives A Rip?" is a fine example of a good evangelism and disciple-ship sermon. The sermon directly reaches out to "the lost" with the good news of God's seeking and healing love — evangelism. But it also chal-lenges those who already believe the gospel to care for the lost world around them by living a life of true discipleship, reaching out to others with God's healing love.

Have you ever struggled with how to present the themes of evangelism and discipleship in your preaching? Have you and your church wrestled with the meaning of the term *evangelism* and the many strategies discussed in the church today? Is "discipleship" a vague or intimidating concept for you or your people?

Gary Downing's sermon "Who Gives A Rip?" is a fine resource for all of us in assessing our thinking about evangelism and considering our understanding of discipleship. This sermon deserves careful reflection. It could be used as the basis for discussion about the meaning and practice of evangelism and discipleship in any local congregation.

Notice the down-to-earth language and style of this sermon. The ser-mon title and theme is itself a slang or colloquial expression which speaks to people right where they are in the everyday "vernacular" of their lives.

"Who gives a rip?" The expression is straightforward and earthy, as the sermon is throughout. There is no lofty, theoretical language here. This ser-mon does not seek to impress with sophisticated theological notions. Instead, the sermon is about the real world of noisy, smelly sheep and the panic of human lostness. The sermon is simple, direct, and urgent. It is "real."

The language and style of such a sermon may not fit every context. But the message, in whatever style, is the same. God cares about the lost. Will this sermon "preach" at Memorial Church, Harvard, or Riverside Church,

New York? Will it "preach" in Blue Eye, Missouri, and Ely, Minnesota? What might it sound like in all those different contexts? You be the judge!

## NEED

In the opening line the preacher asks us to begin thinking about the primary issue of the sermon: "I want to ask you a question this morning. I wonder if you can think back to a time in your life when you were really lost?" He then tells us a story of his own lostness, pausing twice in the story to address us again: "Do you know what that [being lost] feels like?" "Have you ever felt like that?"

With his own story of getting lost along the Mississippi River, Downing draws us as listeners into the question of the day. What is it like to get lost in our lives? He asks us specifically to think of how his story leads us to reflect on our story. The issue he wants to address, of course, is not physical lostness, but lostness of meaning, purpose, and spiritual direction in life.

At the same time, Downing's story gives us an example of a "horn blower," his friend who began blowing the boat's horn to help lead him back to safety. Following the sound of the horn, Downing made it safely back to the boat. His friend cared enough to act decisively to help lead him home.

In this opening story, then, we have the two key images underlying the entire sermon: (1) Downing himself lost in the flooded swampland along the river (anticipating the lost sheep of Jesus' parable); and (2) the friend who sought to help by blowing the boat horn (anticipating the seeking shepherd in Jesus' parable).

As it unfolds, we realize this sermon really addresses two questions: (1) What is it like to be lost? and (2) What does it mean to care for those who are lost? The sermon is about both the lost preacher stumbling along the river at nightfall and the friend frantically blowing the horn back on the boat. The sermon is about both the lost sheep and the Shepherd. You and I are drawn into the question of the sermon first through Downing's own story and then through Jesus' parable.

The use of the preacher's own story is an excellent example of building a sermon around a story drawn from one's own personal experience. This actually happened to Downing. It is a real, personal story, not one drawn from some great person's life. The best stories in sermons are usually stories out of our own personal lives. We can tell powerful stories about Augustine, Luther, Calvin, Wesley, Bonhoeffer, or other great figures in world history. But those stories about someone else are always "out there." The stories that have actually happened to us possess an authenticity and power to proclaim that someone else's story does not always have. Use your own story whenever possible!

Now look back over this sermon and observe how often the preacher asks questions. This is an example of the use of an "interrogative style." Altogether, Downing asks some twenty-five to thirty questions in the course of the sermon. These questions draw us into the sermon by asking us to reflect on our own lives. They also point repeatedly to the ultimate questions — problems, needs, issues — the sermon addresses: Do you know what it feels like to be lost? Why should we care about others who are lost?

In preaching, it is natural to ask questions of our listeners. The Scripture itself makes abundant use of the interrogative. But sometimes we can misuse or overuse this style. One of the common tendencies is to pile up a number of questions in succession in one paragraph, as if the sheer preponderance of questions somehow makes the point.

We need to be careful in our use of questions in preaching. Too many in one section of a sermon can overwhelm the listener! While we're asking the fifth and sixth questions in a row, the listener is still thinking about the first or second question we asked in the paragraph.

Beware of too many questions, especially in succession! In "Who Gives a Rip?" Downing has nicely placed the questions one or two at a time throughout the sermon. The use of the interrogative here gently leads the hearer to reflect on the point being made. Then, a few minutes later, another question is asked. We are never overwhelmed by the questions. But we are properly invited to reflect on our lives. That's good interrogative style.

TEXT

This sermon flows smoothly from stating a question to telling a personal story to engaging the biblical text. The question in the sermon's opening lines ("Have you ever been lost?") is addressed by the preacher's own story of being lost along a river. Probably most of us can identify with Downing in having some story of getting lost.

Just as we have begun to identify with the question and with his personal story, Downing introduces the biblical text by saying: "That [my story] is a picture of what our Scripture is about today. The focus of Luke 15 is on being lost and found" (para. 8). He then proceeds to read Jesus' parable.

This is an excellent joining together of a modern personal story and an ancient text. We can see the parable of the Lost Sheep through the experience of losing our own way and sloshing along a dark riverbank looking for the boat. The story is a picture of the text. The text is a picture of our story. The preacher has helped us to listen to the parable more attentively. He has opened our hearts to let the parable "lead us" in a challenging and transforming way.

In presenting the text, notice how Downing immediately calls attention to the attitude of the Pharisees and scribes in the context of Luke 15: "Later…Jesus begins to talk about the hypocrisy of the religious leaders who are so concerned about religious law and ritual, but don't give a rip about the people they are called to lead." They were challenging Jesus about his welcoming sinners and eating with them.

Here Downing starts getting at the heart of the issue of caring about the lost around us. With this text Downing goes on to say in effect: "Who gives a rip? Many of the Pharisees and teachers of law in Jesus' day didn't give a rip! That's why Jesus told the parables in Luke 15. So this parable of the Lost Sheep is about being lost and found, but it is about more! It challenges each of us to 'give a rip' and to care for those around us!"

PROCLAMATION

Drawing upon the parable, Downing proclaims a number of important truths in the body of this sermon:

(a) God is one who in love takes the initiative to seek the lost. God comes after us and looks for us!

(b) God cares about each one of us and knows when we are lost.

(c) The only solution for being lost is getting found.

(d) God cares, but why should we care? Well, simply because many whom God loves have lost their way. There is great need in the world around us, for many have lost purpose, direction, and connection with God. There is much joy and meaning in reaching out to help them.

Throughout the proclamation section, the sermon focuses above all on the twofold truth that God cares about the lost and so should we. Notice how Downing illustrates the "lostness" in terms of a local poll regarding worship attendance and church capacity in a nearby community; a national poll indicating "you're on your own if you're lost"; and the global reality that "eight out of nine people today do not personally know that God loves them." These citations underscore the reality of the "lostness" and appeal to the listener's willingness to see the need and respond.

Downing is saying that Jesus' parable proclaims our lostness as human beings (the sheep), God's great love for us (the shepherd), and the call to us as people of faith to become "shepherds." The good news is that God loves each and every one of us. As followers of Christ, we are called to care, as God cares, seeking out those who have lost their way and enabling them to find their way home again. As the text in Luke 15 proclaims, we are called to welcome sinners and tax collectors, the poor, marginalized and lost, just as Jesus did. When we do that, there is great joy in heaven: "Rejoice with me, for I have found my sheep that was lost."

## RESPONSE

This sermon extends invitations to two different groups of people to respond or act. First, it invites those who may feel like "lost sheep" to open their hearts to God's seeking love for them.

"I wonder this morning," Downing says, "if maybe there are some of you here who can identify very closely with the lost sheep in this story.... I would encourage you, if you feel lost this morning, just to stop where you are and open your minds and your hearts to the possibility that God is looking for you,…that God wants you to be found, and that you can be found right here this morning." This is an invitation to a saving relationship with God in Jesus Christ. It is almost "an altar call" to come forward and accept the gift of salvation, as some traditions practice. As such, this is a clear expression of an evangelistic invitation which calls upon listeners to accept the good news of the gospel.

Notice, to this first group of people Downing says, "If you do feel you are lost this morning, I'd like you to just ignore the rest of what I'm going to say…." He then turns to a second group of people in the congregation ("the rest of us"), and extends a second kind of invitation. This invitation is to a life of witness and discipleship for those who already believe in Jesus Christ. The invitation here is to become active, caring witnesses of God's love who reach out to the lost around them by introducing them to Jesus and to the good news of the gospel.

In this second invitation to act, Downing says three things: (1) Remember what it feels like to be lost. ( 2) Identify one person who has lost his or her way and wandered away from God. (3) Make an agreement with Jesus to pray for that individual. Ask God to help you "become a horn blower for that person, to help him or her find the way home." Then, ask God how you can help and, as appropriate, share your faith with the person. If we do these things, Downing says, we will discover the joy of being "horn blowers for God" and "giving a rip through the power of God's love."

The two invitations at the end of the sermon are consistent with the twofold theme throughout: being lost sheep, and becoming seeking shepherds. The invitations call both groups of people to act, either by responding to God's seeking love and being "found," or by becoming like shepherds seeking to help lost sheep around them.

Note finally how the closing paragraph of the sermon touches lightly on earlier images of the sermon: "Pharisee," "horn blowers for God," "find the way home," "the joy of coming home." Here Downing's own story about being lost along the river is recalled once more and joined to images from Jesus' parable and its context in Luke 15. The final paragraph of the sermon recalls the opening paragraphs. The sermon is now complete.

The question "Have you ever been lost?" has been addressed by a story and a parable. The text has proclaimed good news as an answer to the question of the sermon. And the proclamation of the text has issued in a call to respond. The sermon has achieved its purpose as an evangelism and discipleship sermon.

## SUGGESTIONS

- Read and discuss this sermon with your Evangelism and Discipleship board or committee. What implications does the sermon have for how you understand and approach evangelism and discipleship ministries in your church? What could you as a church do differently in these areas as a result of reflecting on this sermon?
- Consider preaching a sermon or series of sermons on the themes of evangelism and/or discipleship. What Old and New Testament passages would you use for the sermons? What question (need, problem) do you feel led to address in your church regarding these subjects?
- Preach a series of sermons on Luke, chapter 15. First, give careful study to the context in 15:1–2. How do the parables of the Lost Sheep, Lost Coin, and Lost Son all address the issue in 15:1–2? Why has Luke grouped these three parables together in this chapter? What does each parable say about God?
- Henri Nouwen's book *The Return of the Prodigal Son: A Story of Homecoming* (Doubleday, 1992) is a superb treatment of these themes.

*Gary W. Klingsporn*

# CRUSHED KINGDOMS AND KINGDOM DREAMS

DANIEL 2:24–49

DR. SCOTT WENIG
CENTENNIAL COMMUNITY CHURCH
DENVER, COLORADO

DR. SCOTT WENIG

# CRUSHED KINGDOMS AND KINGDOM DREAMS

### DANIEL 2:24–49

S ometime tonight, about ninety minutes after you're asleep, your brain will come alive with the crack of mental electricity pulsating through it. This electricity will unleash wave after wave of bio-chemicals from the brain stem at the back of your neck and these waves will travel at breakneck speed up toward the top and frontal lobes of your brain. As the chemicals reach their destination, the gray matter in your skull will try its best to sort out the chemicals and the electrical impulses, and by doing so, it will create a series of visions in your mind, some in color and some in black and white. Lying there on your bed for the next six to eight hours, you will experience the process called dreaming.

Those are the dreams of nighttime, and we experience them every time we sleep. But we also have dreams of the day, and those are the dreams that shape our lives, orient our direction, and determine our destiny. All of us here have a dream for our life and what we'd like it to be. So, let me ask you a question this morning: When you dream about your life, what do you dream?

I. Different People Have Different Dreams for Their Lives.

A. Some people dream of creating a better life for themselves and their families.

Many of our grandparents and great-grandparents came to America as immigrants. They sold everything they had and got on those boats and journeyed across a dangerous sea because they had a dream of building a new and better life for themselves and their children and grandchildren.

B. Some people dream of great achievements.

Back in the early 1920s the fastest man in the world was a white man named Charlie Paddock. After he won a gold medal in the 1920 Olympics he went around the U.S. speaking, and on one occasion he came to Cleveland, Ohio. Out in the audience, there was a little black kid who heard Charlie Paddock speak, and after Paddock was done, he went up to him and said, "Mr. Paddock, I want to become the fastest runner in the world like you. How can I do that?" Paddock said, "Son, keep the dream alive. Use the talent God's given you and work really hard." And that little black kid kept the dream alive and worked hard and became the world's fastest man. And in the 1936 Olympics in Berlin, that man, Jesse Owens, personally destroyed Hitler's demonic view of Aryan supremacy when he won four gold medals.

C. Some people dream of great projects to help others.

In the late 1940s a young American entrepreneur stood in a rural area of Southern California and dreamed of making kids happy. He said, "If you dream it, you can do it." And while other people saw only orange groves in those fields, Walt Disney dreamed of the Matterhorn, Space Mountain, Star Tours, Tom Sawyer's Island, and Pirates of the Caribbean in the amusement park named Disneyland.

D. Others dream larger dreams, dreams that encompass entire communities and nations.

On a steamy August night back in 1963 a young black preacher named Martin Luther King, Jr., stood up on the mall in Washington,

D.C., and shared his dream of whites and blacks living together in harmony, "of children being judged not by the color of their skin but by the conduct of their character, of the day that every valley would be exalted and every mountain brought low, the crooked places made straight and the glory of the Lord revealed to everyone."

It's important to have a dream for your life, so let me ask you once again, when you dream, what do you dream?

King Nebuchadnezzar of Babylon dreamed of creating and ruling a monumental empire. And after conquering all of the ancient Near East, he began to make his dream come true.

II. Nebuchadnezzar's Dream of the Babylonian Empire and His Dream of the Statue.

A. He began by building the city of Babylon.

1. It was built with the Euphrates River running through the center of it.
2. The city had 85-foot-high walls which were 30 feet wide at the top.
3. He built over 60 temples in the city to the god Marduk.
4. The king's palace occupied over 11 acres, and in the center of the palace were the "Hanging Gardens of Babylon," one of the Seven Wonders of the Ancient World.

B. But in the midst of turning his dream into reality, Nebuchadnezzar began to dream another dream that we're told of in Daniel 2:31–35:

"You looked, O king, and there before you stood a large statue — an enormous, dazzling statue, awesome in appearance. The head of the statue was made of pure gold, its chest and arms of silver, its belly and thighs of bronze, its legs of iron, its feet partly of iron and partly of baked clay. While you were watching, a rock was cut out, but not by human hands. It struck the statue on its feet of iron and clay and smashed them. Then the iron, the clay, the bronze, the silver and the gold were broken to pieces at the same time and became like chaff on a threshing floor in the summer. The wind swept them away without leaving a trace. But the rock that struck the statue became a huge mountain and filled the whole earth."

C. Nebuchadnezzar dreamed of an enormous, dazzling statue that was awesome in appearance. It had a head of gold, and a chest of silver, and thighs of bronze and feet of iron and clay.

D. But, as awesome as this statue was, it was destroyed by a rock cut without hands which became a mountain and filled the whole earth.

1. And the dream of the statue and its destruction disturbed Nebuchadnezzar.

2. At first it just made him tired and grumpy like Archie Bunker; but then he became angry and sullen; and finally, paranoid and disturbed.

On April 7, 1865, President Abraham Lincoln dreamed that he was visiting the White House and everyone was sad because there was a casket in the State Room. In his dream, Lincoln asked the attending soldier why everyone was so sad, and the soldier replied, "Because the president is dead." A week after he had that dream, Lincoln visited Ford's Theater, where he was shot to death by John Wilkes Booth. Lincoln's dream was a clear premonition of the future and I suspect that Nebuchadnezzar feared something to the same effect.

But the king was unable to interpret his dream and, after a crisis in court (Daniel 2:1-13), Daniel was given a special revelation from God. He told the king his dream and interpreted it for him.

III. God's Word Says: All Earthly Kingdoms and Empires Will Be Forever Displaced by His Eternal Kingdom (Daniel 2:36-45).

A. Daniel said that the statue stood for a series of earthly kingdoms, which would rise and fall, one after another.

1. Now, a lot of ink has been spilled over what these were; we know that Babylon was the first (the head of gold) because the text tells us that in verses 37-38:

"You, O king, are the king of kings. The God of heaven has given you dominion and power and might and glory; in your hands he has placed mankind and the beasts of the field and the birds of the air. Wherever they live, he has made you ruler over them all. You are that head of gold."

2. We don't know what empires the remainder of the statue represents and that's okay because the point of the dream is not who they were, but the fact that they will all be destroyed.

Verses 44–45: "In the time of those kings, the God of heaven will set up a kingdom that will never be destroyed, nor will it be left to another people. It will crush all those kingdoms and bring them to an end, but it will itself endure forever. This is the meaning of the vision of the rock cut out of a mountain, but not by human hands — a rock that broke the iron, the bronze, the clay, the silver, and the gold to pieces."

B. In this passage, God is speaking to Nebuchadnezzar. God is trying to show him that this incredible Babylon that he's building, with its huge walls and the great temples and the Hanging Gardens, is eventually going to be nothing but dust.

1. This would also be true of all the other world empires which would eventually follow: the Hellenistic Empire, the Roman Empire, the British Empire, the Soviet Empire, and even the American Empire.

2. It's hard to believe, isn't it, on this 4th of July, the 217th anniversary of our independence, that someday America as we know it will cease to exist.

Someday, the House of Representatives will be gone, the Senate will be gone, and even the present administration will be gone. Some people, such as Yale historian Paul Kennedy, are already arguing for the demise of America because of its internal problems and its external commitments.

IV. God's Word to Us: Don't Invest Too Heavily in the American Dream Because It Will Not Endure and It Distracts Us from the Eternal Kingdom of God.

A. But, you know what? That statue doesn't just represent political kingdoms or the dreams of kings and rulers. It also represents our own little empires and dreams, whether they're domestic, or social, or financial, or religious.

B. And the dream which that statue represents for most of us here this morning is what we call "The American Dream."

1. The American Dream means different things to different people, but overall, it stands for the aspirations and achievements of someone who has made it and gotten ahead in the society and has acquired all the outward signs of success.

For some, it's a dream for a house in the suburbs, and a house in the mountains for skiing, and great vacations and money in the bank and a secure job and terrific health and a fabulous education for the kids.

For others, it's winning the Lotto jackpot or having enough money to buy a BMW, or the fame, fortune, and romance of a Hollywood starlet.

The American Dream is symbolized by the statements "You can have it all" and "It doesn't get any better than this." That's the American Dream and we're all influenced by it.

I know I am — even in my ministry. I want to be a success, have a big congregation, write books, have people admire me, have a comfortable lifestyle and a good retirement.

C. Now, there's nothing wrong with owning a home, driving a decent car, sending your kids to college, wanting to preach to people or planning for retirement.

D. But let us hear God's Word this morning: It's warning us not to invest too heavily in the American Dream because it cannot endure and it detracts us from investing in what does endure into eternity.

1. The last twelve years of financial prosperity have been bought on credit. America has gone from being the largest creditor nation in the world to the largest debtor nation. The American Dream is being destroyed.

2. And even in those places where people have achieved all the outward signs of the American Dream, it's crumbling from within.

Mill Valley, California, is considered one of the finest places to live in the U.S. Porsches, BMWs and Winnebagos litter the driveways. The schools have the finest state of-the-art equipment. Mill Valley is in a beautiful environment. But, it also has one of the highest alcohol and drug addiction rates in the country; the suicide rate is very high; and family breakups are common.

E. And not only is the American Dream crumbling, but investing too heavily in it keeps us from investing in those things which do endure and which are of importance to God.

Listen to evangelical author Tom Sine in *Discipleship Journal:* "In the evangelical world we talk at great lengths about the 'lordship of Christ in our lives.' But in every church I have visited there is an unquestioned assumption that we all have to get our careers underway, our house in the suburbs, and our upscale living started first. Then, with whatever time or energy is left, we follow Jesus. But the problem is, once we do the whole nine yards of the cultural agenda, we have precious little time, energy, and resources left for anything else — including serving Jesus. Pursuing the American Dream with a little Jesus overlay isn't biblical and it will not impact the world around us."[1]

Are we dreaming the wrong dream? Is it worth our time and our energy and our effort to dream a dream that at best won't endure and at worst can become a nightmare? Isn't it wiser to invest our lives in a dream that's going to endure as a blessing?

That means acting on God's word and investing in God's Kingdom Dream.

V. Let's Act on God's Word and Live for God's Kingdom Dream.

A. According to verses 44–45, that rock which becomes a mountain and fills the whole earth is the Kingdom of God.

B. God's Kingdom is his rule and his reign in the lives of people and eventually over the entire creation.

1. It has come in the life and ministry of Jesus and it is now spreading throughout the whole earth.

My friends, there are some tremendous things going on in the world at the moment. The gospel is spreading like wildfire in South America and in Eastern Europe. In certain places in the U.S., there is genuine revival going on, with thousands of people coming to Christ.

C. 2,500 years ago, God gave this dream to Nebuchadnezzar to show him that he loved him and that the king needed to repent and align his life with the Rock which would fill the earth.

1. This passage is teaching us the same thing today: To hear and act on God's word and dream the eternal dream of his kingdom, rather than wasting our time and energy on the American Dream which cannot endure.

2. And we have people here in this church doing that to show us the way!

There's Greg Preston, serving as a deacon and teaching the four-year-olds in Sunday School every week.

There's Libby Bergstrom, investing her life in the fifth graders.

There are a lot of people in this church who are giving of themselves weekly to seniors in the Seniors Ministry.

There are Bob and Jan Williams who moved downtown to help others and minister to them in the Inner City Health Clinic.

Lisa Harmon works every Friday and Saturday night at the Coffee Shop on East Colfax with street people.

And many of you have given sacrificially to the Somalia project to feed the starving millions there.

So, let me ask you once again, when you dream, what are you dreaming? Your dream determines the course of your whole life and shapes the impact you have on others before you die.

## CONCLUSION

And we need to think about that because someday, every person in this room is going to die. I know that we don't like to think about that and we may want to deny it, but someday, we're all going to die. And let me tell you what's going to happen when we do, because I've been to a lot of funerals in my life and they do the same thing at every one. When we die, they are going to take our body, drop it in a hole, throw some dirt on it, and then go back home and eat chicken and potato salad and chocolate cake.

Now, the day we were each born, we were brought home in that soft, white blanket, and we were the ones crying but everybody else around us was happy because we were born. But the important question is this: What's it going to be like when we die? When we die, are we going to be happy and leave everybody else crying?

The answer to that question depends on what we do with our lives NOW! If we dream that American Dream and use our lives to get stuff and honors and success, that's not going to make much of an impact on anyone around us. But if we dream God's dream of his Kingdom, then we'll make a huge impact on other people and they will really miss us when we're gone.

When we die, are people going to look at all the stuff we've left behind or are people going to be crying because they feel like they've lost their best friend? Will there be an obituary telling how successful we were, or will there be people crying in sorrow about how we ministered to them, impacted them, and made a huge difference in their lives? The dream we dream now, today, will answer those questions.

So let's make sure that we're dreaming God's dream of his Kingdom, not the American Dream, because God's dream lives beyond us into eternity.

Notes
  1. Tom Sine, "A Different Discipleship," *Discipleship Journal* 49 (January-February 1989), p. 6.

COMMENT

A sermon grabs when it opens with "sizzle." Scott Wenig's sermon "Crushed Kingdoms and Kingdom Dreams" opens with a vivid word picture describing the key word *dream*. He then asks the rhetorical question "When you dream about your life, what do you dream?" Using a play on words, he moves from life dreams to night dreams as a way of introducing the text. Giving four examples of life passions that changed people's lives, he makes the transition to King Nebuchadnezzar and his dream. Here is the center of the sermon.

Throughout, Wenig lets the "narrative-prophetic" text of Daniel 2:24–49 inductively challenge his hearers to reconsider their life dreams. He concludes by challenging his audience to be sure they're dreaming God's eternal Kingdom dream rather than building their lives on the transient American Dream. This sermon gives us one approach to dealing with a difficult text and a sensitive subject: how our cultural and material values compare to the vision and values of biblical faith.

## FORMAT

Wenig uses a narrative outline as the format for his sermon. While much of the text is included, he does not completely fill in the blanks. He gives us the chance to see the structure of the sermon as he goes. It would be possible to take this outline and change the illustrations but keep the flow of his exposition of the Scripture.

Wenig begins by weaving his hearers into the theme by describing the biological process of dreaming. He gives four examples of dreams some people had for their lives. The dreams of better lives, great achievements, and great projects drove these people. It was the same passion that drove the biblical character in Daniel. Nebuchadnezzar experienced the ultimate human dream of conquest, fabulous wealth, and virtual divine status.

This is where the focus shifts from life dreams to a night dream which Nebuchadnezzar found very disturbing. Wenig uses the "dream" play on words as a thread to connect the hearers to the text and Daniel's interpretation of the king's dream.

Notice how Wenig uses the story of Abraham Lincoln's premonition of the future in a dream he had prior to his assassination. This creates some understanding of the emotional state King Nebuchadnezzar was in as a result of his terrifying dream. Daniel is called upon to tell the king the meaning of this bizarre premonition.

Wenig uses this biblical story to challenge his hearers to a similar understanding of God's Word across the ages to another empire and another dream — our American Dream. He concludes by offering alternatives to our dreams for conquest, wealth, or even eternal life.

## TEXT

Wenig refuses to get trapped in an elaborate system of textual interpretation that attempts to predict the future based on numerology, typology or analogies to King Nebuchadnezzar's nightmare statue. Instead he cuts right to the main point of the biblical text: "Empires will be destroyed: therefore don't place your faith in life dreams or driving passions that are American but not of God's Kingdom."

Here is an important principle for preaching. We may be tempted to read into a text our system of interpretation along with a potential timetable for the future. That may be suitable for a seminar on the "end times" but does not allow the hearer to interact directly with the key point in the passage. Preparation for preaching often requires cutting out material that may be fascinating but is not explicitly in the text we seek to interpret. We want the Bible to speak to our hearers as directly as possible so that people can interpret and apply the truths to their lives. We want our hearers to be equipped to read the Bible for themselves without requiring a manual or interpretive workbook setting forth an elaborate and complex system which may represent only speculation about the future.

This is not a polemic against pondering the future. It is, however, a good reminder to all of us to let the Bible make its own point and not impose our viewpoint on the text. This temptation to systematize Scripture to fit our worldview has been a problem over the past 1900 years for well-meaning preachers. We may have to exercise the same discipline to ask the Holy Spirit for interpretation as Peter did in his daytime dream of the clean and unclean animals lowered in a sheet. Rather than leap to hasty conclusions, it is better to invite our hearers to join us in the exploration of a passage that might appear obscure or hard to understand.

This is what Wenig does in this sermon. He leads his hearers to the key point of the king's dream. "The point of the dream is not who they were, but the fact that they will all be destroyed."

## PROCLAMATION

Despite the fact that earthly kingdoms all end, God's Kingdom will never be destroyed. This becomes the good news of the sermon. We are to place our trust in God, not in the American Dream. Wenig describes different aspects of the dream, such as having a house in the suburbs, winning the lottery, or even being considered successful in ministry. Then he asks the question "Are we dreaming the wrong dream?" He challenges his hearers to act and live according to God's Kingdom dream. Through specific examples of people both within and outside the life of the congregation, Wenig shows that living out the vision of the Spiritual Kingdom can take place here and now. Wenig also puts the dream question into ultimate context when he has us look at death. At the point of death, the point of life becomes very important. "Are we dreaming the right dream?" is always an essential faith question to ask ourselves.

## RESPONSE

Through many illustrations and rhetorical questions Wenig overcomes some of the objections his audience might raise. He does not minimize their dreams or responses. Rather, he elevates the audience to a higher perspective to see reality from an eternal perspective. This makes it easier to respond than if the preacher had induced shame in the hearers for their pursuit of the American Dream. In this way he doesn't come off sounding shrill or "political."

By motivating and challenging the audience to live their lives according to God's eternal Kingdom rather than by temporal human kingdoms, Wenig provides a biblical exposition of a practical alternative to often-dominant contemporary American cultural values. The sermon draws hearers into the text to make their own heartfelt, Spirit-inspired evaluation of the Lordship of Christ in their lives.

## SUGGESTIONS

- When you approach a "narrative-prophetic" text like the one here in Daniel, try to write down your own particular preconceived ideas about the text. Set them aside. Then on a blank piece of paper write down the straightforward conclusions contained within the text. If the text doesn't say it, don't assume it. Then compare the two. Which of your assumptions are supported directly by the passage and which ones require using other texts or elaborate interpretations from other sources? Consider preaching the simple, straightforward text and saving the more complex interpretations for a seminar or teaching setting more conducive to such material.

- Take a single word like dream, as Wenig has done. Write down all the various ways the word can be used in different contexts. Look for plays on words that might be interesting to use to illustrate biblical themes. Sometimes lyrics to songs (especially country western music) use these double-meaning words or phrases to give a new twist in applying these words to our lives.

- Wenig does an interesting thing when illustrating the application of the biblical truths. He uses real, live people who are actually doing what the Bible is talking about. This has the double effect of illustrating the text and affirming those who are mentioned. Be careful not to focus only on a particular group or use only spectacular examples.

C O M M E N T

Sometimes the quiet, behind-the-scenes person illustrates the point in a way more of the audience can relate to than unbelievable examples that seem unapproachable.

*Gary W. Downing*

COMMENT

# LOOK AT YOUR LIFE

1 SAMUEL 3:1–18

REV. JOHN ACKERMAN
BRYN MAWR PRESBYTERIAN CHURCH
MINNEAPOLIS, MINNESOTA

# LOOK AT YOUR LIFE

## 1 SAMUEL 3:1–18

O nce upon a time, which is to say, at every time, there was a king who commanded one of his subjects to bring him an apple every day for a year.

The subject who brought the apple was a wise old woman who grew apples. The king had quite refined tastes, having been educated in the upper crust, so he looked down his nose at this ordinary apple. He had one of his advisors throw it into a shed.

One day, before the apple was thrown out, the king's monkey went into the shed, took the apple, and ate it. When he got to the core, out dropped a large diamond. The king was astounded. He yelled at his advisor who ran out to the shed, and there, in the rotting pulp, were many, many diamonds. Amazing.

*The Moral:* Though your taste may be refined, you have the gift of days, of people, of your experience. And if you're not too proud or lazy to look, God gives you a jewel in everything. Will you look and listen to your life?

But who does? We think the answers are out there in more money, in being well liked or respected, in having everyone happy. We spend our time in front of the television looking at the news of the world, or we read books or newsletters, as though the good news were there. We read about the Bible or we turn through it for insights.

*And, we utterly disdain the apples, the gifts, that God daily gives us, and throw them away in a back room of memory.*

Listen to your life.

When Jesus says, "Consider the lilies of the field," or, "The kingdom of God is like a woman who swept her house," he's asking his hearers to pay attention, to wake up to the tremendous realities that are at hand.

One way to wake up is to look at our life in faith.

When in your childhood did the word *God* become something real? When was the holy and mysterious source of the universe part of your experience?

When I think back, it is usually to church, at communion. I am sitting with my parents, and they are uncharacteristically silent. The minister is talking and there is organ music and light comes in through the windows. There is something special about the silence and the fact that my extended family is all there. There is what I would now call a reverent silence, a sense of the holy. I don't know what was going through my mind then, but my body was uncharacteristically still and I was what I would now call centered and prayerful. That's in a religious context.

If I were to ask the question not religiously, but spiritually — where did I feel at home, centered, connected — there would be several answers: The bathtub, a place of great solace. It was warm, comforting, and made me feel good. Lying in the sun. I remember, once in the summer, doing that and feeling warm — not just physically warm, but connected, with light going through me. Quite ordinary, yet one of those apples that God gave me, which I look back on appreciatively now.

What do you remember about being connected, or longing to be connected? Listen to your life.

As an adolescent, when I was sent away at fifteen, I remember being lonely. I remember singing nightly with the men's choir in chapel, and doing what now would be called male bonding. I remember the mystery of communion again.

I can remember the pain of doubting and yet wanting to pray. I can remember trying to medicate my pain with several substances, none of which seemed to take the pain away long term. Even girls didn't take away the agony of being a person and being lonely. I can remember loving sad music like the melody of the well-known spiritual: "Sometimes I feel like a motherless child, a long way from home." And I was.

Can you hear your pain somehow, as set to music, as a cry to the universe to be at home — as one of the best prayers you'll ever say or feel?

Were you ever aware of being lonely or in pain or depressed? It's too bad if you never were, or if you put it out of sight.

It's like throwing the apples away.

I have an older friend who is filled with longing. He has a rich and full life. But he is acutely aware of how much he longs for God. And he is acutely aware of the gift of his wife, his students, the day, his experience, as a daily gift from God.

I don't think we really can find the core, the jewel, until we are aware of our hunger, our longing for the gift.

I encourage you to write your own holy history. We've got to see the big stuff before we can notice the little things, more than likely. You might ask, "What question is my life asking me?"

My response is, when are you going to relax and be at home? Suppose you have moved and can now settle in. You have a new parish and now can be at home. When will you see that God is at home in you? When will you let that reality color all you think and do?

Think of your holy history as another testament God is writing — another text beside the Bible. How can you read it to see what God is saying? How can you read the Bible to hear what God is saying now?

How can you write your story?

For many, writing is done literally by writing. For others, it is done symbolically, by drawings or remembering symbols like a rock or picture to recall what God has done. For some, it is done musically.

And how do you know where God is?

You need help. The story of little Samuel is the story of us all. We are awakened from our literal sleep, or our symbolic sleep, by God's voice. God calls us by name: "John, wake up, wake up." Have a spiritual awakening.

But we don't get it. We don't get the significance of the noises in our lives, much less the message of our dreams.

So we need to go to someone like old Eli and say, "What does it mean?" "How do I get in dialogue with my life, with God?"

Eli doesn't give the answer, but he suggests how Samuel might get the answer: *by asking.*

Do you have an Eli, someone you can be in touch with? You may have a group that you share your literal or symbolic dreams with. Someone to tell your story to.

And I will be glad to listen to your story and tell you what I hear. That's what a pastor is for.

I'll be going to every one of our leaders this summer and asking them what God is saying in their life.

What an exciting thing that can be. For my experience is that it's helping notice the jewels in the apples we've been receiving but throwing away.

# COMMENT

John Ackerman's sermon "Look at Your Life" is a study in the power of simplicity. The sermon is brief and to the point. It speaks directly to us. It is
easily remembered. Like the truth it proclaims, the sermon is simple, but
not simplistic. It invites us to look at our lives and to listen for God. Yet it
acknowledges that this is not easy to do. God's presence is often hidden —
the voice of God overcome by the noise in our lives. So we need help to
see and to hear.

The tone of this sermon is personal, intimate. It feels like a quiet conversation with a friend sitting in the park by the lake on a summer afternoon. It engages us by asking questions throughout: "When has God been
real to you?" "How do you know where God is?" We walk away from the
conversation reflecting on what our friend has said and has asked. Rather
than speaking to us, the sermon invites us into a conversation in a very
effective way.

One of the great temptations in preaching is to say too much in a sermon. We are often tempted to say everything we can about the need, the
text, God, the human condition, ourselves, and our listeners, in the hope
of somehow connecting with people. But John Ackerman's sermon is elo-
quent testimony that, often in preaching, "less is more." This sermon simply tells a story, makes a point, and tells another story. That's all that is needed: the power of simplicity.

## PROBLEM

The introduction to a sermon is crucial. In the opening lines, we can either
gain a hearing from our listeners, or lose them to a thousand other competing thoughts. Ackerman opens this sermon by telling a story about a
king and apples with jewels hidden in them. The story engages us. We ask,

"Where is he going with this?" and "What on earth does this have to do with faith or anything in the Bible?"

A good introduction arouses curiosity and makes the hearer want more. Time spent developing the introduction, finding just the right story, words, or image, is time well spent. The introduction to the sermon can sometimes take more time to conceive and prepare than other portions of the sermon.

In the opening phrase of the sermon, when Ackerman says, "Once upon a time, which is to say, at every time…," he signals that this story is universal. It is not simply about the past. It is your story and my story: "So listen up! I'm talking about us!" And if this strange story of kings and apples and jewels is about *me,* I want to know why and how. I want to listen.

But the opening story does far more than gain a hearing. It goes right to the heart of the sermon by laying before us the question which the sermon addresses. In the style of Aesop's fables, Ackerman concludes the story of the king and the apples with the "Moral": "God gives you a jewel in everything. Will you look and listen to your life?" That's the whole point of the sermon: to listen, and to look for God in the ordinary events of our lives.

"But who does?" is Ackerman's next line. That's the problem. We look for answers and meaning everywhere else in life, but we overlook or ignore the gifts of God in the everyday experiences of life. The sermon's opening image of the king tossing apples into a dark shed day after day puts the problem on the table. The king missed it all. And we so often miss that which we need so desperately: the loving presence of God.

## PROCLAMATION

This sermon proclaims the biblical truth that God speaks to us in the ordinary events of life, in the high moments as well as in the pain, darkness, and loneliness of life. The challenge is to take nothing for granted, "to wake up and to pay attention to the tremendous realities that are at hand." But notice, after the introduction, Ackerman does not immediately turn to the biblical text, the story of Samuel and Eli. Instead, he deftly sprinkles the words of Jesus on the king and apples story: "Consider the lilies...." "A woman swept her house...." The words of Jesus invite us to "consider," to look at our lives in faith, and they anticipate Samuel and Eli at the end of the sermon.

In the body of this sermon, to proclaim the truth of God's presence, Ackerman turns to his own personal experiences of God and shares them with us to invite us to "consider the lilies of the field." Notice how Ackerman relates his experiences of God as a child in church, in a bathtub, or lying in the sun. Relating these experiences, he repeatedly asks us, "What do you remember about being connected with God in your life?" "Can you hear?" "Do you see God's presence?" Here Ackerman is personal and self–revealing. He gives us permission to think about our lives by willingly sharing his life. He lets his own experience proclaim the reality and presence of God in the world as he has known this presence. But he always invites us as hearers to reflect for ourselves on that proclamation by trying to identify our own experiences of the gifts of God.

The experiences of pain, darkness, and loneliness can especially be times when we encounter God, says Ackerman. As a lonely, doubting adolescent he experienced that. Indeed, we "find the core, the jewel in the apple, when we are most aware of our hunger, our longing for the gift." We can hear God in the pain. The Scripture proclaims this repeatedly in the experiences of the psalms of lament, in Job, and in many other passages. "God speaks to us" is the simple proclamation of this sermon. How utterly biblical! But Ackerman does it without repeatedly quoting the Bible throughout the sermon. Sometimes "less is more."

## RESPONSE

From beginning to end, this sermon invites us to act. Notice the large number of questions Ackerman addresses to us in the second person: "Will you look and listen to your life?" "What do you remember...?" "Can you hear...?" "How can you write your story?" "Do you have an Eli?" The invitation is not only to reflect in faith ("Listen to your life"). It is to read God's story, to "write your own holy history," and ask others to help us see the presence of God in our lives. At the end of the sermon there is a beautiful pastoral invitation for members of the congregation to tell their story. "I will be glad to listen to your story and tell you what I hear," says Ackerman. "What is God saying in your life?" That is the whole point of the sermon.

## TEXT

As we noted, Ackerman saves his reference to the biblical text about Samuel and Eli (1 Sam. 3:1–18) until the end of the sermon. Presumably, his hearers have heard the story of Samuel read prior to the sermon. They know this sermon is somehow related to Samuel and Eli. But Ackerman waits with the biblical text until the effective moment — in this case, the end of the sermon.

A common tendency in preaching is to tell a story or give an introduction and then go immediately to the text and spend the remainder of time on the biblical text. When we do that, no matter how powerful the text or how good our exposition of it, we sometimes lose listeners because of their familiarity with or distance from the biblical text. Ackerman refrains from doing this. Not only does he save the text for the end of the sermon; when he reaches it, he treats it sparingly. That has a profound impact. He allows the biblical story to draw the sermon together and leaves the listener thinking about Samuel and that other question, "Do you have an Eli?"

It is not necessary in every sermon to retell the biblical story or recapitulate the text in detail line by line. In some sermons that is appropriate and quite necessary. But it's important sometimes simply to rely upon the listeners who have heard the story read in worship. We can trust them with the earlier hearing of the story and achieve a more powerful effect by allowing the story, as in this case, to "clinch" the sermon. Had he chosen, the preacher might have played a little more with the line in the text, "Speak, Lord, for your servant is listening." But perhaps that is for another sermon.

When Ackerman reaches the text, he utters a small but important statement: "The story of little Samuel is *the story of us all.*" That's a good phrase to use in preaching. This story is our story. It is yours and mine. We all need to be reminded of that so we can more readily enter the world of the text.

In closing the sermon, Ackerman makes the point that we all need an Eli, someone to help us look and listen for God in our lives. This offers us help along the way. We can do this. But like Samuel, we don't have to do it on our own. Others can guide us; as Eli said to Samuel once long ago, "It is the Lord."

C O M M E N T

## SUMMARY

This sermon is about ten to twelve minutes in length, depending on one's rate of delivery. It is a study of economy in preaching. The sermon simply tells the story of a king. It makes essentially one point. Then it closes with Samuel and Eli and restates the point: We *can* see the jewels in the apples we've been throwing away.

## SUGGESTIONS

- Work on developing sermon introductions in which the reader isn't sure where you're going or what your sermon is about, but wants to find out by listening.
- Preach a one-point sermon sometime, limited to ten or twelve minutes.
- Try saving the text for the end of your sermon.

*Gary W. Klingsporn*

# NOT ALONE

REVELATION 1

REV. EARL PALMER
UNIVERSITY PRESBYTERIAN CHURCH
SEATTLE, WASHINGTON

# NOT ALONE

## REVELATION 1

I am going to begin a brand new series of sermons today. These are going to be biblical studies of people in the Old and New Testament — how God meets them; how God uses people in the Bible; and how he uses them in the lives of other people. In a way, this is a sequel to the sermon series I did last fall on the early chapters of Acts called "Ambassadors for Christ — In a World That Waits." There we tried to understand our ambassadorship. In this series we are going to look at the ambassadors themselves and see ourselves and how God meets us and uses our lives to touch other lives, and how he uses other people's lives in our lives. I have entitled this series "Not Alone."

Let us pray together. *Lord, we thank you that we are not alone. We thank you that we can come to you today in this time of worship and be with you and be with one another and have this experience of focusing our eyes on the gospel of Jesus Christ and see all the rich and wonderful implications of that in our lives. Bless us today in this time. In Christ's name we pray. Amen.*

God knows us very well. He knows what makes us tick; he made us. And one thing he knows about us is that we should not be alone too long. Sometimes a little bit of aloneness — but not too much — can help to clarify our thinking. It is no surprise, when you come to think about it, that in imprisonment experiences, the one thing a prisoner dreads most of all is solitary confinement. To be alone doesn't actually clarify; after awhile it muddles your head and confuses you. In fact, one of the first steps in brain-washing is to isolate the victim so that he or she is alone. This is the way it is, and this is the way God made us.

So a little aloneness, but not too much, is all right; that can be seen from the beginning of the Bible straight through to the Book of Revelation. Genesis, chapter 2, has this very incredible line, that God saw man and realized it was not good that he should be alone — one of the first statements in the Bible about us. And when God saw that it was not good that we should be alone, he made a helpmate for man — woman.

I have been reading a book by a political scientist, a Harvard professor named Robert D. Putnam, a premier authority in understanding the American scene. The book that has made him so famous right now, *Making A Democracy Work*, is really a book about Italy. Putnam, who studied Italy for a great number of years, focused on two provincial areas of the country, in the North and in the South. What he reports in his book is fascinating for me to read. Through his study, he discovered that democracy won't work if people are alone, and apart from each other. In one province people tended to be isolated and frightened — almost as if they were reacting to a jungle experience of the supremacy of a few powerful people over everybody else — they couldn't make a democracy work. In the other province, the people were highly organized in small communities like church associations and family groups and interest groups that had a sense of civic interdependence and responsibility. They *were* able to make democracy work.

Now the reason Putnam's book is such a bombshell is that we in the American experiment of democracy pride ourselves on our rugged individualism. Putnam, in an article called "Why Men Bowl Alone," says there are no more bowling teams; everyone is bowling alone now. He is beginning to worry about America because of our intense pride in our rugged individualism, since, according to his study, democracy won't work in that setting. It doesn't work when we are suspicious of everybody and everybody is our potential enemy or rival. It may work in some businesses, he says, but it doesn't even work very well there. And individualism doesn't help make democracy work. Because we were not meant to be alone, it goes contrary to the way we were designed.

I believe we are going to see a lot in public debate on this subject now. We need people as friends, we need people as mentors, and we even need friends who are friendly mentors but also antagonists. (Yes, we even need those.) Friendly antagonists help us by keeping us in community, and they remind us that we are not alone.

Now, it may surprise you that I tell you we need antagonists. You say, "I need that — more antagonists — like I need another hole in the head." But, maybe antagonists *are* good. Martin Luther writes about John Eck, another theologian, his nemesis. He is always battling Eck. But Luther at one point paid tribute to John Eck, when he noted this in a diary: "Eck made me wide awake." So he acknowledged his debt to John Eck, his friend and archrival, even though they didn't agree on anything. These friends knew each other. Eck kept Luther wide awake.

G. K. Chesterton, an Englishman who is one of my heroes, was a great Christian writer of this century. One of his very best and longstanding friends was George Bernard Shaw. If you are a Chesterton fan, you know that there existed all kinds of correspondence between Chesterton and Shaw. The two of them, like Luther and Eck, were good friends, but they didn't agree on anything either. Still, they stayed loyal friends right until the very end. In a sense they were not alone toward each other and thus they helped each other. I know that Shaw helped Chesterton and I really think that Chesterton helped Shaw. Their relationship is very intriguing.

As you know, I am very interested in C. S. Lewis. And one of the marks of C. S. Lewis's life, as the movie *Shadowlands* brought out, is that Lewis had these longstanding debates and arguments with some of his best friends. They never gave in to each other; they too were antagonists all the way to the end. Probably Lewis's best friend was Owen Barfield. In fact, Lewis dedicated *The Lion, the Witch and the Wardrobe,* his first novel in the Narnia series, to Owen Barfield's daughter, Lucy. Lewis was godfather to Lucy Barfield, and yet her father and Lewis agreed on hardly anything, always struggling with each other about theology, politics, and everything else. Nevertheless, they were friends: they were not alone toward each other. And they were a help to each other.

Okay, it seems certain therefore that it's God's will to put people into our lives. He puts them into our lives to encourage us, and he puts us into other people's lives to encourage them. His ordinary way of encouraging us is with people.

Now before we look at Revelation 1, I want you to look at one other text, chapter 28 in the Book of Acts. I want to read the last scene, which deals with the Apostle Paul. Paul is one of the two great heroes in the Book of Acts, and in the very end of the book, Luke has this to say about Paul in a very tender sentence (which we will read in a moment) as he is describing Paul's arrival at Rome. Paul comes there as a prisoner — remember, he had been on a prison ship, and he finally reaches his destination. We discover from Philippians and 2 Timothy and from other early church documents that this is Paul's final imprisonment. He will never get out of prison there; this is where he is going to die.

But in Acts 28:14, he finally arrives in Rome, and he is probably pretty discouraged. "And so we came to Rome. And the brothers and sisters there when they heard of us, came as far as the Forum of Appius [a small town near Rome], and Three Taverns [that is a kind of dubious-sounding town — does that mean they came from the town with three bars? I hope it wasn't just people from Three Taverns — another town near Rome] to meet us."

Now listen to this telling line. "On seeing them, Paul thanked God and took courage." Paul was discouraged, but what was it that gave him courage when he got to Rome? It wasn't some great mystical experience; it was meeting brothers and sisters, Christian friends in Rome who welcomed Paul. Paul had never been to Rome so these were people he had only heard about. They met him there and he took courage. And so Paul came to Rome, and was allowed to stay by himself with the soldiers who guarded him. And that is the end of the Book of Acts, though it seems just to stop without really having an ending. But Paul at last is in Rome.

Well, we can see that God sends people into our lives to encourage us. And that is his ordinary way of encouraging us himself. I chose this passage to start the series with because it shows this pattern so clearly, and in all the rest of the series we are going to deal with people. But in this first sermon I also want you to see that God himself is the first encourager.

Open to the first chapter of Revelation. This chapter describes John who writes this book, the last book of the Bible. And we believe it's John the son of Zebedee, the youngest of the disciples, now an old man — he is the Bishop of Ephesus and the Bishop of the seven churches. In fact, he writes this book to the seven churches. He is their bishop, he loves them, and he has now been imprisoned in Ephesus, a terrible place.

I had the chance to visit the Isle of Patmos a couple of years ago, and it's a quaint little island now. But, believe this, it was a grim island for John. There was virtually no rainfall on Patmos. In fact, to this day they have to bring water in by ship to supply the island. There are all kinds of elaborate cistern systems to catch the rain, when it does rain. But it happens to be a totally leeward island with hardly any rain at all. So the Romans decided to use it for something they thought it would be good for, and that was for prisoners. They put prisoners on it to quarry stone, because there was a lot of stone on the island.

Prisoners were kept in virtual solitary confinement while they were on the Isle of Patmos. So John, this beloved bishop, is being expunged by the Romans, not only with hard labor, at this late point in his life, but also with isolation. He is put where there are no friends, such as Paul had. When Paul got to Rome the Christians could come from Three Taverns, but there are no Three Taverns near Patmos. There is nothing there. There are no friends that can come to comfort John. So God comforts him himself. Have you ever had that happen?

Now you are going to see it happen, in the first chapter of Revelation — watch it! You heard it in the song earlier in our service; now listen to it in the text. John decides to address his churches, the seven churches in Asia. (He means the province of Asia, which is modern-day Turkey.) "Grace to you and peace from him who is and who was and who is to come [John loves this kind of boundary language because he sees all of history as boundary; to him it is a terribly important point that the history of our lives has boundaries at the beginning and at the end], and from the seven spirits who are before his throne, and from Jesus Christ the faithful witness, the firstborn of the dead, and the ruler of kings on earth."

It helps us to know that the first thing John does after greeting his readers is to remember the good news about Jesus Christ. "To him who loved us and has freed us from our sins by his blood and made us a kingdom, priests to his God and Father, to him be glory and dominion forever and ever. Amen." Remembering positive things like the good news of the gospel is a good thing to do when you are alone. Remember the great truths.

Our closing song today is from the Book of Lamentations. Jeremiah, who was totally alone in Lamentations, said, "I will remember the faithfulness of God." This is what John does in Revelation. He starts to remember the goodness of God. "Behold, he is coming with the clouds and every eye will see him, every one who pierced him; and all the tribes of the earth [the nations, all of us], will wail on account of him [when we think that this One was slain in our behalf]. Even so. Amen." Listen to the rest. "'I am the Alpha and the Omega [the Beginning and the End],' says the Lord God who is and who was and who is to come, the Almighty." Alpha and Omega are the first and last letters of the Greek alphabet. We have them right here on this altar cloth. One of the oldest signs of Christendom is Alpha and Omega. It is the great affirmation that God gives boundaries to everything — the beginning and the end.

Now listen as John speaks autobiographically. "I John, your brother, who share with you in *tribulation* [the word in Greek means intense pressure] and the kingdom [that is, I share with you the intense pressure but also the kingly reign] and the patient endurance [stay-in-there, hang-in-there endurance] of Jesus Christ, was on the island that is called Patmos on account of the word of God and the testimony of Jesus. I was in the spirit on the Lord's Day [another way of saying I was alone, I just had my own spirit, no friends worshiping with me], and I heard behind me a loud voice like a trumpet" [notice the word *like* because the rest of this passage is John trying to describe a vision he had, and he has to say what the vision was *like* because the experience was too big for his words to express]. This trumpet-voice was saying to John, "Write what you see in a book and send it to the seven churches [which are in Asia], to Ephesus..."[then he lists all seven churches of which John is the bishop, the people John loves so much].

"Then I turned to see the voice that was speaking to me, and on turning I saw seven golden lampstands [this is one of the rare images in Revelation that is actually interpreted to us in the Scripture itself, at the end of this chapter, where the seven lampstands are identified as the seven churches — that is one interpretation I can make with assurance] and in the midst of the lampstands [seven churches] one like the Son of Man...." In other words, I saw Jesus Christ walking among you. Don't you love that? I have found that when people are alone and worried, their minds are filled with questions like "I wonder what my children are doing right now; I wonder if they are all right; how are they doing?" In John's image you see the seven lampstands. (Do you have seven children? Well, then this is a text for you.)...John saw the seven churches and Jesus Christ, the Son of Man, walking among them. Isn't that great! He was taking care of them.

So "I saw the seven lampstands and in the midst of the lampstands [I saw] one like the Son of Man, clothed with a long robe and with a golden girdle round his breast; his head and his hair were white as white wool, white as snow; his eyes were like a flame of fire [notice this is all *like* — an image that is too big for him], his feet were like burnished bronze, refined as in a furnace, and his voice was like the sound of many waters. In his right hand he held seven stars, from his mouth issued a sharp two-edged sword [in other words, when he spoke it was with incredible power that cut in two directions], and his face was like the sun shining in full strength. When I saw him, I fell at his feet as though dead." This is easy to relate to: when John saw him he did what anybody would do, he was terrified, so he fell as if he were dead. Maybe that's what you would do too; I'm sure I would. Something like that is a little too much for our imagination to handle.

And now comes an incredible surprise: "But he laid his right hand [the hand of authority] upon me, saying, 'Fear not. I am the first and the last, and the living one; I died, and behold I am alive forever more, and I have the keys of Death and Hades [the place of death]. Now write what you see and send it to your beloved churches.'" And that's the beginning of the Book of Revelation.

I would call that quite an experience, wouldn't you? A moment of wonder in which you have the mixture of the awesome power of God and then the surprising kindness of God. Maybe this is where England got the idea of knighting — when the king or queen knights a soldier or a great hero of the realm. Do you know what happens in knighting? Have you ever thought about the odd mixture that is present in the knighting of a man or woman? The great hero kneels in front of the ruler — today it would be the queen — and a sword (a very sharp sword). And if she were just a little careless or didn't particularly like this hero, she could just whack off his head. She has that kind of power: she is the queen, and she has all this authority. Then the queen takes this sword (and this is the great moment of the knighting)...and instead of chopping his head off, or stabbing him, or saying, "That's enough of you; let's have another one"...instead of that, she puts the sword on his shoulder (just like it happened to John, when the right hand — the hand of power — was put on his shoulder);...she puts the sword on one shoulder, then passes the sword over his head and puts it on the other shoulder and says, "I knight you, and you are now Sir Lancelot."

It's a big surprise. John would probably describe it to us this way. "I had this incredible power in front of me, and now this omnipotent One tenderly says to me, 'Don't be afraid; I'm for you.'" That is encouragement — really, a definition of encouragement.

Now there may be a big question on the minds of some of you. Let me see if I can bring that question to the surface. The big question that many people ask, and maybe you have asked it yourself: "If God can be so vividly present with John on the Isle of Patmos, then why can't he do it on Mercer Island? Or Whidbey Island?" Or some other island in your life.

Heaven knows Mercer Island needs it. If you watch "Almost Live" then you know that they have the Mercer Island Mission trying to take care of those poor folks. If God can meet John on the Isle of Patmos in this dramatic way, then why can't he do it with you or me? Maybe some of you have had that experience, but most of you haven't. Why doesn't he do it? Well, he can if he chooses and if you need him. But, ordinarily, it is clear in the Bible, he will help you and assure you with people. If he can't find any people, he will do it himself.

I'll prove that to you. When Paul got to Rome he was comforted by people from the town of Three Taverns. (The Three Cafes?) The people from the Three Cafes came to comfort Paul, the hero of the Book of Acts. No angels. No nothing. Just people. The court official who was going to carry the gospel to the Queen of the Ethiopians — that man was reading the Book of Isaiah, and he was wide open and wanted to meet God. And how did God meet him in Acts 8? He brought Philip, and Philip joined him on his chariot. And Philip baptized him.

Cornelius the centurion, a Roman official who could do a lot for God, is a good man and he wants to meet God. In Acts, chapter 10, how does God meet Cornelius? Well, he does waste two angels. He has an angel go to Cornelius. Cornelius is so open that you want to zap him right there and make him a converted Christian and get him on with his job. Instead, guess what happens: the angel comes to Cornelius — you can read it for yourself in Acts 10 — and says to send men to go get a man named Peter down in Joppa. Then he sends an angel to Peter (wasting two angels — God is not very efficient). Peter is a slow learner. The angel has to have all kinds of things happen to Peter to get him ready to go with the messengers that Cornelius will send and to go to a Gentile's house, which Jews are forbidden to do. So God sends another angel to Peter so that Peter will go to Cornelius and share the good news. Why not go directly to Cornelius? Because, ordinarily God does not do that. He could. And if there is no one to come to help you, God will do it himself.

John Bunyan experienced that in prison. There may be some of you who have had a lonely hour in the night when there was nobody that could come to you but you were comforted by God. But, ordinarily…ordinarily he will do it with people. That doesn't mean that God cannot use mysterious ways. He does. I believe in angels. The Book of Hebrews gives us an interesting and wonderful statement that says, "Be careful, to entertain strangers, because some have entertained angels unaware." So, you never know what God is doing. But, ordinarily God uses people in our lives.

J. R. R. Tolkien, the man who led C. S. Lewis to Jesus Christ, actually convinced Lewis of the reality of Christ. But Tolkien later would write in his own journal this statement: "The unpayable debt I owe to C. S. Lewis was not influence as it is ordinarily understood, but sheer encouragement. He for a long time was my only audience, and only from him did I ever get the idea that my stuff could be anything more than a private hobby." Tolkien is describing *The Lord of the Rings*. Lewis encouraged Tolkien to publish *The Lord of the Rings*. He played that role in Tolkien's life. There are people ready to play that role in your life, and you must be ready to play that role in other people's lives.

Now what is it that God wants us to know? Let's look at the text. It is clear what God wants John to know. First, he wants John to remember the great facts of grace and victory. John says, "I remember the fact that Christ died for me and that he rose and conquered death." Then God wants John to know that he is not alone. And also — and I love this — John needs to know that his churches are not alone.

I have talked to lots of people who were dying, and I want to tell you the one thing I have discovered about people who are at the end of their life, who are gravely ill: they are not so much concerned about themselves. After all, they are going to be okay. They are really concerned about the ones they love. When I get a chance to pray with someone who's critically ill, I always pray in his or her presence that God will bless this person. But I always go on to pray (still in his or her presence): "O Lord, bless the ones that this brother (or this sister) loves." Remember the seven lampstands. Help those gravely ill individuals to know that Jesus is walking among those seven lampstands. And he is.

John needed to know that, and the Lord assured him of that. Then

John needed to know that the Lord who is among the lampstands reigns. He needed to know that this reigning Lord loved John. Finally, John got to know that Jesus loved John's churches. And that is why he put his hand on John's shoulder.

Brothers and sisters, you are not alone. You need to know that.

*Heavenly Father, thank you for this day. Thank you that we are not alone, because we need to know that. And we need also to know that you are going to use our lives as you have used other people's lives to assure us of this and to assure others that they are not alone. Thank you for this, Lord. In Jesus' name we pray. Amen.*

# COMMENT

"Alone." A chilling word in a culture that pretends everybody has someone you can reach out and touch in an electronic moment. Earl Palmer challenges that myth in his sermon "Not Alone" and offers a biblical alternative to loneliness. The sermon addresses a widely known, strongly felt, and therefore motivating need in our society. The need for people in our lives who are there and really care drives us to try all kinds of strategies — some even spiritual — to fill our personal sense of loneliness and isolation.

Palmer takes a different approach than one might expect from a cultural analysis, psychological explanation, or self-help seminar. He teaches the Bible. But he teaches the Bible in such a way that people can relate to the text regardless of their spiritual maturity. This quality is distinctive of this particular sermon.

Palmer demonstrates a real knack for communicating on several different levels. He uses graphic word pictures. He includes exposition of the text. He also makes creative use of what might be called "teaching tangents." The hearer comes away with a sense of Palmer's deep love and respect for the Scriptures. The hearer also feels encouraged to act on the theme the text highlights as an invitation to overcome loneliness.

## FORMAT

Palmer begins this first in a new series of sermons by referring to his previous sermon series. Then he continues with prayer. The nonverbal implications remind the hearers they are already "not alone." They have received a personal revelation — a "love letter" if you will from God — and they are invited to listen as Palmer simply talks to God, who is present in the same room.

The preacher's opening phrase is meant to be reassuring. "God knows us very well." For some hearers it may be quite intimidating to think that God does know what makes us tick. But Palmer immediately focuses our attention on the problem of too much aloneness. Quoting from one of his many "teaching tangents," he reminds us of the long, incredible history of God's loving understanding of our need for relationships.

Moving to theory, Palmer "culturalizes" this felt need with a reference to an obscure study done in Italy by a Harvard political scientist, then applies it practically with a "bombshell" explanation of the growing phenomenon of solo bowling in America. Many of the hearers may have engaged in the "sport" during just the previous week.

Palmer captures the tension between rugged American individualism and our need for friends. He clarifies those friends as those who might even be antagonists. Palmer begins one of his "teaching tangents" which are charateristic of his style of preaching. These tangents allow him to accomplish a number of things without departing from his central theme or biblical text.

First, Palmer's teaching tangents allow his personal passions to come to expression. It becomes obvious that the preacher has a love for the life of C. S. Lewis. He has studied Lewis and understands more about him than he can put in a series of sermons. At the risk of trying the patience of those parishioners who do not share his admiration for this great Christian apologist, Palmer can still use the tangent to illustrate the point of his sermon.

Second, the biblical tangents in the sermon become a means of engaging hearers at different levels of awareness and spiritual maturity without "derailing" the entire sermon on a theme which may not be of as broad an interest as his title designates.

For example, Palmer uses the story of Paul's arrival in Rome as an apparent tangent to teach the importance of having friends. He later uses a tangent on angels to illustrate just the opposite. What happens when a man like John in exile on the Island of Patmos has no friends? Angels come to minister to him. The point is that Christians are never abandoned to total isolation even when earthly friendships are cut off.

While these teaching tangents may appear at first to be excursions away from his central theme, Palmer weaves them into his sermon in such a way as to invite hearers, who themselves may have wandered away, back into the center of the sermon again. There is "method to his madness" especially if we recognize the human capacity to process information faster than we normally speak. The teaching tangents give hearers an opportunity to reflect on some other thoughts until the preacher brings them back to the theme at hand.

As a communicator, you can use the tool of the "teaching tangent" in similar ways. You can make a subpoint without having to elaborate. Or you can address a topic of special interest to a particular part of the listening audience. But it is important to use such tangents deliberately in preaching. Of course, we must always beware of digressions which go nowhere and often result from inadequate preparation or discipline. If you make a tangential point in a sermon, always ask youself, "Does this point serve some meaningful purpose? Is it important or necessary?" Feedback from trusted reviewers of our sermons will give us a good idea if our tangents are accomplishing their desired ends.

## TEXT

Palmer is a gifted Bible teacher. He chooses to address his assigned New Testament text midway through the sermon. He helps the hearers understand the context of the passage by creating a number of word pictures that help us visualize the setting of the text. This gives more of a three-dimensional perspective and connects music they heard earlier in worship to the experience of being alone in the text of Revelation 1.

Palmer then proceeds with a line-by-line expository section of biblical teaching that conveys the intensity of the text and of Palmer's preaching style. He interposes personal questions or exclamations that help create a feeling of excitement about actually reading the Bible for yourself. He involves the hearer in the text by communicating his own anticipation of what God is saying as he rephrases the text in first-person English.

Notice that Palmer does not get into numerology or systematic theology in this sermon. He allows the text to interpret itself and points out places where it does. This allows the hearer to feel better equipped to revisit the passage to receive truth without having to rely on the preacher to do the exegesis professionally. For example, quoting from the first chapter of Revelation, Palmer shows how the passage where the seven lampstands are interpreted as the seven churches illustrates the biblical principle of allowing Scripture to interpret Scripture. He underscores this approach by indicating his confidence in the interpretation John makes within the text. In light of the text Palmer makes an important application that Jesus is walking among his churches, and with us.

Palmer also teaches some good pastoral care in this sermon. He points out a dimension of need when people are all alone in their concern for their children. Later he comes back to this little "gem" to show how caring visitors can reassure and encourage people who are facing extreme loneliness or the possibility of death by using this word picture of Jesus' seven children as lampstands or churches. At the conclusion of this sermon, Palmer has given the family loving tools to say and pray in circumstances that call for spiritual encouragement when the preacher can't be at the bedside of a gravely ill person. Preaching is one way of equipping Christians to care for lonely, ill, and anxious people with whom they may come in contact.

## PROCLAMATION

In this sermon the multiple biblical word pictures of encouragement become "gospel" for hearers who confront their own loneliness. Palmer summarizes his sermon by asking one of his rhetorical questions, "Now what is it that God wants us to know?"

First, God wants John to remember the facts of grace and victory. Second, God wants John to know that both he and his churches for whom he was the bishop were not alone. Palmer's closing prayer thanks God that we are not alone. This sums up the good news for John and for us from Revelation 1. The sermon ends on a high note that would lend itself to a great worship theme which Palmer foreshadows in the middle of the sermon, "Great is thy faithfulness."

### RESPONSE

One can picture the hearers personally stirred by the powerful scriptural truths they have just experienced. Lonely people in the congregation may go away feeling better because they have heard the tremendous reminder of God's loving presence. Others may go away feeling more confident they could respond to a friend in need. Seekers may have been given a different glimpse of the nature of God than they received when they were growing up. Palmer lets the Holy Spirit speak through the words of Scripture at different levels in different ways.

This is one reason this sermon is effective. By giving hearers multiple ways of responding to the truths presented, Palmer gives them great freedom to apply the encouragement to their daily lives. For some, this might be too open-ended. Except for a brief reference to a mission in a nearby community, he does not direct people to get involved in ministry to the needy in any particular way. Not every sermon need focus on practical application to the same degree. But over time in preaching to a congregation, it is important that we be as specific as possible in challenging people to live out the faith in practical ways.

It is hard to find the balance between direction and freedom. Our culture seems distracted and people are pulled in many different ways. Often we need to become more specific in our application — to help people "get it" — and not assume most will respond with concrete action steps on their own.

In this sermon, Palmer's use of a brief illustration of application in the middle of another "tangent" on queenly authority is just what was needed to convey the practical need to apply biblical truths to Christian lifestyle and ministry. Palmer creates the word picture of the knighting of a hero. You can see the queen standing with her sword having the power to take an ear — or your life! He ties the illustration together by suggesting if God can empower John on the Island of Patmos, then we can be empowered to minister in the settings we find ourselves instead of feeling alone.

## SUGGESTIONS

- Notice how Palmer teaches "pastoral care" in this sermon. Reflect on some practical tools your congregation could use in dealing with people in need with whom they will have contact. How can you incorporate biblical applications to caring skills as a regular feature of your preaching?

- Palmer has a knack for making faraway places and distant times in history seem contemporary. How can you enter "into" the text so you can create word pictures that will draw your hearers in with you? Perhaps you can take key words, phrases or concepts from the text for your sermon and list particular experiences in your life that will "contextualize" biblical ideas for your hearers.

- Think about "tangents" you might be tempted to make — planned and unplanned — in your preaching. How do they help or hinder your attempts to communicate a key point or concept in your sermons? If necessary, how can you become more intentional about your tangents so they don't distract from your effectiveness in preaching? How can you use them to allow your hearers different ways of engaging your sermon at different levels?

- What is your understanding of expository preaching as a preaching method? How can we preach the Word without turning our sermons into seminars? In what ways, if any, do we need to "root" our preaching more in the biblical text?

*Gary W. Downing*

C O M M E N T

# INVESTING IN FUTURES:

## THE LIFE OF BARNABAS

ACTS 4:32–37

REV. PETE BRISCOE
BENT TREE BIBLE FELLOWSHIP
DALLAS, TEXAS

# INVESTING IN FUTURES:
## THE LIFE OF BARNABAS

ACTS 4:32–37

When I was a teenager, my dad and I had a conversation that was a turning point in my life. Dad's first words put me on red alert for real trouble when he said, "Pete, sit down. I want to talk with you."

I said, "About what, Dad?" He said, "I want to teach you how to invest your money." I said, "Dad, I don't have any money." "Yes, but someday you may have a little to invest, and I want to teach you some principles." "Great," I said, "let's go." So we sat down and he started talking about a long-term plan. He started talking about aggressive investments and stable investments. How you had to have most of your money in stable investments and a small amount of money in the aggressive ones. "But, Pete," he said, "the most important thing you need to understand is this — you need to find someone who is an investment expert, and you need to get their advice. You need to be able to trust them, and you need to take their advice carefully so that they can lead you through the process." That made sense to me.

Then Dad said, "Peter, let me talk to you about something a little different. I want to talk to you about your life. In the same way that you can either spend your money or invest it, you can spend your life or invest it too." "What do you mean, Dad?" He said, "We've all seen people that just spend their life. They spend their time, they spend their money, they spend their talents, and they just spend their life. And a lot of them are pretty happy folks. Then we see people that go about life in a different way. They invest their life. They see things a little differently. They invest their time, they invest their treasure, they invest their talents so that they might make a difference, not only for this world, but for the future world as well."

Now we were getting to the real point. "Peter," he said, "this is your mom's and dad's prayer for you — that you be a young man who *invests* his life, instead of simply spends it." That had a powerful impact on me. Then he said, "Pete, you need to find someone who will be an expert on how to invest your life. Then you need to follow their advice. By the way, there are a lot of them in Scripture."

### THE LIFE OF BARNABAS

[Pastor Pete begins his sermon.]

Today we start a new series entitled "Investing in Futures." This morning I'm going to introduce you to a person I consider to be the greatest example of an investor in futures that has ever lived. In fact, he is going to preach to you today and share with you some advice on how to invest yourself in futures. While I go to find him, Tom is going to lead you in prayer and have you look up a Scripture passage to read together. In the meantime I'm going to find the expert and he'll come and share with you. Thanks for coming up, Tom.

[Pastor Pete leaves.  Tom comes to the pulpit to pray and read Acts 4:32–37.]

*All the believers were one in heart and mind. No one claimed that any of his possessions were his own but shared everything they had. With great power the apostles continued to testify to the resurrection of the Lord Jesus. And much grace was upon them all. There were no needy persons among them. For from time to time those who owned land and houses sold them, brought the money from the sales and put it at the apostles' feet, and it was distributed to anyone as he had need. Joseph, a Levite from Cyprus, whom the apostles called Barnabas (which*

*means Son of Encouragement), sold a field he owned and brought the*
*money and put it at the apostles' feet.*

[A man from Jesus' time, dressed in the garb of the day, steps up to the pulpit to speak with the congregation.]

I have never done this before except for the other two services this morning. I'm not a real preacher, but Pete said to me, "Barnabas, of all the people in biblical history, you're the one person I think really epitomizes someone who has his life invested in futures. I don't agree with what you just said about not being a preacher, since your friend Luke contradicts that right here in the Book of Acts where he wrote about you." Well, I checked in Acts and, sure enough, Luke did write about me. There are a number of stories there about how I invested my life. So here I am, and I'll share with you nine principles that really govern my life and help me to invest my life in people — in futures, instead of just spending my life.

Now, I don't know how to do an introduction, so let's just start. Here's the first thing I would encourage you to do:

1. *Invest financially.* In the passage from Acts 4 that you just read together, notice that I sold a piece of land and I gave the money away. Now at this time in the early church there were some very, very poor people. In fact, most of us were extremely poor. Then there were some other people who had a little bit of property. The problem was that so many of the poor were really hurting. The apostles said that if any of us could sell anything and bring some money to help meet these people's needs we should feel free to do so.

I may have been the first person who did, and perhaps that's why I got mentioned in the Bible; I'm not sure. But I had a piece of property in Cyprus (where I originally came from), which I sold. I brought the money and laid it at the apostles' feet. "Here," I said, "please use this." I gave something of my own because I remember Jesus saying on one occasion, "You cannot serve both God and money."

That really created a tension, a struggle in my heart, because I wanted to serve Jesus, but I knew I was serving money at the same time. Jesus pulled me aside one day and said, "Barnabas, what do you think is the best thing to do with money? Buy a house? No. Put your kids through school? It's a good thing but it's not the best thing." He went on, "Barnabas, the best thing to do with your money is to give it away." I said, "What?" "That's right," he said. "The best thing you can do with your money is to give it away."

I never forgot that talk with Jesus. So, as I went through life, every time I came into some money I tried to give it away. And you know, he was right — it *is* the best thing you can do with your money. It brings more joy than anything else you do with it. So I encourage you to invest financially. That's principle #1.

As I said, I am not a preacher and I don't know how to do transitions, so let's just go on to principle #2.

2. *Invest courageously.* Let's find Acts 9:26 in your scrolls. I'd like to read you another story good brother Luke wrote about me. It's about what I think is probably the best investment I ever made in my whole life. I had to do it courageously; it was risky. Many of you have heard of Saul. In the early days of the church Saul was its greatest persecutor. He went around throwing Christians in prison and having them killed for their faith. But, then one day on the road to Damascus, Saul met Jesus Christ, and he was changed instantly. It was amazing. Remarkable. Later I saw him preaching Jesus in Damascus, and that's where we pick up the story, in Acts 9:26: "When he [Saul] came to Jerusalem he tried to join the disciples, but they were all afraid of him, not believing that he was really a disciple."

Understandable, isn't it? Saul had been killing disciples and then all of a sudden he shows up at the door of the church and says, "Hi, I'm one of you guys." Yeah, right! They were having trouble accepting Saul.

"But Barnabas [that's me] took him and brought him to the apostles. He told them how Saul on his journey had seen the Lord and that the Lord had spoken to him, and how in Damascus he had preached fearlessly in the name of Jesus. So Saul stayed with them and moved about freely in Jerusalem, speaking boldly in the name of the Lord."

Ah! This brings me great joy, just thinking back to one of the great moments in my life.

Investment strategists today will talk about something called the risk-reward trade-off. If you make a really small risk in your investment you will probably get a very small dividend. But, it's when you take massive risks that you make massive dividends. When I looked at Saul of Tarsus, I realized that I was looking right into the eye of a risk. I could take him to the church of Jesus Christ and he could be lying and he could slaughter all my brothers and sisters. That was a distinct possibility. I could lose not only my reputation, but I could lose my friends and my brothers and sisters in Christ. I looked at that risk and it was massive.

But then I looked at the potential of this young man, Saul. Oh, he had the brightest mind — he was the sharpest man I ever met. And, could he think! He knew the Old Testament inside out. Not only that, he was a great preacher. (I wish he was here today instead of me.) I'm not a preacher; Paul was the preacher. And he loved Jesus like no one I'd ever met.

So I saw the great potential in Saul, and the great risk, and was weighing what I should do. Finally, I chose to invest courageously. I took the risk and introduced him to the church. Just look at the dividends that we have from that investment! There in your scroll are thirteen New Testament books written by this man Saul, who became Paul. One of those books, Romans, is probably the greatest theological treatise of our times. The three greatest missionary journeys of all time were accomplished by this man. He introduced Jesus Christ and planted churches in the five major areas of the ancient world — in fact, all across the ancient world — in less than ten years. He went from Syria to Italy, and, many of us believe, on to Spain as well, telling people about Jesus all the way to the coast. Not only that, but he is the one that really explained to us the concept of grace. If it hadn't been for Paul, we probably wouldn't understand grace the way we do today.

So you look at the dividends of that investment and you look at the risk and you say, "Man, I'd take that risk a thousand times."

Now, over the next few weeks and months, you'll be thinking about risky investments that you may make in the church of Jesus Christ in a lot of different forms. You will be struggling, asking yourself, Should I do this, or should I not do this? Should I invest this way or should I not? It might be something of a risk for you. But my advice to you is to remember — the bigger the risk the bigger the dividend. I'd encourage you to do it. Or the way we said it in ancient Israel — just do it! Do you still say that now? You do! Okay, just do it!

3. *Invest in the Body.* What I am talking about here is the church of Jesus Christ. That is the best investment that anybody can make. Look in Acts 11:22. Let me give you a little context here. There was a church growing up in Antioch, north of Israel. The people in Jerusalem, my church, were very nervous because the members up there were Gentiles and we were all Jews. (And you know we were always a little nervous about those folks.) So we were not quite sure what was going on up at Antioch.

So we come in on Acts 11:22. "News of this [the church in Antioch] reached the ears of the church at Jerusalem and they sent Barnabas to Antioch." Now let me say something here: historians who know about the church will tell you that this — my trip to Antioch — was possibly the most important moment in the history of the church of Jesus Christ. You know why? Because when I came back with my report to Jerusalem I could either say yea or nay as to these Gentiles coming into the church. If I had said nay after this trip, you folks wouldn't know about Jesus today. Pretty important, wasn't it?

But, that's not what happened. Look what does: "When Barnabas arrived [oh, that sounds easy — it wasn't; it was a 325-mile journey on a mule with a wooden saddle. Think about that for a second.]… When he arrived and saw the evidence of the grace of God he was glad and he encouraged them all to remain true to the Lord with all their hearts. [Now, Luke says a little something about me in here that's a bit embarrassing, so I'll read it quickly.]

"He [Barnabas] was a good man, full of the Holy Spirit and faith, [this is the good part] and a great number of people were brought to the Lord." The word *brought* means "added." What I'm talking about here is all the people that came to know Jesus. I sent a note back to Jerusalem: "Hey, there's nothing to worry about. This is what a church really should be like. There are people coming to know Jesus all over the place." So I made an investment in the church of Jesus Christ in Antioch. I chose to go and spend some time up there, even though I had a business and a family and things to take care of at home.

Keep reading with me. "Then Barnabas went to Tarsus to look for Saul." Now, Tarsus is another hundred miles on my wooden saddle on my mule, but I went anyway, because I knew I needed Saul's help. Saul had been off the scene, having fled Israel to Tarsus a number of years earlier in fear for his life. And he hadn't been seen for ages. I knew he was in Tarsus somewhere, and I went to look for him at his parents' home. They didn't know where he was. But I knew I needed Saul. Verse 26: "And when he found him he brought him to Antioch. So for a whole year, Barnabas and Saul met with the church and taught great numbers of people. The disciples were called Christians first at Antioch." Notice, we stayed there a whole year. Deciding to invest myself in the church of Jesus Christ in Antioch was a good investment. The Scripture says that the followers of Jesus were first called Christians in Antioch. I remember the pagans of the city saying *"Christos! Christos!* All they ever talk about is *Christos!"* So they called us *Christosians* — Christians. I thought that was what a church should be like; all we ever talk about is Jesus! Jesus! Jesus!

Now why is the church of Jesus Christ the best investment that anyone can make? Here's why. Investment advisors today will tell you that there are two kinds of investments: stable investments and aggressive investments. Stable investments last a long time and don't fluctuate a whole lot — your investment is always there. Well, the church is the most stable investment you can make; it's been around for 2,000 years now. How many of you are investing in any companies that have been around that long? Probably not any of you. You know what else? That investment's going to last through eternity. That's a long-term investment. Long, long term. As stable as it gets. It's lasted 2,000 years and it's going to last forever.

But, you know what makes it a *great* investment? The fact that not only is it a stable investment, it's also the most aggressive investment you can make. There's nothing like the church of Jesus Christ, anywhere in the world, when it comes to activity, and reaching its mission. Thousands of people will come to know Jesus Christ this morning in church services across the face of the earth. The church of Jesus Christ is the best investment anyone can make, and it produces the best dividend too. That's why I poured my life and everything I was into the church of Jesus Christ.

4. *Invest in an understudy.* I spent my life doing this. Saul was my first, and as you can imagine, I'm very proud of what happened to him. We are introduced to another, John Mark, in Acts 12:25: "When Barnabas and Saul had finished their mission, they returned from Jerusalem, taking with them John, also called Mark." This was my boy, not my son; I wanted to invest in him so I kind of adopted him as my understudy.

Now the first thing I want to share with you about Mark is that he was a *follower.* We first see him in Scripture in Mark 14:51, where the story has it that Jesus was in the Garden of Gethsemane and a young man wearing nothing but a linen garment was following him. Apparently, Mark jumped out of bed, threw a linen garment around himself, and ran after Jesus. "When they seized him, he fled naked, leaving his garment behind." Here's the first streaker in scriptural history! Not a very auspicious introduction for young John Mark, but there it is. The important point is not that he was streaking through the Garden but that he was following Jesus, whom he passionately loved. And that's what really attracted me.

Second, Mark was a *church member.* Acts 12 tells about the time a group was praying in the house for Peter to be released from prison. While they are praying, Peter is miraculously released and goes to the house, knocks on the door, and the servant girl who responds, but doesn't open the door, says, "Peter's here." The other people inside say, "Can't be Peter; he's in prison," even though they'd been praying to God for his release. Remember that? Here's how it goes, "When this had dawned on Peter [that he'd been rescued by an angel] he went to the house of Mary the mother of John, also called Mark, where many people had gathered and were praying." It was John Mark's house where this was happening. They were one of the good families of the church; John Mark was one of the kids that grew up in the church — like all our kids upstairs right now. He was a follower of Jesus and a member of the church.

Third — and this may surprise you — Mark was a *quitter.* Acts 13:13 says: "From Paphos, Paul and his companions sailed to Perga in Pamphylia, where John left them to return to Jerusalem." No details are given there, but let me fill them in for you. John Mark walked up to me and Paul one day and said, "I've had it, I can't do it anymore, I'm tired, I wasn't cut out for this. I'm going home to Jerusalem." Oh, Paul was angry! I was pretty angry too, but I still saw potential in that boy. Like I did a long time before in the young man Saul. I couldn't give up on him.

Next, I want to point out that Mark became *an investment.* The next time we see him mentioned is in Acts 15:36. "Some time later Paul said to Barnabas, 'Let us go back and visit the brothers in all the towns where we preached the word of the Lord and see how they are doing.'" Verse 37 tells that "Barnabas wanted to take John, also called Mark, with them. But Paul did not think it wise to take him, because he had deserted them in Pamphylia and had not continued with them in the work. They had such a sharp disagreement that they parted company. Barnabas took Mark and sailed for Cyprus, but Paul chose Silas and left." This Scripture is so nicely worded, "sharp disagreement." It was a lot worse than that. We had a knock-down, drag-out fight. I wanted to invest in this boy and Paul said he was not coming with me and I said are you making me choose between you and him and Paul said, "Yeah." I said, "Fine, I'll take John Mark." I chose John Mark over Paul the apostle. That's how badly I wanted to invest in that boy.

This is the exciting part. After Mark became an investment with me and went with me to Cyprus and on a missionary journey, Mark became a worker. 1 Peter 5:13 says: "She who is in Babylon chosen together with you sends you her greeting and so does my [Paul's] son Mark." Mark had been brought back into the apostles' group and worked with them. Mark also became a contributor. In my favorite verse in Scripture, 2 Timothy 4:11, Paul says to Timothy, "Only Luke is with me. Get Mark and bring him with you because he is helpful to me in the ministry." Yes! Isn't that great! The Apostle Paul finally came around and admitted that Mark was helpful. But, folks, if I hadn't invested in him, Paul would never have said that. Paul would never have given him another chance, because he was so angry. Luckily I saw the potential in that boy, so I invested in him. It's really exciting that Mark also became an author. The Gospel of Mark in your scrolls there is written by him. It is one of the four great accounts of the life of Jesus Christ. Oh, am I glad that I invested in that boy! What a wonderful minister he was.

Pastor Pete was telling me before I came out to preach today that when his son Cameron was born he got a phone call from a friend in Chicago, Don Sweeting. Don said, "Pete, you are a pastor and you've got a lot of people that you are discipling, but I want you to remember one thing that is very important: Cameron is your #1 disciple. Never forget that. Pour your life into him; invest your life in him. So Cameron will be Pete's #1 disciple. But I am also going to have other people who will be my investments. My question to you this morning, Other than your kids, who should be your #1 investment, who are you pouring your life into? Who's your John Mark? Anyone? That's one of the ways you can invest in futures.

5. *Invest personally.* A lot of the time many of us just expect everyone else to do all the investing in the church. But the way it's supposed to work is that everyone does his or her part. Acts 13:1–3 tells about an amazing event in my life. We were still in Antioch teaching (remember, I stayed there for a year to invest in the church): "At the church in Antioch there were prophets and teachers. Barnabas, Simeon called Niger, Lucius of Cyrene, Manaen (who had been brought up with Herod the tetrarch), and Saul. While they were worshiping the Lord and fasting, the Holy Spirit said, 'Set apart for me Barnabas and Saul for the work to which I have called them.' So after they had fasted and prayed, they placed their hands on them and sent them off." Get the picture here — I just went up to Antioch for a weekend trip, so to speak, to find out if everything that was going on up there was okay. I saw the tremendous need, went to get Saul, and brought him back, and we stayed there a whole year to teach and train those people. During that year they decided it would be good for us to go off on a mission trip. But we really felt it was the Lord telling us to do that too, so we went.

From that moment on I invested the rest of my life in mission work; I invested myself personally. Now a lot of you may say, and a lot of people over the centuries have asked me, "How did you make a sacrifice like that?" Well, I tell them about the day that I will never forget. As long as I live eternally, I will never forget that day. It was dark and gloomy — just a depressing day to begin with. Jesus had been tried, the verdict had come down, and he had been convicted of what we had no idea. They never told us, but he had been convicted anyway. He was flogged and beaten. He came out into the streets of Jerusalem carrying the crossbar of his cross. He walked through the streets, and everyone was throwing things at him and spitting on him. They were cursing him and mocking him — "King of the Jews." We were following him, quite a way back to be safe, but we were following him because he was our Savior.

They took him up to the top of Golgotha, the place of the skull. It was a ghastly place, a garbage heap. There the Savior of mankind was laid upon that piece of wood and they pounded a nail through his wrist. Folks, it doesn't say anywhere in the Bible, but that man screamed. I will never forget that sound as long as I live. They nailed his other hand, and they nailed his feet and they dropped him into the hole, dislocating every major joint in his body. We were cowering back, but we could see him. I've got to think that the pain dulled or numbed after a while because he stopped screaming and crying, but you could just see the anguish in his eyes. He looked down at his accusers and said, "Father, forgive them; they don't know what they are doing." I thought, What kind of man is this?

Then he said these words: "It is finished." He told us about those words before he died. What they meant was that the sacrifice had been completed. As soon as he said those words, it reminded me — oh yes, Jesus has died for my sins. I fell at the foot of the cross and said, "Jesus, forgive me," and Jesus said, "Barnabas, you are forgiven. It's a done deal. My blood has washed you clean." In the awe of the moment, I looked up and said, "Jesus, I will do anything for you, anything." I remember Jesus' head bowing, and the breath going from him as he died.

The most amazing thing happened three days later. I ran into Jesus alive. Wow! Was that wild! He pulled me aside and said, "Barnabas, remember that promise you made to me at the cross? That you will do anything for me?" "Yes, Jesus." "I'm going to take you up on that. There are not enough people saying that today. I'm going to ask you to sacrifice your life for me, Barnabas." I said, "Jesus, I will do whatever you want me to do."

Now here is my advice for you this morning. If you have fallen at the cross of Jesus Christ; if he has saved you and washed you clean; if you have said those words, "Jesus, I'll do anything for you" — watch out, because he's going to take you up on it. He will expect you to fully sacrifice yourself for him and his work, and, like me, you will find inexpressible joy in that. Because that's the only way to live as far as I am concerned. So invest yourself personally. Don't expect everyone else to "do it."

6. *Invest wisely.* In Acts 14:12, Paul had just done an amazing, incredible miracle. I wish you could have seen some of Paul's miracles. As miracles go, he was good, and this was a doozy! Everyone thought we were gods because of the miracles he had done. Verse 12 says, "Barnabas they called Zeus and Paul they called Hermes." They called us gods. But here is the part I want you to see. They called Paul Hermes because he was the chief speaker. But who was it that introduced Paul to the church at Jerusalem? It was me, Barnabas. Who was it that took him under his wing, trained him and taught him? It was me, Barnabas. Who was it that went and found him at Tarsus and brought him back to Antioch? It was me, Barnabas. Who was it that took him on his first missionary journey and said, "Come on, Paul; I'll take care of you?" It was me, Barnabas.... What's happening here?

If you go back to Acts 13 you will see the most amazing thing. At the beginning of the chapter it says Paul and Barnabas came to such and such a place and Paul preached, Paul talked, Paul did this and Paul did that. Then at the bottom it says, "Then Paul and Barnabas left." Then the Scripture does it again. It says, Paul and Barnabas arrive here and Paul does this and Paul does that — Paul, Paul, Paul — then Paul and Barnabas left. At the beginning of Acts it's Barnabas and Paul. At the end, it's Paul and Barnabas. I don't know if you ever noticed that switch.

What happened? Why was that? I'll tell you. It was because of a talk Paul and I had one day. It's not in Scripture but I can tell you about it today — how fortunate you are. We sat down one day and I said, "Paul, you're the preacher, I'm not. I have gifts of encouragement and administration. Let's go together. I'll go and get all the plans worked out, the itinerary set up. I'll find us a place to stay. I'll figure how we are going to work for our food, and I'll pray for you. I will encourage you. I'll take care of everything. You just get out there and preach to the people." Paul said, "Sounds good to me; that's my gift." So he exercised his gifts and I exercised mine, and, oh, what a good team we were.

The thing I want emphasize to you this morning is to invest wisely. Invest where your gift is. In fact, very few of us should be Pauls. All of us need to be Barnabases. We need to look at our gifts, figure out what our talents are, and then invest them wisely. What a great joy we had and you can have serving each other together.

7. *Invest humbly.* As we've already noted, in Acts 14, Paul and Barnabas heard the crowd calling them by the names of gods; Barnabas they called Zeus and Paul, Hermes, because he was the chief speaker. Verse 14: "When the apostles Barnabas and Paul heard of this, they tore their clothes and rushed out into the crowd, shouting: 'Men, why are you doing this? We too are only men, human like you.'" You see, they were calling us gods and we wanted them to know that we were not gods, but just people like them.

We learned a very valuable lesson that day too. You know what it was? That when you start to invest yourself wisely in ministry and the Holy Spirit works through you, you will see success. If you make yourself available, you will see success in ministry. But success in ministry is a very, very dangerous thing. Not only do other people start seeing you as a god, but you also could start seeing yourself as a god. And you could start taking all the credit.

Do you think it was Moses who split the seas so the Israelites could go through? No, it wasn't Moses, it was God working through Moses. Do you think Mary was responsible for the supernatural conception of Jesus Christ? No, it was the Holy Spirit that came upon Mary; she was the vessel. Do you think Peter was such a great preacher so that on the day of Pentecost 3,000 people came to know Jesus, and then 5,000 more?

No, it's because the Holy Spirit came and worked through him. Any time you see ministry happening, it's because the Holy Spirit is working. But he works through people. So the thing I want you to understand today is this — it's God's money, it's God time, it's God's gifts he has given you. It's God's power that makes ministry work. Don't ever, ever take credit for it yourself. You are just a vessel. I'm just a vessel. Paul was just a vessel. We are just human like you. So invest yourself humbly.

8. *Invest yourself freely.* In 1 Corinthians 9:6, Paul said, "Is it only I and Barnabas who must work for a living?" This is just one phrase in a whole chapter where Paul goes on and on about the fact that he and I never got support, especially money support, from churches. We always had to work and do the ministry on the side. We made tents all day and sold them in the market. Then at night we did our ministry. But the point of the chapter is: that's the way we wanted it. We didn't want to be tied down, and we didn't want to feel like we were getting something in return for our investment.

This morning I would like to share this principle with you: never expect anything in return for your investment. Here is where investing in money and investing in futures is different. When you invest money, you expect to get something back someday. When you invest in futures, you are just doing it for what we call the joy of the process. The joy in the Christian life is in the joy of giving, the joy of ministering, the joy of sacrificing in the process. That is where full Christian life is found. Don't worry about what you're going to get out of it.

Over the next few weeks, some of you might be planning to give a large financial gift to the new building campaign. Now I can say this because I'm Barnabas; your pastor Peter couldn't get away with this. That's why I'm here today. If you are looking forward to someone patting you on the back for the large gift you are planning to give to the campaign, don't hold your breath. Pete told me before the service that nobody here knows how much anyone gives except the person that counts the money. No one knows. So if you are looking forward to giving a big gift and getting a building named for you or getting a letter of thanks, it's not going to happen. In fact, I'll say this (I have to talk with Pete afterwards anyway to see if it's okay) — if you are going to do it with that motive, don't do it at all. If you are giving for the wrong motive anytime, don't give anything at all. It's wrong.

We invest freely. We give of ourselves just for the joy of giving — giving back to Jesus in response to what he has given us, not so that we can expect something in return in this earthly life. So invest yourself freely. With the correct motives. The way I can put this is, if you're looking for credit, invest in a credit union. But, if you are looking for eternal significance, then invest freely in the church of Jesus Christ.

9. *Invest eternally.* This is the most important principle of all. It's the one that all the others fall out of. This is where I get the term "investing in futures." I remember the day that Jesus preached what I thought was his best sermon. It was up on a mountainside. He had the people in the palm of his hand that day. It's called the Sermon on the Mount. In the middle of that great sermon he says this. Listen carefully. "Do not store up for yourselves treasures on earth, where moths and rust destroy, and where thieves break in and steal. But store up for yourselves treasures in heaven, where moths and rust do not destroy, and where thieves do not break in and steal. For where your treasure is, there your heart will be also" (Matt. 6:19–21).

When he said those words, I just couldn't get them off my mind. That's when I realized there are two ways you can live: you can store up treasures on earth, or you can invest your life storing up treasures in heaven. The reason I gave that land that you read about in Acts 4 is because I wanted to invest in those people, because they last forever. The reason I went to Antioch for a year was to invest in those people, because they last forever. And the reason I went on the mission field for the rest of my life was because I wanted to reach people for Jesus. Because I knew they would last forever. I wanted to invest in John Mark because I knew he would influence people that would live forever. Everything I did was for the purpose of investing in things of eternal nature: I was investing in futures instead of just spending my life.

There you have it. I hope it's helpful for you — these nine principles from my life that helped me invest in people's futures. Now let me go find Peter, and he'll be right back. I don't know how to conclude a sermon either. So, Tom, come on up and share with the folks and I'll go find Pete. Pete will be right back.

[Brother Tom fills in at the lectern to wait for Pete's return.]

Thanks, Barnabas, for those very encouraging words. Amen! Isn't it amazing how much Barnabas looks like Peter?

[Pete arrives, a little out of breath, stroking his hair back into place.]

Let me finish our service with this story. I want to compare Larry Bird and Bud Schaffer. Larry Bird was drafted #1 by the Boston Celtics out of Indiana State University. He became an All-Star, League MVP, won many championships, and made a good deal of money before he had to retire with a sore back. He spent his life well.

Bud Schaffer was the Larry Bird of his day. In 1951 or '52 he was the #1 draft pick of the Boston Celtics. He said no to the Celtics and put ten basketballs in a bag and went to the Philippines. He hopped into a Jeep and went wandering around from one little town to another, challenging the five best players of the town to a game of basketball. Never lost a game, one player against five. By the end of the game, the whole town was watching and laughing at all the good players because this American guy was beating them.

Bud told them all to sit down, and they all sat down. He told them of the wonderful and blessed story of Jesus Christ. And people came to Christ all over the place. He got them into the churches, and a real revival began in the Philippines. From this originated a program called "Sports Ambassadors."

A number of years later, after the Philippines had this thing really going, Bud found a young man named Tom Randall, who became Bud's John Mark. Bud took Tom under his wing. Tom, who averaged 43 points a game as a senior in college, was drafted in the NBA too, but he chose to go with Bud instead, to the Philippines. The ministry expanded into Southeast Asia, South America, and Africa as well. Now all over the world there are baseball teams and basketball teams and gymnastics teams telling people about Jesus Christ.

Tom Randall met me one day in Minneapolis and said, "Pete, I want you to come to the Philippines." I said, "I will." I went to the Philippines to play basketball and tell the people about Jesus in a small town called Ba Holong. I met a small young pastor with five people in his church. That guy had an incredible impact on me, so that later that night I said, "Lord, I want you to use me however you want, and I think you want me to be a pastor."

By the time I came back from that trip, I knew I was going to be a senior pastor. I knew that was what God wanted me to be. I came back, went through schooling, came here, and I am now your senior pastor. So if the Lord has ever used me to minister to you in any way, you can say thank you to Bud Schaffer for saying no to the Boston Celtics in 1951. You may say, "Pete, that's stretching it a bit." But just consider: If Bud had not gone to the Philippines, Tom Randall wouldn't have gone to the Philippines and I wouldn't have gone to the Philippines and I wouldn't have met that pastor and I wouldn't have had that turn in my life. And, for some of you, you wouldn't be here today either. That's the difference. Larry Bird spent his life well. He has had a good life. Bud Schaffer has reached thousands of people for Jesus Christ. Same gifts but totally different results.

My prayer is that over the next few weeks you would invest your life as well.

# COMMENT

COMMENT

"Investing in Futures" is a creative sermon on stewardship. Many pastors are reluctant to encourage the congregation they serve to give generously. They know parting with money will make some people very defensive. They know their role as the messenger will leave them open to accusations of seeking to line their own pockets. They may cringe as they imagine, or remember, someone saying, "All the church ever wants is money." Yet they know for the good of the church and the people they serve, as well as the effectiveness of the gospel, they must encourage a generous spirit.

Pete Briscoe has avoided these pitfalls with his good use of a first-person sermon. He has the congregation hear Barnabas draw upon the whole of his life as recorded in the Scriptures, in order to testify objectively to the value of giving in a wide variety of ways.

## STYLE

The most apparent aspect of style here is the choice of a first-person sermon. What makes such a style work?

First-person sermons recognize how much our culture is accustomed to dramatic presentations. By speaking in the language of the people, first-person sermons are helpful in convincing an audience to listen to an extended amount of material about a biblical character or episode.

In a sense, the entire first-person portion of this sermon is an illustration: the life of Barnabas. If we allow ourselves to think as if it truly were Barnabas delivering the sermon, then we can see that the stories he gives from his life — creatively embellished — are capable of being preached with the same type of attention-holding depth of feeling we can have when we tell dramatic stories of what really happened to us, if we do the work of truly entering into our character. Briscoe has done this especially well as he tells the story of Jesus' Crucifixion during the fifth point of this sermon, "Invest personally."

Outside of the first-person portions, there is just one illustration, the concluding story about Barnabas. But it is well chosen. It enforces the primary point of the message: Invest your life in what will last, the Reign of God.

## PROBLEM

"Are we going to spend our life or invest it?" is Briscoe's particular wording for the question a thoroughly Christian understanding of stewardship leaves us with. The closing illustration presents one outstanding basketball player who might be reasonably understood as having spent his life, contrasted with another who invested his. Another way of phrasing the question is Psalm 116:12: "What shall I return to the Lord for all his bounty to me?" (NRSV).

## TEXT

Acts 4:32–37 is listed as text for this sermon because it introduces Barnabas to the Bible's cast of characters. But in actuality, the entire New Testament record of Barnabas's life is in view.

If we truly believe in preaching the Scriptures in context, whenever we are convinced that our responsibilities in rightfully handling the Word of God compel us to proclaim the biblical understanding of a specific subject or individual, then there will be times when we cannot be satisfied merely to read a single passage of the Bible. Whether the subject is a word study or a biographical sermon, it will become important to present a fair representation of what is said throughout the Canon.

Exegesis for a first-person sermon places a strong emphasis on the context. Briscoe has repeatedly asked himself questions like "What did the world look like to Barnabas? What did it feel like? What was the social-political flavor of the times?"

Asking those kinds of questions led Briscoe to tell his audience what they needed to know in order to "feel with" Barnabas. They could thrill to Paul reaching every region of the known world with the gospel. They could share a chuckling agony at the idea of riding a mule with a wooden saddle, and appreciate the sacrifices, or investments made on behalf of the gospel by the first Christians.

Briscoe is addressing the subject of stewardship as he describes how Barnabas's life was marked by generosity of time, talent, and treasure. Notice how Barnabas, as portrayed by Briscoe, contradicts the assumptions of modern American suburbia. Instead of building one's career, the sermon promotes a priority of time to family and personal ministry, along with sacrificial financial support of the Kingdom of God. Instead of surrounding ourselves with people who have already "made it" and can help us, the preacher calls us to look for those we can help, and can invest ourselves in as understudies. What we have received from God we hold in trust for his service.

## PROCLAMATION

God giving his Son to give himself for us calls us to give of ourselves for and to God. Briscoe brings the proclamation of the cross into the equation vividly when he says of investing personally: "If Jesus has saved you (given himself for you) are you willing to do anything for him?... He will expect you to fully sacrifice yourself for him and his work." Briscoe has had to make the assumption that Barnabas was present at the Crucifixion in order to portray this point effectively, but having made that leap, it makes this a climax in the sermon. Asking ourselves what the Atonement teaches about our subject will keep us on track theologically, and add power to the message.

## RESPONSE

This sermon asks for several responses: at least one for each of the nine ways to invest in "futures." The sermon is the more effective because Briscoe outlines a practical response for each subtopic. When asked to give financially, we are told the best thing we can do with our money "is to give it away." When the topic is investing in an understudy, we are asked, "other

C O M M E N T

than your kids, who should be your #1 investment, who are you pouring your life into?" Calling for a practical response with every point will keep your audience with you and reinforce the connection between faith and life at every point.

Overall, what makes this sermon effective is that when Briscoe, at the end of the message, asks the congregation to "learn to invest their lives," they know he is asking a lot, but they are beginning to understand why and how they should do it.

## SUGGESTIONS

- Try a first-person sermon, especially if you have never done one. Read all you can about the character, and put yourself in his or her shoes. What are the life lessons of the character that your audience would benefit most from learning? How would this individual from the pages of the Bible — or from history — teach you that lesson from their life?

- If you have done first-person sermons before, add to the effectiveness of this sermon style by doing one from memory. For some people, "how-to" sermons like this one are among the easiest to do without notes of any type. Since precise sentence structure would almost harm the special quality and effectiveness of this sermon, the preacher, beyond having a solid understanding of his subject, need only memorize a list of nine ways to invest, and have a copy of the Scriptures handy.

- The publishers of *Church History* magazine have produced an excellent film series. Their motion picture on John Wesley is an excellent example of a first-person sermon.

- *The Challenge of the Disciplined Life: Christian Reflections on Money, Sex and Power* by Richard Foster (San Francisco: Harper/Collins, 1985) is an excellent treatment of many of the topics Briscoe addresses in "Investing in Futures."

*Peter J. Smith*

# I WAS
# IN THE
# CROWD

MARK 11:1–11; MATTHEW 21:1–9;
LUKE 19:28–38

REV. DR. GARY WHITBECK
MEADOWBROOK UNITED METHODIST CHURCH
FORT WORTH, TEXAS

REV. DR. GARY WHITBECK

# I WAS IN THE CROWD

MARK 11:1–11; MATTHEW 21:1–9;

LUKE 19:28–38

I t was such a beautiful day that day. I remember the deep blue of the sky broken only occasionally by fluffy clouds that slowly drifted with the gentle breeze. The air was somewhat brisk, but there was an excitement, a fascination, that made me forget about the chill. The talk was that a certain prophet was coming to town. Not that that was all that unusual for Jerusalem. There were always religious leaders coming to Jerusalem. After all, it was one of the greatest religious centers of all times. Many great teachers and proclaimers of the Pentateuch resided here, in fact. Indeed, we had the great temple where people from all over journeyed many miles to bring their offering and make homage to God.

But the people kept saying that this prophet was different from the others. I remember how word had gotten around about this man they called Jesus from the little town of Nazareth — that he had spent much time walking the roads and visiting the towns of Judea and Galilee, preaching a message of compassion and true worship of God. Some even claimed that he referred to God as "Father" as if he were his son. At first we all laughed about that but as the stories of his miracles, his kindness, his genuine love of everyone, rich or poor, continued to reach our ears, we began to think otherwise about him. Maybe he wasn't just another hustler trying to get a following for some political purpose. Seems somebody was always trying to use religion or the temple to promote their own welfare.

Then, Zera, one of the most faithful and devout men I ever knew, remembered how he was taught as a youth that some day the Son of God would enter Jerusalem to bring peace and release from the trials of life. He thought it was the great prophet Zechariah who proclaimed this would happen. We didn't think much about it because that was so long ago. Why would a man at the peak of his life take a chance with disrupting the leaders of Jerusalem when they pretty much had things the way they wanted them?

Some speculated that this new prophet was coming because he wanted to appeal to the nation, who had solemnly gathered for the festival. They predicted he would try to get them to follow his way and so make possible the establishment of the kingdom of God on earth. Others reasoned that he was coming to confront the leaders of the nation with the claims of that kingdom, so that they would either repent and follow its righteousness, or exhibit themselves as disobedient. Still others thought that he was coming because that's the way he'd always done his ministry. They said he was simply carrying on his work and had no different objective from what had been his concern in Galilee.

As you can see, no one really knew why. We only knew that this was the day he had chosen for Jerusalem.

The closer the time got, the more stories began to pour in about this man they now were calling the "Son of David." All the stories seemed too good to be true. How he forgave people their sins, how it made him angry when people didn't treat each other fairly and honestly. Heck, I know in Jerusalem most of us believed in God, but we had a life to live. We had to scratch out a living any way we could, and if that meant some of our friends got their feelings hurt, why, they would just have to get over it. Besides, the law had always taught us that if we were offended we had the right to do the very same thing back to the offender. But word was that this Jesus also forgave the women of the streets, and that he even had tax collectors and liars following him around daily. People all over were drifting into

Jerusalem, and the streets were crowded. I remember overhearing one woman tell another about the day she sat on a mountain at the prophet's feet as he spoke a beautiful message about how those who are sad and those who really try to find righteousness will someday be rewarded.

I was intrigued with this Jesus. I went home to prepare myself for his arrival. I had decided that I too was going to see and hear him. I had no sooner gotten to my door than I heard loud shouting coming from the main gate of the city. I knew he must be in sight. I started running toward the growing crowd. People were carrying myrtle and willow branches and palm leaves, spreading them before a man on a donkey. Some were even taking off outer garments and placing them before the donkey. This was the kind of thing they would do for a king. But all the kings I knew about strutted in on fine horses which illustrated their might as warriors. I inquired of a man next to me if this was Jesus and why in the world he was riding a donkey. He said it *was* Jesus and that he had heard that Jesus was coming to be a different kind of leader — that he professed peace and had no intention of exercising force. That sounded strange amidst the shouts of "Hosanna," which meant "Save now!"

The people must have believed as I did that when the Messiah came he would bring peace and save us from the oppressors such as Rome and others who always kept our faces in the dirt. It made me sick at my stomach to have to be obedient to those in high office who used my tax money to raise their salaries and throw orgies at my expense. Even some of the higher-ups in Jerusalem held us at financial bay by keeping us ignorant of the law. They were the only ones allowed to have law books, and they interpreted to us what they meant; if anyone began to get wise, they engaged in double-talk among themselves. There was no way to get ahead because the rich, who were in the minority, always seemed to bend the laws and the leaders to their way of thinking. It was unreal what money could do in Jerusalem. But this Jesus was saying that it wouldn't do a thing for a man's eternal life. I liked that kind of talk, and I began to understand what they meant about his preaching good news to the poor.

I wanted to get a closer look, to see this Jesus face to face. I grabbed a palm branch that someone had dropped on the ground and ran to catch the donkey. It was so hard: people kept shoving me and stepping in front of me. Guess they wanted to see him as much as I did. I finally worked my way down the street and jumped up on a brick column where I could see. He was just passing by. The first thing I noticed was his face. Oh, that face. He had such a calm look about him. People were grabbing at him and hollering at him, and yet he had a smile. But I sensed that smile had meaning — kind of like a smile that said, "I hope you can keep this spirit." He didn't have the same air about him that other leaders had when they were greeted in such a triumphant manner. I had no impression from him of conceit or any feeling that he thought he was better than anyone. Riding on the donkey proved that to me.

As he passed by I decided to follow him. Oh, there was no way he could have noticed me with all those people around him. But I was really curious. I remember that some people went home afterwards, but many continued to follow him.

He went straight to the temple. I thought he was going to pray or perhaps teach. But he began to shout at the people selling pigeons and at the money-changers. He even turned over the tables. I can remember hearing the coins rolling down the steps and ringing round and round on the stone. I thought it was kind of funny, especially when the birds landed on people's heads. But I also knew that this must be a fearless man who stood up for what he believed. I guess that session at the temple made a believer out of me.

I know a lot of people think anger is wrong and that people of God don't get mad, but I learned that if you are angry for the right reason it has a valuable side. Our religious leaders had allowed this bartering to go on until it had finally gotten inside the temple itself. Jesus drew the limit on real religion that day. If some people didn't understand why he could be pushed to anger, then they probably would never really understand the idea of the temple anyway, outside of a superstitious fear that kept them coming. Guess they believed in God only because they were scared of him, not because he loved them, as Jesus taught. I had to agree that by selling their wares in the temple they were making a mockery of God and the people who honestly believed. Especially when they were cheating the people who came to worship. I hoped inside that this would forever teach mankind that cheating one another was not God's way. I guess my thinking was even a little utopian when I hoped what Jesus was doing would ease the tax situation.

I noticed that right away many people began coming to him and his composure changed so quickly. You could see a real compassion when the lame and the blind came to him. He couldn't turn them away. It was amazing to see people's lives changed right before my eyes. One old man, with his hands shaking and a tear running down his cheek, thanked Jesus over and over again. Jesus simply patted him on the arm and wished him well. Oh, I just wish you could have been there to see those people. It was the way life was supposed to be. It gave me an idea of the joy that will be in heaven.

As I was standing there I saw some chief priests and scribes talking among themselves. At first, I thought they were amazed as I was, but then I noticed a frown on their faces and one man pounding his fist into his palm. As I got a little closer I could hear that they were indignant about him. In fact, they were just flat jealous: he was stealing their thunder. But it was more than that. Jesus was teaching what they didn't have the guts to teach, and they knew he was right. They were afraid that he would expose them and they couldn't have that happen. It would ruin their lives.

It was getting late. The sun was setting, and I was getting hungry. But I had vowed that this day I was going to follow him until he rested for the night. As he went back out of the city, not nearly as many people followed now — just a few stragglers like me and several men. I counted twelve of them circled about him. He went to Bethany to spend the night.

Once again I got to see his face. It was a time of meditation and when he would lift his eyes toward heaven, you could see — no, you could *feel* — his sincerity. Just watching him, I felt in the presence of God, and I wanted the whole world to feel what I was feeling. If only they would stop warring against one another. If only they would stop disbelieving in God and come to their senses about what life is all about. It was all free, but you had to have the eyes to see it.

If only those money-changers at the temple could see him as I did, they would realize that the real treasure of the kingdom is here. Perhaps they might understand why some give more than their fair share to the temple. If people could see him now we'd never have to beg for money or have special drives and requests for the ongoing work of his church. No, I think they would see and be happy to give whatever they had. I hoped this message would come across during the time he was there, for the word was that he was staying in Jerusalem the entire week. I vowed right then and there to leave work early every day and go listen to him.

As I began returning home for the night, I thought of all the events of the day. How it started out just right, the excitement of the coming of the Messiah, the people, the shouts. I looked down at the dusty road he had traveled and in the dim light I saw a palm branch. I stepped over and picked it up. It was broken in the middle where the donkey had stepped on it. It drooped in my hand. I had a strange feeling that this was an omen, but chased that idea from my head. This man was too good for anything bad to come to him. The things he said, the actions he took were all for good means. Even when he was angry, he had a godly purpose. Surely nothing would happen. Look at the support the people had given him. Wasn't that a vote of confidence today? Hundreds and hundreds of people cheering and demonstrating their enthusiasm.

As I reached my step I turned and looked at where my day had begun. A few short hours ago I had hardly heard of this Jesus of Nazareth and now I felt as if I had known him all my life. Why, I hadn't even talked to him. Do you suppose people will believe him if they don't see and talk to him? Will they ever be able to catch the spirit he brought today? It was so good, so pure, so fresh. We all need it.

I could smell the food my wife had prepared for our supper. As I turned to go into the house, a thought struck me that I had never considered before. I don't know where it came from but it was something to the effect that if I really believed in what I saw today then I for one ought to be responsible to tell someone else about it. How else will this word get out into the world?

Just then my wife shouted, "Where have you been so long?" That to me was the question all of us had been asking of God all our lives. Today it was answered for me. I went in to tell my wife this incredible story. I wanted her to know about him too.

# COMMENT

Years ago, Walter Cronkite used to do a television program on historical events called "You Were There!" This sermon, "I Was In The Crowd," presents the Palm Sunday story in the form of a first-person dramatic narrative that is reminiscent of that old show. Gary Whitbeck recasts the gospel story in order to tell it afresh and bridge the gap between text and listener.

It's too bad we cannot see, hear, and experience this sermon rather than simply read it. In this style of sermon the delivery is as important as the content.

## PROBLEM

On one level, the problem in this sermon is quite simple. It is framed in a question near the end: "Do you suppose people will believe him if they don't see and talk to him?" That is, we were not there. How will we know?

The answer comes next. "Just then my wife shouted, 'Where have you been so long?' That to me was the question all of us had been asking God all our lives. Today it was answered for me. I went in to tell my wife this incredible story. I wanted her to know him too."

In this final dramatic exchange, we learn that the central question is not just about telling, but knowing. What is necessary for us to experience in order to be able to tell the world who Jesus is? And the answer is, "We must follow Jesus until we understand who he is, and then we will be able to tell the world about him."

## TEXT

A real strength of this sermon is the way Whitbeck adapts the form he uses to the nature of the story itself. He doesn't make the mistake of attempting everything in the sermon. It is tempting to tell the entire story, much like the tiresome gospel songs that try to say everything and get to heaven by the fourth verse!

His form retains a humility that resembles the story he tells. He begins and ends with a note of ambiguity, which is exactly where this section of the Easter story begins and ends.

Jesus enters Jerusalem amid the buzz of multiple expectations (and resentments!). He stirs great excitement in the crowd, but also (according to the synoptic gospel accounts) creates an uproar by driving the money-changers out of the temple.

At the end of the triumphal entry story (Palm Sunday), we do not have the whole story. Things will turn in a new and terrible direction. But Whitbeck is able to imply this by means of a very effective image. He looks down at the dusty road where the procession had earlier passed. There, in the dust, was a single palm branch: "I stepped over and picked it up. It was broken in the middle where the donkey had stepped on it. It drooped in my hand. I had a strange feeling that this was an omen, but chased that idea from my head."

In this moment, he is able to point ahead to the cross without going into great detail. He allows the listener to make that connection imaginatively. Fred Craddock has always reminded us to allow the congregation to be a part of the sermon. We can consider the presence of their minds and hearts in the listening and allow room now and then for their own imagination.

We do not have to state every truth. We can imply them, suggest them, evoke them. If the congregation knows the story, they will make the connection. If not, they might wonder about it until next week when we tell the rest!

A dramatic narrative style of sermon imaginatively draws the hearers into the scene. So, one of the key points about a dramatic presentation is the issue of who we decide to be — which character? For it is our character with which the people most likely will identify (if we do well!). Will we be Jesus? One of the crowd? One of Jesus' enemies?

If done well, the characterization brings the text alive. If done badly (and I have seen more of these!), it will have the effect of calling attention to itself. Little thoughts like, "Gee, the pastor doesn't really sound like somebody from there!" Or the mind may drift off to something else.

C O M M E N T

The devil is in the details, as they say. And the preacher who does not pay attention to the details in a dramatic monologue will find that what he or she gains in realism may be sacrificed in authenticity. We may "transliterate" certain images or ideas into contemporary terms.

To Whitbeck's credit the narrative is credible, tight, and effective in moving the listener along. The focus stays where it should — on the fast-breaking events of the Passion and on Jesus.

This whole matter of "transliteration," however, raises a question. While narrative or story-telling seems more immediate and less complicated, it is just the opposite. Faithful exegesis is even more necessary if we are to comprehend the distance that must be bridged between text and listener. If we do not understand the expectations, mindset, and cultural setting of the original hearers, we will simply convey impressions and prejudices that listeners already hold. The result may be entertaining, but it will not be biblical. And if, on the other hand, our "transposition" into the story does not connect with real issues today, then it simply becomes an exercise in biblical illustration.

Whitbeck illustrates the diversity of understandings that existed in Palestine in accepting Jesus. He does this narratively by telling things that others have said to the narrator about Jesus, or events that have happened, or telling us what the narrator thought about something.

He is also effective in his use of description. A good narrative sermon should drip with vivid, concrete images. None of that "He went across town" stuff! Tell us what he sees, what he smells, and who he talks to. What are people wearing? What is their facial expression?

An example is the scene when Jesus cleanses the temple. "I can remember hearing the coins rolling down the steps and ringing round and round on the stone." The hearer has listened to that sound before, perhaps has even spun a coin around by flicking it when he or she was a child. Tapping into those sensate memories is a wonderful, involving technique.

Concreteness has another advantage. Many studies of ministers' personality temperaments (as in Myers-Briggs), indicate that while most ministers are intuitive types who can pick up symbols and connections rather easily, the majority of the people sitting in the pews are much more earth-grounded and more oriented to immediate and obvious things. This is especially important in preaching, where the connections and implications are clouded by the communication gulf. Concrete images, familiar experiences, and sensate realities can bridge that gap, making ideas present to us experientially. They also help by making the sermons more memorable.

## PROCLAMATION

What does Whitbeck do to encapsulate the Gospel? He recounts the various experiences of people with Jesus and shows him "preaching a message of compassion and true worship of God." In his persona as a member of the crowd, Whitbeck tells us that "some even claimed that he referred to God as 'Father' as if he were his son." Whitbeck observes that "...his miracles, his kindness, his genuine love of everyone, rich or poor, continued to reach our ears...."

The remembrance of Zera about the prophecy of Zechariah weaves into the story the idea that the triumphal entry "is the fulfillment of Scripture." The storyteller notes "how [Jesus] forgave people their sins...." "This Jesus even forgave women of the streets, and had tax collectors and liars following him around daily." He can put many affirmations about Jesus in the mouths of the minor characters.

Equally important in a dramatic narrative is the order in which it is told. Structurally, "I Was in the Crowd" has only one main point — that once we know who Jesus really is, we will want to tell others about him. But there is a more subtle structure intentionally embedded in the narration which builds in dramatic intensity until the ending. In that structure, we also find the proclamation of the Gospel call, "Follow me!"

This dramatic heightening is particularly important when we are presenting a familiar story. Notice how Whitbeck presents the story. The framework goes something like this:

a. Jesus, who was the talk of the town, was coming to Jerusalem and there was excitement in the air.

b. People expressed a lot of different opinions about what this visit really meant, but there was little agreement.

c. I decided to go see him. I got there just as the procession arrived.

d. I moved closer and for the first time saw him closely; his demeanor had a great impact on me.

e. I decided to follow him to the temple, where he shocked us by driving the money-changers out in a fit of anger.

f. Yet when people in need came to him afterward, there was no anger. He was gentle and compassionate.

g. Still, I noticed the chief priests and scribes, angry.

h. It was late, but I determined to keep following, this time to Bethany, where I watched him pray and felt myself in God's presence. If only everyone could understand!

i. Now I returned home, thinking about what had happened, when I came upon the road he had traveled and found a broken palm branch. Was it an omen of things to come?

j. I was back where I started, but I wasn't the same.

k. As I reached home, it dawned on me that I had to tell others about him or else they wouldn't know. I realized in my wife's question to me that he was what I had been looking for all along.

Notice the movement; both geographically and spiritually, he follows along, at each step understanding Jesus at a deeper level. At the end, he returns to where he began, but not as the same person. The movements in the story correspond at a deeper level to the movements taking place in his heart and life.

The question is, "How do we come to know who Jesus is?" and the answer is, "By following him." The movements within the story are the pointers which help answer the larger question: How do we know who Jesus is and what difference does it make? It makes all the difference in the world, a difference worth telling the whole world about.

It is a very fine turn of phrase at the climax of the sermon when his wife asks the unintentional truth question: "Where have you been so long?" That, says Whitbeck is THE question we have all been asking God. And today it is answered.

So the Gospel word is not "We ought to tell people about Jesus so their lives will improve and they can join us in telling people." Rather, it is about Christ. The motive for telling is not external, but intrinsic. Whitbeck makes that point with great strength. And at the end, the narrator is moved enough to walk in and begin to do what he knows deserves to be done. He is about to tell his wife, for "I want her to know about him too."

This is where he leaves us. He does not spell out where people are going to go, whether with Philip into the desert to find one Ethiopian eunuch who is searching, or with Paul to the uttermost parts of the earth, or simply back to their own office to risk themselves in friendship a little more with a co-worker whose life is in disarray. But it is clear what response is called for here. We are invited to consider who Jesus is, to feel (which is the dominant word he uses throughout the sermon) the personality and presence of Christ, and to act on that feeling.

In short, we have returned here to the motivational core of Christian living. We have touched the presence of Christ. If we love him, we will serve him in the world. The question, the deeper question, is, "Have we understood him? Do we love him?"

## RESPONSE

So what is it that this indirect approach asks us to do? Whitbeck is effective in making the present connections. People have to be told about Jesus or they won't know. But here we meet once again the advantage of the story. The listener can identify without being coerced.

I am a Baptist, and we are well inoculated to such pleas; they are part of our "language of Zion" at denominational meetings. Our eyes glaze over when someone reminds us of our obligation to witness. Too, there is a secretly held cynicism among many in the pews: "Is this really about witnessing, or do we just need more people to help prop up the budget?"

Whitbeck's sermon returns proclamation to its center, the person of Jesus Christ. There is really no other reason to tell the Gospel except to point others to the dynamic, living presence of the Lord Jesus.

This is the climax of the sermon. No "musts," "oughts," or "shoulds," to rain down on the guilty listener. Just drawing the eyes of the listener back to Jesus and then, in the device of sudden realization, the hearers realize, too, that this wonderful story deserves to be told and told well.

This indirectness sits well with today's better-educated, questioning listeners. Notice how many exhortations Whitbeck is able to work in through the characters and their thoughts. All are made more accessible because they are served to us in a story where we are allowed to experience the conviction and consider it rather than react to it. A preacher can afford to give the congregation some credit for being able to think and respond. Perhaps we can set the platter of great convictions of the faith out on Sunday and serve it like a fine meal rather than strapping on the bib each week and trying to talk a reluctant toddler into accepting one more force-feeding of pureed asparagus.

## SUGGESTIONS

- Try doing a dramatic interpretation sermon like this one. For your first try at it, select a story that lends itself to it, like one of the great stories of the Old Testament (Joseph remembers his reunion with his brothers, or Moses tells about his call on the mountain), or perhaps in the New Testament (Simon the Cyrene is drafted to carry Jesus' cross, or Pilate's wife or the woman at the well), the possibilities are endless!

- Practice your descriptive abilities. Write out a detailed description of some experience you had or something you observed. Try to stay away from clichés. What did you notice? Smell? See? Hear? Touch? Taste? What did the experience bring to mind?

- Take a familiar Bible story and outline its dramatic structure. A good place to start is with the story of the blind man in John 9. Notice the growing awareness reflected in the telling of the story. "Play around" with the structure: how else could the same story be re-told? Who are all the characters who appear in the story? What viewpoint would each have in telling what happened from their particular angle?

*Gary Furr*

# SECOND-CHANCE RELIGION

JOHN 21:1–19

REV. MAURICE A. FETTY
THE CONGREGATIONAL CHURCH OF MANHASSET
MANHASSET, NEW YORK

REV. MAURICE A. FETTY

# SECOND-CHANCE RELIGION

## JOHN 21:1–19

I t is one of the more tenderly dramatic scenes of the Bible. There they are, seven of them, in the peculiar silence of day's early light, sweating, throwing the nets and retrieving them — these three professional fishermen and their four confused, discouraged companions. If professional fishermen long to get out onto the water for the good of the soul as well as the good of the pocketbook, so do amateurs.

But unlike professionals, amateurs don't care as much if they catch anything. They need the water, the escape, the tranquility. They need the time to smell the salt air and feel the moist breeze on their brows. A sunrise over the water can be good for the soul, and if nothing else, amateurs can always talk about the one that got away.

But not professionals. Peter and his brother Andrew, along with James and his brother John, had been in the fishing business on the Sea of Galilee from day one. James and John had a partnership with their father, Zebedee, along with hired servants. Apparently, they had been making money. Peter and Andrew knew the sea or lake — 12 miles long and 7 miles wide — and probably were doing all right financially.

Except today. Except this morning after Easter. Except this all-night fishing expedition to gain a catch for the morning market. Peter, sweaty and tired, is stripped to his loin cloth. A familiar blend of hunger and weariness came over the man as the light began to rise over what today is the Golan Heights.

There is a strange quietness about that time of day — a time when the light is peculiarly soft in the early morning haze, a time when the world has not quite awakened to hustle and bustle, a time of dreams fading back and forth into wakefulness, a time when birds are clearing their throats to announce the mystery and miracle of a new day.

There may have been a faint whiff of charcoal smoke in the air that first aroused their curiosity. Someone might have caught a glimpse of a figure on the beach, dismissing it as an early morning apparition. But it was the sturdy voice across the waters that arrested their attention. "Friends, have you caught any fish?"

Amateur fishermen don't mind such a question, since they are not necessarily expected to catch any fish. But professionals? Well, professionals are different. It's like asking, "Did you men fail today?"

Before they had time to grumble a reply, the stranger on the beach suggested in a confident voice, "Throw your nets to the starboard side, to the right." It is difficult enough for professional fishermen to accept suggestions from amateurs, and even more difficult to accept advice from a landlubber stranger, who, of all things, might even be a carpenter. What do carpenters know about fishing?

In a mumbling, half-resigned "Oh-what-could-it-hurt, we'll-try-anything" attitude, they cast the net to the right side of the boat. And there it was — the success they dreamed of all night, now arrived in dawn's early light at the suggestion of a supposed rank amateur. Been fishing to the left side of the boat all your life? Try the right for success — the success of the second chance, says the stranger.

I.

However, the second-chance fishing and second-chance religion and second-chance anything imply something we may not wish to acknowledge or to admit. They imply a judgment.

"Peter, Andrew, James, and John, before you answered Jesus' call to follow him to become fishers of men, you were professional fishers of fish, right?" "Right!" "And reasonably successful fishers of fish?" "Right!" "So how does it feel to have someone you don't know tell you, in effect, that you've been doing it all wrong, all night? Try the other side." "Well, it feels like an insult, a judgment, like we don't know who we are or what we're doing. A second chance implies we failed at the first chance."

The truth is, that is what had happened to all these seven disciples in the boat — the four professional fishermen and the three amateurs. But we're not talking about fishing here. We're talking about living up to ideals and commitments, about following through on promises and agreements. We're talking about keeping one's word and maintaining one's loyalty. We're talking about promises made to God in our youth. We're talking about vows taken in late-night religious consciousness, about commitments made at baptism and confirmation, and covenants owned when we joined the church.

As often was the case, Peter was the impulsive one in this scene. If it was the intuitive and perceptive John, the one whom Jesus loved the most, who first recognized the stranger on the beach, it was the impetuous Peter who jumped into the water to swim and wade the 100 yards to shore. The others came in the boat, dragging behind them the untorn net with 153 fish.

And with them all, there is a hesitancy — a hesitancy of mystery and curiosity, but also a hesitancy of judgment. They did not dare to ask if it was the Lord, risen from the dead; they knew it was. Yet, like pilgrims approaching a holy man, they kept, for a moment, a respectful distance. Would he judge them? Will he judge us?

Their minds flooded with memories of their three years together. As their movement grew, as the campaign picked up momentum, as the expectations heightened that Jesus just might be God's man of the hour to lead them again into the Golden Age, their personal hopes and private aspirations soared. Judas, as treasurer of the group, had dreamed of the fabulous wealth he would oversee in the new realm. He now had hanged himself.

James and John had asked to be second and third in command in the new empire. All debated as to who would be greatest and have the most influence in the new monarchy. "We're with you, Jesus. We're with you all the way, Jesus. We'll never forsake you. We can smell victory and power; they are all so close." So said they all.

But at the Last Supper, he had predicted the powers-that-be would strike the shepherd and the sheep would scatter. Nonsense, they said. "Peter," said Jesus at the Upper Room table, "before the rooster announces the dawn you will have denied me three times." "Absurd," said the stalwart, impulsive Peter. "Though they all deny you, I will never forsake you."

On this mystical morning, Peter had jumped into the water to get to shore first, but now we can imagine a hesitancy — a hesitancy born out of memory and regret, a hesitancy arising out of a sense of judgment and an onrush of guilt, a hesitancy to approach again the one to whom he had made such a boisterous promise. "Though they all forsake you, I will never forsake you."

But it was cold that night a few weeks earlier. Peter had drawn his sword in Gethsemane's Garden ready to fight for the Cause. He followed along as they dragged his hero and liberator before the cynical authorities of the time. But the dreams were evaporating that strange night. The hopes and aspirations not only of a lifetime but of centuries were being shattered. The visions of glory were quickly becoming a nightmare of misery and short-circuited revolutionary power.

In the nighttime cold, he drew near to the charcoal fire in the courtyard. Soldiers were there. And outside the high priest's house, a maid was there, and in the flickering light, she recognized Peter and announced that he had been with Jesus. Peter denied it. Later she said Peter was one of the revolutionaries. That he also denied vehemently, claiming he never knew Jesus.

But she wouldn't let it rest. Like a prosecuting attorney on a righteous cause, she asserted, "You are certainly one of them. Your Galilean accent gives you away." Peter cursed, saying, "Damn it all, lady, I told you I don't know the man. Don't implicate me with him."

He had hardly finished the words when the cock crowed, announcing the first light of dawn. And Peter went out and wept bitterly. Because, as French existentialist Albert Camus used to say, the fall comes in the morning, the knowledge of wrong in the light of dawn. Guilt is heaviest then, for in the morning the conscience convicts of sin and the deeds of darkness are exposed, and judgment rests in the depths of the soul as surely as our efforts to cover it or deny it only reinforce it.

II.

That is why, after rushing to shore ahead of the others, Peter approached the risen Christ cautiously. He was aware of a deep sense of judgment and guilt. And that is why, when we hurriedly, frantically, belatedly, eventually rush off to church, we get there only then to hesitate, to wait, to hold back, to keep our distance, to refrain from too much holiness, because holiness implies judgment of unholiness, and that implies change, throwing the net on the right side of the boat in place of the left.

We keep our distance from the risen Christ because, like Peter on this post-Easter beach, we too are guilty about images we had had of Christ. Some of us had wanted a Christ to give us success and victory, fame and glory, as James and John envisioned.

Some of us have envisioned a Christ who coincides with our views of the American Way of Life, or who wholeheartedly embraces a pseudo-religious, exploitive capitalism, or a Christ who espouses a paternalistic socialism, or a Christ who champions a strident feminism, or a Christ who clearly endorses a radical, dictatorial fundamentalism, or a Christ who embodies the ideals of a Renaissance man or the achievements of an Enlightenment woman, or a Christ of a migrant worker advocacy, or a Christ of academia which allows him to speak only the words they put into his mouth, or a Christ who serves primarily as a cheerleader for self-help psychology, or a Christ who fits neatly into the New Age Pantheon, or a Christ who really belongs to my denomination, but not yours, or a garden variety kind of Christ, thoroughly domesticated, controllable, and transplantable to wherever we need him in our inward soulscape.

That's why with Peter we shuffle hesitantly in the sand toward this

post-Easter Christ on the beach. Because his new reality judges every earlier reality into which we have molded him. When, with Peter, we behold
the reality of the risen Christ in dawn's early light, we become newly aware
of our deeds of darkness, newly aware of our fall from grace, newly aware
of our manipulation of Christ into our image, into a usable, manageable
Christ, to aid us toward the fulfillment of our dreams and aspirations.

Will he give us a second chance?

## III.

This is the gospel, the good news — beyond every judgment there is forgiveness, and after every fall, there is grace, and after every night of death,
there is a resurrection to new life.

"Yes, Peter, there is a second chance. Throw your net to the right side
of the boat. Yes, Peter, there is another opportunity. Draw near. Here, take
some charbroiled fish. You must be famished." He acted as host again, this
risen Jesus, giving out second chances with the food. He broke the warm,
toasted brown bread and gave it to them. The crispy-brown charbroiled
fish was theirs to crunch too. It was a sacramental meal, when once again
in sacred oath the human was bonded to the divine in grace and love.

Could it be Peter would live up to his new name after all? A year and
a half earlier they had been up near Caesarea Philippi, near the large cliff
beneath which the melted snows of Mount Hermon gushed out of their
underground streams to become the beginning of the Jordan River. When
Jesus, midway in his three-year campaign, asked them who they thought
he was, it was Peter who blurted out, "You are the Christ, the Son of the
living God."

Jesus blessed him for this revelation God had given him and then gave
him a new name — *Cephas* in Aramaic, and *Petros* in Greek, meaning
"rock." You are to be a rock for the church with faith like that, he told Peter.

Some rock. When the chips were down in a dark night of the soul, he
buckled under the accusations and mockery of a maid. "Damn it all, I told
you I don't even know the man!" Peter — *Petros* — *Cephas* — Rock. Some
rock, thrown around like a pebble in a three-times denial.

Jesus' timing, like God's, is always exquisite. It was after breakfast, after the needs of the body had been satisfied, after the initial fear and apprehension had mellowed into familiarity, that Jesus addressed the needs of the soul. "Simon, son of John, are you my friend?" "Yes, Lord, you know I'm your friend." "Then feed my lambs."

Another bite of the remaining fish and bread, and the question comes softly across the charcoal fire again. "Sy Johnson, do you love me?" "Yes, Lord, you know I'm your friend." "Then tend my sheep."

There was, as we say today, a pregnant pause; a moment in history was waiting to be born. Something new was about to appear. There was a hush, a reverence around the fire as the eastern light broke over the hills. "Sy Johnson, do you know me; do you love me?"

Simon, Son of John (Sy Johnson), John's son, also named the Rock (Rock Johnson), thought back to that terrible night a few weeks earlier when the maid's accusations came across the charcoal fire. It grieved Peter that Jesus asked him about love and loyalty the third time, but it was to Peter's everlasting credit that he knew he had it coming. He had denied him thrice. Jesus is wondering, will he affirm him thrice in this dawn of the new age? "Lord, you know everything. You know that I love you." And Jesus said, "Feed my sheep."

And Peter did and does, even to this day. Yes, it was Peter, Rock Johnson, leader of the twelve — Peter, whose faith was the rock foundation of the church — who became a chief shepherd of souls. It was Peter, who by the risen Christ, was transformed from guilt and remorse and self-reproach to become Peter, the hero of the faith and the martyr for the Cause, crucified upside down, outside Rome. Yes. It was Peter. A second-chance disciple casting his net on the right side of the boat for divine success after human failure.

So this risen Christ invites us now to the early morning, post-Easter beach. Come near the gentle charcoal fire. Let all the guilt and judgment, regret and remorse be acknowledged and confessed. And when he says, "Do you love me?" let us answer, "Oh, yes, Lord, we do love you." And he will say, "Let's start all over again. Because this is Resurrection Day."

Let's start all over again in the marriage, in the family; let's start over again in the church, in the job; let's start over again in the failed career and the discouraged, depressed soul; let's start over again with a life which seems to be ruined, because this is Resurrection Day. Every day you awake is Resurrection Day. Because Easter religion is the religion of the second chance, and the third and the twenty-third. "For I am with you always, even to the end of the world," to give you the second chance. *Amen.*

# COMMENT

"Second-Chance Religion" by Maurice A. Fetty is a superbly and beautifully crafted literary sermon. It has the quality of great literature. It is a "story" or "narrative sermon" in which the preacher simply retells the biblical story. But in so doing, he allows the story to proclaim powerful truth through vividly painted word pictures and keen emotional and psychological insights.

Hearing this sermon, we are there on the shore of the Sea of Galilee in the early morning mist. We smell the damp, fishy air. We hear the small waves lapping on rocks at the water's edge. We catch the whiff of charcoal smoke in the air. We can see the human figures moving through the fog, their voices muffled by the shroud of heavy mist. Oh, in this sermon we are there.

The story is recreated in such an effective way that the sermon needs no other quotes, poems, illustrations or stories outside the text. The sermon lets the biblical story do it all! Here the text states the problem, proclaims good news, and invites us to join the circle with Jesus around the early morning fire. Because we are there with Peter and the others, we see and hear and feel it all. As Peter is "restored" and given a second chance, so are we!

The sermon has a vividness and simplicity about it that can only be experienced. Words of comment or analysis will always fall short of capturing the true essence of such a sermon.

## TEXT

The story of Jesus' post-Easter appearance to seven disciples by the Sea of Galilee in John 21:1-19 comprises the text for this sermon. Since the story itself constitutes the sermon, Fetty introduces the text in the sermon's opening line: "It is one of the more tenderly dramatic scenes of the Bible...." Thereafter, he proceeds to tell the story bit by bit, interspersing pieces of biblical narrative with quiet interpretive comments and keen psychological insights.

Fetty begins the story at John 21:3 with the disciples fishing all night and catching nothing. By the end of the sermon he has reached the specific focus of his text, the words in John 21:17: "And [Peter] said to [Jesus], 'Lord, you know everything; you know that I love you.' Jesus said to him, 'Feed my sheep.'" Between these beginning and end points of the sermon we are carefully taken back through the story of Peter's bitter denial of Jesus and the journey that has brought Peter to this moment on the shore of Galilee. A series of flashbacks makes this possible. The technique is effective.

A key element in the effectiveness of this sermon is Fetty's juxtaposition of "second-chance fishing" alongside "second-chance religion." Throwing the nets to the right side of the boat after catching nothing on the left side (John 21:6) is placed alongside Peter's earlier denial of Jesus (John 18:15–27) and his opportunity this day to be restored to full relationship with Jesus. The text in John 21 is commonly interpreted as the "restoration" of Peter after his denial of Jesus. But the juxtaposition of the "second-chance fishing" image alongside Peter's "second chance" is an additional unique and powerful insight into the text.

Casting the nets successfully on the other side of the boat thus becomes an image in the story which interprets and proclaims Peter's second chance. The miracle of the catch on the other side of the boat becomes an image of hope for all of us who fail in our commitments or relationships and need a second chance. On more than one level, then, the text proclaims the good news that God is a God of second chances!

## PROBLEM

The first clear indication of what this sermon is really all about comes when Fetty says: "But we're not talking about fishing here...." (pt. I, para. 3). What a nice signal this is for the listeners! Up until now the sermon has dealt with professional and amateur fishermen, a failed fishing expedition, a suggestion to cast nets elsewhere, and finally, a successful catch. We have been standing there on the shore watching it all.

Suddenly, everything shifts: "But we're not talking about fishing here...." Hearing that one pregnant phrase, we lean forward, listening attentively, thinking to ourselves: "Okay, so if we're not talking about fishing, then what are we talking about?" In other words, what is this story about? What is this sermon about?

Fetty does not leave us hanging here. He goes on to tell us what it's about: "We're talking about living up to ideals and commitments, about following through on promises and agreements. We're talking about keeping one's word and maintaining one's loyalty. We're talking about promises made to God in our youth. We're talking about vows taken in late night religious consciousness, about commitments made at baptism and confirmation, and covenants owned when we joined the church."

Now we may be getting uneasy, but at least we know what this story is about. It's about us! It's somehow about our lives and our failed promises and commitments. At this point in the sermon we're not altogether sure how the catch of fish, Peter, and the disciples fit into all this "second-chance" business. But we do know that the sermon is about us and not just about those Galilean fishermen.

Notice how Fetty goes right on with the story of Peter jumping into the water and swimming to shore (21:7). We have to wait to hear more about the question of living up to our commitments and ideals. Fetty keeps us wondering, keeps us thinking. He lets the story carry the sermon and introduces the question to us piece by piece.

In preaching, there is often a tendency to "say everything at once" and get it all out. Fetty's technique here is instructive. He gets us thinking about how the remainder of this fishing story might speak to the promises and commitments we make in our lives. As a result, we listen more carefully. We're wanting to see where all this is going. We want to know the connection between the story and ourselves.

Good preaching exercises restraint not only in the length and verbosity of sermons, but in the timing of what we reveal in the course of a sermon. Help your hearers get involved in your sermon by asking them to think and listen carefully for where you are leading them. Arouse their

interest, as Fetty has done, but don't give them the whole point of the sermon at one time until well into the sermon or near its conclusion! Lead
your hearers along with you.

Fetty's sermon is an excellent example of this kind of preaching technique. Here we learn the text, the question, and the proclamation of the
sermon piece by piece. And only when the sermon is done do we have the
full picture. It is our picture because we have worked to get there. We have
had to follow the sermon and put it all together piece by piece. We have
invested ourselves in the sermon. When that happens, there's a much
greater chance the message will stay with us!

By the time we near the end of this sermon, we are aware that the problem it addresses is our "first-chance failures" in life. So confidently we confess faith in Jesus when all is well. So proudly we make promises and enter
into commitments. But then, with Peter, when the chips are down, we say,
"I never knew this Jesus," or we fail in our commitments to each other.
Judgment and guilt ensue. We keep our distance from Christ. We begin to
refashion our image of Christ into a safer, more self-fulfilling version of
"god." The problem is that again and again we fail, we fall, we die.

How can we ever go on? We need a second chance! We need to hear
the good news of the gospel spoken to us once again!

## PROCLAMATION

Toward the end of this sermon (pt. II, next-to-last paragraph) there is a
beautiful passage in which Fetty summarizes the human problem his text
addresses. He says, "That's why with Peter we shuffle hesitantly in the sand
toward this post-Easter Christ on the beach. Because [Christ's] new reality
judges every earlier reality into which we molded him. When, with Peter, we
behold the reality of the risen Christ in dawn's early light, we become newly
aware of our deeds of darkness, newly aware of our fall from grace, newly
aware of our manipulation of Christ into our image, into a usable, manageable Christ to aid us toward the fulfillment of our dreams and aspirations."

Following this there is a clear statement of the message the text proclaims: "Will God give us a second chance? This is the gospel, the good

news: Beyond every judgment there is forgiveness. After every fall, there is grace. After every night of death, there is a resurrection to new life." This is a fine example of proclamation directly addressing the problem of human sin and brokenness.

With this statement we have reached the point in the sermon where the text (Peter's "Do-you-love-me?" encounter with Jesus) proclaims an answer to the need addressed in the sermon (Will God give us a second chance after our failures?). The answer is, "Yes, Peter, there is a second chance. Throw your net to the right side of the boat. Yes, Peter, there is another opportunity." The preacher will go on to say to all of us listening to the sermon, "Yes, for all of us, there is a second chance!"

As Fetty proclaims, the gospel draws us back into relationship with Jesus Christ. It can overcome our burden of judgment and guilt. It reaches out to us across the distance we have created in fleeing from God. The gospel overcomes our hesitancy and says, "Come to me." We need to hear that good word in our lives.

Note Fetty's simple phrase announcing the proclamation: "This is the gospel, the good news." It is good to use this or a similar phrase in every sermon when we are ready to proclaim the Christian gospel. Such phrases as "Today the good news of the gospel is…" or "The good news this morning is…" are important for at least three reasons. First, such a phrase keeps ever before us and our people the reminder that preaching is ultimately and supremely about proclaiming the *evangelia*, the good news of our redemption in Jesus Christ.

Second, regularly using such a phrase in our preaching signals to our listeners that at this point we are stating the core message, the most important point of the sermon. It is as if we are saying, "Okay now, listen up! Here's the point of all this today! Here's the good news!" People will listen for this announcement of the gospel and hear it better if we introduce it with familiar language week to week.

Third, using such a phrase in our sermons is an important reminder to ourselves as preachers that the gospel is always about good news! Regularly using such a phrase is a means of checking ourselves, a way of asking, "Do I really believe every sermon is ultimately about the good news? Am I reflecting this faithfully in my preaching? What is the good news in the text this week?"

## "GOOD NEWS"

It may be hard for some of us to imagine, but, as preachers, it is possible for us over time to lose sight of this important truth — that the gospel is always good news. We can become so overwhelmed by the pervasiveness of sin, violence, and injustice in our world that the good news begins to take second place. It may even fade into a faint echo or die out in our preaching. It's possible for us to get so caught up in confronting sin and evil in the world that, without realizing it, our primary emphasis shifts to the prophetic challenge of sin, injustice, and oppression.

To be sure, in our ministry it is always critical to confront evil and injustice. The gospel is not about cheap grace. It is about the challenge to change. But in and through it all, we must never lose sight of the fact that the gospel always represents good news. In every situation, however dark it may be, we are called to ask ourselves, How does the gospel's good news speak a word of transforming grace and hope in this situation?

"The good news of the gospel" is therefore a critical phrase in preaching. It holds us accountable to the basic *kerygma* or "proclamation" of the entire biblical tradition: "God is merciful and gracious, slow to anger, and abounding in steadfast love and faithfulness" (Exod. 34:6). "God so loved the world that he gave his only Son…" (John 3:16). If for any reason you are not regularly using a phrase like "the good news of the gospel" in your preaching, begin doing so! As preachers, we all need to hold ourselves accountable to the discipline of proclaiming this fundamental truth at the center of the Christian faith.

## INVITATION

From the beginning of this sermon we are invited into the story. We are invited to breakfast with Jesus, Peter, and the others there by the sea. As we have observed, Fetty's skillful painting of the scene and unfolding of the story puts us there with Peter, amid the smell of the charcoal fire, the damp morning air, and the lapping of the water on the rocks.

As the sun finally begins to rise, we are right in front of Jesus when he asks, "Do you love me?" We know it is a question addressed to us! Out of our own darkness, failure, and denial, we are invited to answer with Peter, "You know that I love you."

This invitation to respond is specifically found in the closing two paragraphs of the sermon: "So this risen Christ invites us now to the early morning, post-Easter beach. Come near the gentle charcoal fire. Let all the guilt and judgment, regret and remorse, be acknowledged and confessed.... Jesus will say, 'Let's start all over again, because this is Resurrection Day.'"

Fetty concludes by applying this invitation to our lives: "Let's start all over again in the marriage, in the family...in the church, in the job...in the failed career and the discouraged, depressed soul.... Every day you awake is Resurrection Day. For Easter religion is the religion of the second chance, and the third chance, and the twenty-third chance...."

What a beautiful invitation! What a beautiful sermon! How beautiful is the good news of the gospel!

## SUGGESTIONS

- Try writing a narrative sermon like this. Begin by choosing a vivid story from the Old or New Testament. Read it a number of times. Then close your Bible and write the story in your own words, placing yourself among the characters and imagining what the setting of the story might have been like (sights, sounds, smells, etc.). Imagine also what the internal emotional and psychological experiences of the primary character(s) must have been. During this process, ask yourself what questions, problems, or needs the story addresses. Experiment with the technique of interspersing applicational comments between the parts of the narrative and leading your listener gradually to the point of your sermon. Work at it until you have it!

Then enjoy preaching it and let God use the sermon in the life of your people as he wills!

- Ask yourself: Why is the gospel of Jesus Christ "good news"? Sit down and write out a list of all the specific reasons you can think of from Scripture and from your experience. Then take these and preach a sermon or series of sermons from your list.
- Take Fetty's theme, the God of the second chance, and go to the Old Testament. Identify at least three to five different Old Testament passages in which this theme occurs. Preach a sermon or series of sermons on these passages. Prophets like Isaiah, Jeremiah, Hosea, and Jonah are good possibilities here. Also, think about Jacob and Joseph, Moses and David. The possibilities are endless.

*Gary W. Klingsporn*

# ON GETTING A FAIR DEAL IN YOUR CAREER

MATTHEW 20:1–15

DR. CALVIN MILLER
PROFESSOR OF COMMUNICATION
SOUTHWESTERN BAPTIST SEMINARY
FORT WORTH, TEXAS

# ON GETTING A FAIR DEAL IN YOUR CAREER[1]

MATTHEW 20:1–15

He who labors as he prays, lifts his heart to God with his hands," wrote Bernard of Clairvaux in 1130 A.D. He might have written, "...in his calloused hands." It is ever as the old Latin truism says, *"Labor omnia vincit"* — "Work conquers everything." Our work, our jobs define our lives and tell us in part why we're in the world.

Jesus' work was a redeeming work. On the cross, Jesus was not only faithful in providing eternal life, but Jesus also remains faithful in providing for us those material goods which we need to endure and to live every day of our lives. "Every good and perfect gift [and every material gift]," says James, "comes down from the Father above" (James 1:17).

Many of the most popular songs across the years speak of how important our jobs are! Some years ago there was a country and western song — a kind of crass song — whose opening line was "Take this job and...." Well, you know the rest, of course. Obviously the song writer was not happy with his job. The chorus of another song, popular when I was in high school, said, "Yip yip yip yip, boom boom boom boom, get a job! Sha la la la, sha la la la."

Or, there was the ever-popular campfire sing-along song which went:

I've been working on the railroad
All the live-long day....

. . . . . . . . . . . . . . . . . . . . . . . . . . . .

Can't you hear that whistle blowing?
Rise up so early in the morn.
Can't you hear the captain shouting
"Dinah, blow your horn!"

And about five o'clock in the afternoon, that song changes to, "Dinah, won't you blow? Dinah, won't you blow?" Haven't we all felt a little like that, waiting for that whistle sometimes?

Remember that old black slave in *Showboat*, who stood looking out over the Mississippi and sang "Ol' Man River"? The lyrics of this Broadway classic talk about weary, pain-wracked bodies of the workers, of getting "sick of livin'"and "scared of dyin'," while Ol' Man River just "keeps rollin' along."

One of my favorite bumper stickers amends the song of the Disney dwarfs to say, "I owe, I owe, so off to work I go!" It happens day after day.

When Pearl Bailey was doing the black *Dolly* on Broadway, she would often finish her performances by sitting down on the circular ramp face-out to the audience. There she would sit and talk with the crowd. One night somebody asked her, "Miss Bailey, why do you do this every night? Why don't you just sing your role and go home?"

"You know," she replied, "these people work hard all week long. Somehow when they come here on Friday night, I feel if I can just make them laugh and forget how heavy and hard their work week has been, I'll feel a little like Jesus, when he said, 'Come unto me all you who are weary and heavy laden, and I will give you rest.'" (Matt. 11:28).

What a great gift it is to have a job, to work till we're "sick of livin' and scared of dyin'" and then to come to Christ's church and be the people of God together. Both being at work and being the people of God are most necessary to think well of ourselves. I read of a little boy who finally had found a reason to think well of himself in a crazy world. The boy took a baseball and bat into his backyard and cried, "I'm the greatest batter in the world!" and tossed the ball into the air. He swung mightily. Just as he missed it completely, he cried out "Strike one!"

He tossed the ball into the air again and said, "I'm the greatest batter in the world!" Once again, he swung, missed, and cried, "Strike two!"

After looking over the ball and bat, he tossed the ball in the air and reminded himself: "I'm the greatest batter in the world!" One last time he swung with all his might, and missed again. "Strike three!" he exclaimed. "Well, I guess I'm the greatest pitcher in the world!"[2]

You know, every day we get up and we try to think of what we're best at and what the world really is about. Some days we don't want to go to work, and some days it doesn't seem that work helps us to think well of ourselves in the least. I've always appreciated the tale of the mother who woke up her son and said, "Son, it's time for you to go to school."

"I don't want to go to school today, Mom," he argued back.

"Son," she replied, "you've got to go for three reasons. First of all, school is important for the development of your life. Second, you do not have one good reason for staying home today, and third, you're the principal."

There are some days when we can hardly wait to get to work. There are other days we get up and go because we've got to do it. Perhaps the most degrading change that can come to any person is when the word *career* changes to the word *job*. *Job* is a nasty little three-letter word that says, "Your toil is to get the bucks and feed your family and keep the roof fixed." But the word *career* says, "I've got a life dream. And I'm planning with my employer how to live out my employment years in such a way that my life will have meaning to me. I'm going to spend most of my life at this place. I've got a career." I've always believed that if you start playing by the rules of self-aggrandizement where you work, you deserve whatever you get. Remember the proverb: "Even if you win the rat race, you're still a rat."

A few months ago, Barb and I bought a house in New Mexico where a good many retired people also live. One of the fringe benefits about this community of seniors was that they immediately started calling Barb and me the "young people" in the neighborhood. That sounded so good. But you know what I really liked about those people? I found in them a people who were genuinely in love with life. After years of the rat race, they found themselves retired.

For the first time in their lives, they didn't have to go to work, and they were free to explore what it meant to be fully human. Suddenly they didn't have to compete for a desk that was three inches longer than the desk of the guy in the next office. They no longer had to compete for the best carpet in the office suite. Once they quit competing, they somehow became real. Praise be to God, they found they were even happy. Some of them began taking square dance lessons. All their lives I think they had wanted to square dance, but they had to work, and once off work they had to go to church (and remember, you don't square dance if you're a Baptist).

Every time I think about these happy, liberated square dancers, I think, Oh, the liberation Barb and I are going to have someday. And I've already confessed to you tongue-in-cheek that somehow, when we get out of town, we always say that we're going to smoke and dance. We've never done it yet, of course, but who knows? Someday... To be honest, we'd have to take smoking lessons, too, because we don't know how to do that. But it all accentuates the misery that comes upon all of us when we work all day long, trying to please other people. And then we walk into a church where we've got to please other people? The drudgery of work, coupled with the drudgery of legal expectations, all but destroys the deepest, most authentic joys of our lives.

In Jesus' story, the early-hired are grumpy for three reasons.

They were all working and were as happy as could be. Then they went into a churchlike mode of mutual envy and began to compare salaries. "I wonder how much she makes?" "I wonder how much he makes?" "Why doesn't God ever bless me like he does old so and so?" Such comparison is an endless and losing game.

When are we most mature as believers within the church community? Could it be when we can bless our fellow church member who gets a better job or buys a bigger house than ours? If there's any time I don't like church people, it's when they look across the congregation and see someone who just bought a nice new car and say, "Hm! He's either doing something dishonest or maybe he's making payments with his church tithe." We are most demonic when we lose the ability to bless our peers as God blesses their circumstances.

## I. THEY FORGOT THE CURSE OF NOT HAVING A JOB

The early-hired in Jesus' parable made three mistakes. First of all, I think they forgot how bad it felt to have no job. Here in Matthew 20:3, it says they were just standing around anyway, and an employer hired them. In so doing, the employer gave them dignity and a place to fit in life. He gave them a salary and the glorious self-esteem of having an honest, earned wage at the end of the day!

My mother, to the last day I knew her, always bought more groceries than she really needed — mostly extra canned goods. She'd buy those canned goods and she'd stick them under the bed, or over in the corner by the chimney. And I used to say to her, "Mom, why do you do that?"

"Well, son," she'd say, "things could get tough."

What made her think that? Well, things had been tough. I was born at the end of the Depression in 1936, but we Millers really stretched the not-so-great Depression on into the '40s. I can remember Mother saying things like, "Things can get tough. We've got to save some of this food."

I would ask, "Mom, what do you think about the Depression?" She'd say two rough words, "Herbert Hoover!" A song in the musical *Annie* takes off on this image as it recalls Hoover's promise of "a chicken in every pot." The trouble was that hardly anyone during the Depression even had a pot!

That's how Mother felt about it. But during those "dirty thirties," she taught me that God is most gracious when he gives us a place to go to work. What line of work was Mom in? She was a laundress. You can't make a real living as a laundress, but she didn't know that. You can't raise nine kids on a laundress's pay. She didn't know that, either. So every morning, I'd see her go off to work with her hair up in a bun, and she looked great. But at night when she came back after working over tubs of hot water all day long, her hair was straight and limp from the humidity of her calling. But she taught her children a million miles of truth in her example. Her truth was simple: how good it is to have a job!

When Barb and I first married, I moved to Kansas City and left Barb in Hunter. I couldn't afford to take her to Kansas City. I had Barb and no income. Once in Kansas City, I went to apply at Hallmark Cards. I had about thirty or forty dollars in my pocket. I had to pay all that to the guy to rent the little apartment that afternoon. Then I applied for that job, and they said, "We just can't tell you. You'll have to call back later and see if you got the job." So I had my next interview at Ford Motor Co. in Claycomo. I want you to know that it is possible to walk from Hallmark Cards to Claycomo, Missouri. You can walk about four miles in an hour if you hurry.

I walked there and applied. On the way, I got caught in the rain. By the time I got there for the interview, I didn't look so good and I felt even worse. I applied but didn't get that job. Before I left Claycomo, I called back to Hallmark Cards and said, "How about the job?"

And they said, "We'll give it to you if you can come back this afternoon and fill out the papers." I walked all the way back to Hallmark Cards. You can do it if you hurry. But do you know what I felt that night? That night I went to bed and I thought, "Lord Jesus, I haven't got any money, and I haven't got much to eat, but I've got a job!"

To all of you who are working today, fall to your knees in some quiet moment on Monday and say, "Hey, this is Labor Day! I have a job. I am blessed!"

## II. THEY FORGOT TO BLESS OTHERS

The early-hired also forgot to bless others. When they looked around and saw what everybody else had, they began to grumble. "When they received it, they began to grumble against the landowner. 'These men who were hired last worked only one hour,' they said, 'and you have made them equal to us who have borne the burden of the work and the heat of the day'" (Matt. 20:11–13).

Those who had a reasonable wage forgot to bless the Joneses, simply because it seemed to them that the Joneses had an even better wage.

When you look across the congregation and see any brother or sister whom God has blessed (even if he appears to have blessed them more generously than you), just go up and throw your arms around them and say, "I'm grateful God has blessed you." Every time I see God financially bless any member of this church, I hug them and I tell them I'm happy for them. And I truly am happy. How great it is to see people get the blessings of God. I feel I must walk up and say to them, "Congratulations. God loves you. I'm grateful and I'm glad about your good fortune, Mr. Jones!"

### III. THEY COULDN'T CELEBRATE THE GENEROSITY OF GOD IN THEIR OWN LIVES

The third thing the early-hired couldn't do was celebrate the generosity of God in their own lives. Do you know what their real sin was in the vineyard? They didn't take God to work with them that day. You're not going to make many friends for Jesus if you go in there grumbling over how short your desk is when someone else has got a bigger one. All you really make clear is how you are failing to take God to work with you.

George MacDonald was defrocked by the Scottish church. Once "fired," he nevertheless continued to go into his study and (for many years of his life) write sermons. Those sermons, which were never ever preached in anybody's church, were called "The Silent Sermons." In one of those sermons he wrote this: "The man to whom business is one thing and religion another is not a disciple. If he refuses to harmonize them by making his business religion he has already chosen Mammon; if he thinks not to settle the question, it is settled. The most futile of all human endeavors is to serve God and Mammon."[3]

One man in our church has his Bible lying on his desk. When I walk into his office and I see that Bible lying out there, I just want to say, "Hey, look everybody, here's a man who takes his commitment to Jesus Christ to his job and he's not ashamed of who he is in Christ."

When John the Baptist was preaching in the wilderness, he cried: "'Produce fruit in keeping with repentance. And do not begin to say to yourselves, "We have Abraham as our father." For I tell you that out of these stones God can raise up children for Abraham. The ax is already at the root of the trees, and every tree that does not produce good fruit will be cut down and thrown into the fire.' 'What should we do then?' the crowd asked. John answered, 'The man with two tunics should share with him who has none, and the one who has food should do the same.' Tax collectors also came to be baptized. 'Teacher,' they asked, "what should we do?' 'Don't collect any more than you are required to,' he told them. Then some soldiers asked him, 'And what should we do?' He replied, 'Don't extort money and don't accuse people falsely — be content with your pay'" (Luke 3:8–14).

I know sometimes there are all kinds of injustices out there. But I somehow believe these verses are just as real. I think God ever wants us to be moral examples when we go to work. He wants us to be good workers. But he also wants us to talk about our faith and who we are.

How frequently the Bible speaks about our job and its material obligations. In 1 Timothy 6:10, the Bible says, "The love of money is the root of all evil." Paul says earlier in 1 Corinthians 16:2, "Now on the first day of the week, let every one of you lay by him in store as God has prospered him." One of my favorites is in Habakkuk:

> Though the fig tree does not bud,
>      and there are no grapes on the vines,
> though the olive crop fails
>      and the fields produce no food,
> though there are no sheep in the pen
>      and no cattle in the stalls,
> yet I will rejoice in the Lord,
>      I will be joyful in God my Savior.
>
> (Habakkuk 3:17-19, NIV)

Psalm 37:3–4 has always been a favorite of mine. It says this: "Trust in the Lord and do good; dwell in the land and enjoy safe pasture. Delight yourself in the Lord and he will give you the desires of your heart."

And listen to this, also from Psalm 37: "I was young and now I am old, yet I have never seen the righteous forsaken or their children begging bread" (v. 25).

God is out to take care of us. Our strong hands and backs and his goodness form the trinity of the workplace. God is always taking care of his people.

One of the stories that circulated about Fiorello LaGuardia, then mayor of New York, tells of those terrible depression times when a man was arrested for stealing a loaf of bread to feed his family. LaGuardia, a very short man, was very tall in his sense of justice. When the poor man was brought into the court, LaGuardia looked down at him from the bench and said, "I fine you ten dollars." Then LaGuardia stood from the bench, reached into his pocket, and extracted his wallet. He took out ten dollars and said, "I pay your fine." Then he turned to all the watchers in the court and said, "I fine everyone in this room fifty cents for living in a city where a man has to steal bread to feed his family."

Consider the graciousness of God: "I am old; I've been young, and I have never seen the righteous forsaken nor his seed begging for bread" (Psalm 37:25). You see, God's big accusation in the parable at the beginning of the 20th chapter of Matthew is "Are you mad at me for being generous?"

I first encountered this passage in Matthew when my sister was dying. Not knowing if she'd ever received Jesus Christ as her Savior, I went from Omaha down to Oklahoma for the express purpose of asking her before she passed on if she'd really come to eternal life. I will never forget the experience of going into a hospital room and seeing her in this very sick condition. She could hardly speak. Her voice was soft and pleading. When all the others had vacated the room, and the time was just right, I asked her, "Sis, have you ever asked Jesus Christ into your heart, and do you know his wonderful gift of eternal life?"

She whispered and I drew my ears as close to her as I could. I heard her say, "You know, Calvin, there's a story in Matthew 20. It's about people who went to work in a vineyard. Some of them worked all day long and they got a penny. And some of them came in at the very last minute, and they also got a penny. I'm glad you asked, but what is so wonderful to me is to know that those of us who come at the very last moment receive the same ultimate gift of life, just like those who came at the first."

This is the generosity of God. This is the grace of God. Let's go to our workplaces and magnify Christ, in here, out there, wherever we serve. Let us remember that he who saved us from sin did it with a cross. He who saves us from a lack of bread and the depravity of dependency does it with our jobs.

## Notes

1. This sermon previously appeared in the September/October 1992 issue of *Preaching*. Gratitude is expressed to the publisher for permission to use the sermon in this volume of *The Library of Distinctive Sermons*.
2. Wayne Rouse, *Preaching* (July-August 1991), p.35.
3. George MacDonald, *The Closet Sermons* (Wheaton, IL: Shaw Publishing, 1974), p. 82.

# COMMENT

Calvin Miller's sermon "On Getting a Fair Deal in Your Career" has taken a difficult parable of Jesus, the Laborers in the Vineyard, and enabled us to see its implications for understanding both our human labor and the generosity of God.

Illustrations and stories make the sermon lively and engaging and keep it moving. To gain our attention early, Miller quotes from Bernard of Clairvaux and alludes to some well-known songs and lyrics from Broadway musicals that help us identify with a variety of attitudes and expressions about the nature and importance of human work. At its best, work can be a wonderful and fulfilling gift which gives us vitality. At its worst, work becomes drudgery which takes away much of the joy of living. Who cannot identify with these descriptions of work as either blessing or curse?

The quotations and illustrations throughout this sermon are practical, down-to-earth expressions about "the work of our hands." Here the preacher engages in no soaring flights of esoteric theological imagination. The focus is rather on the day-to-day human experience of getting up and going to work and coming home again. "Our work, our jobs, define our lives and tell us in part why we're in the world." Being at work is necessary "to think well of ourselves." To "have a career" is to find meaning and purpose in life. At the best, Miller says, "what a great gift it is to have a job...." These varied expressions of ideal attitudes toward work prepare us to experience the strong contrast in the attitudes of the grumpy laborers in Jesus' parable who, upon payment, grumble against the landowner. If work is so wonderful, what has gone wrong? Why these attitudes?

## PROBLEM

When all is well with our work and our attitude toward it, life is gift. But when things go wrong and we lose sight of work as gift, compare ourselves to others, and become envious and resentful, then our work becomes a painful expression of our human sin and brokenness.

Miller says that in Jesus' story "the early-hired are grumpy for three reasons": 1) They forgot the curse of not having a job; 2) they forgot to bless others; and 3) they couldn't celebrate the generosity of God in their own lives. Each of these three points describes part of the problem of the sinful human condition. We so easily forget the past and lose perspective. We fail to rejoice in the good others experience and instead view it as injustice toward us. And we fail to perceive the ever-present generosity of God in our lives. Biblically, sin is about forgetting the past, coveting what others have, and failing to acknowledge the goodness of God.

Notice in the middle portion of this sermon how Miller relates the three points about the parable to people in the church as the community of faith. For example, he says the grumpy laborers "went into a churchlike mode of mutual envy and began to compare salaries." Then he asks, "When are we most mature as believers within the church community? Could it be when we can bless our fellow church member who gets a better job or buys a bigger house than ours?....We are most demonic when we lose the ability to bless our peers as God blesses their circumstances."

Here Miller is speaking directly to some of the issues we face in an affluent, materially oriented culture. He brings Jesus' parable right into the congregation and gives it relevance when he identifies the grumpy-laborer attitude among contemporary people of God: "If there's any time I don't like church people, it's when they look across the congregation and see someone who just bought a nice new car and say, 'Hm! He's either doing something dishonest or maybe he's making payments with his church tithe.'" It's tough straight talk. It's a good example of contextualizing the parable in a modern setting. And of course, it's important in preaching to work continually at contextualizing the truth of Scripture, applying it to people's attitudes, problems and needs. It requires staying in touch with our people, knowing their attitudes and values, their needs and struggles, and then being able to see and articulate the connections between the Word of God and their lives.

## TEXT & PROCLAMATION

Notice the language in the three main points: "They forgot...," "They forgot...," "They couldn't celebrate...." As Miller explores these points, notice how in each case he uses the negative example of the laborers to proclaim an important truth about the positive attitudes and actions of faithful people of God. The positive teaching of Jesus' parable may be understood as the exact reversal of each of the three points about the grumpy laborers. God's faithful people are called to remember the curse of not having a job. They are to rejoice when good things happen in other people's lives. They are always to recognize and celebrate the goodness of God in their own lives.

What begins to emerge as one moves through this sermon is an increasing emphasis on the grace and generosity of God. By the time one reaches the conclusion, God's generosity is the primary point of proclamation, exemplified in such statements as: "God is always taking care of his people." "Consider the graciousness of God...." "This is the generosity of God. This is the grace of God." Miller obviously considers this the key to a proper understanding of the parable of the Laborers in the Vineyard. The owner of the vineyard has been gracious in giving work to all. He is willing and has the freedom to exceed conventional practices in paying the later-hired equally. His goodness is nonetheless apparent to all.

Let's take a moment to observe how effectively Miller uses stories to illustrate this sermon. In the first point ("They forgot the curse of not having a job"), he tells how during the Depression and afterward his mother always valued having a simple job. "During those 'dirty thirties,' she taught me that God is most gracious when he gives us a place to go to work." She was a hard-working laundress with a low-paying job, but "she taught her children a million miles of truth in her example. Her truth was simple: how good it is to have a job!" Miller then tells the story of the day he got a job at Hallmark Cards (after much walking!). He concludes with the bedtime thought, "Lord Jesus, I haven't got any money, and I haven't got much to eat, but I've got a job!" These stories not only illustrate the point of the sermon but offer inspiring models of faith and piety. They proclaim, "God wants us to be like this, rather than grumpy laborers."

C O M M E N T

RESPONSE

In a number of statements placed throughout the sermon the preacher calls us to respond in faith and action. At the end of the first point, for example, he says: "To all of you who are working today, fall to your knees in some quiet moment on Monday and say, 'Hey, this is Labor Day! I have a job. I am blessed!'" In the second point he urges his listeners to go to others in the congregation who have been blessed and "throw your arms around them and say, 'I'm grateful God has blessed you.'" And at the end of the sermon Miller urges us to "consider the graciousness of God," then "go to our workplaces and magnify Christ...wherever we serve."

In a sermon like this with three developed points in the body, it is usually best to place invitations to respond along the way in relation to each point. Miller has done that here, rather than holding all the calls to faith and action until the end of the sermon.

Notice also how Miller has emphasized the need to connect Sunday's faith and worship with Monday and the real world. We are called to go to our workplaces and glorify God there, not just in church on Sunday morning. This needs to be a frequent emphasis in our preaching in a day when the tendency is to separate faith from life and the sacred from the secular. As people of faith we need to see ourselves as part of the "priesthood of all believers" who have ministries not just "at the church," but precisely in our daily activities, where we live and work and play.

Miller's sermon moves in a lively way from the nature and meaning of labor to the problems of human sin often associated with our work and our attitudes. Drawing upon Jesus' parable, the preacher connects the human problem to the biblical text and its proclamation. The quotations, stories, and illustrations put flesh on the truths of the sermon. The call to respond is clear. We are invited to come away from the sermon with a new appreciation of our common everyday labor, and most of all, to see it as a gift of God's generosity.

This sermon can make getting up the next morning and going to work a whole new experience, viewed now through the eyes of faith. Isn't that what preaching is about? The Holy Spirit can use preaching to give us new eyes, enable us to see, and then follow Jesus.

## SUGGESTIONS

- Study this parable (Matthew 20:1–16) in its literary and structural context in the Gospel of Matthew. Examine what immediately precedes the parable in Matthew 19 and what follows in Matthew 20:17–34. How do you think the parable relates to its context? Develop a sermon relating the parable to Peter's statement in Matthew 19:27, Jesus' passion prediction in 20:17–19, and the request for a place of honor in 20:20–28. How does Jesus' saying, "The first will be last, and the last will be first" (19:30; 20:16), fit into all of this?

- Develop a sermon or series of sermons on "work," "vocation," and "leisure". What issues do you feel need to be addressed among your people on these subjects? What biblical texts speak to these needs?

- Develop a sermon or a series on "Celebrating the Generosity of God in Our Lives." What topics can you address? What biblical texts apply? How do the psalms speak to this subject?

*Gary W. Klingsporn*

COMMENT

# THE CHRISTMAS LIGHT

ISAIAH 49:1-6

REV. DR. MARK D. ROBERTS
IRVINE PRESBYTERIAN CHURCH
IRVINE, CALIFORNIA

# THE CHRISTMAS LIGHT

ISAIAH 49:1-6

N ot long ago the Arkansas Supreme Court ordered a Little Rock
resident to "reduce substantially" the size of the Christmas display in his front yard. That's right — the Supreme Court of the
State of Arkansas told a man he has to take down some of his Christmas
lights!

"Government intrusion into personal freedom!" you may protest.
"How extreme and invasive!" Maybe so. But this was no ordinary front yard
Christmas display. For many years Little Rock resident Jennings Osborne
had literally covered his mammoth suburban home with red Christmas
lights and glowing Christmas figurines. These figurines weren't a few little
snowmen, but an eighteen-foot high Santa along with similarly sized rein-
deer and elves. And we're not talking about a few strands of Christmas
lights. In 1993 Osborne used over three million red lights, a setup that
required special power lines coming to his home. Three million lights.
That's 30,000 boxes of 100. Quite a few trips to the local department store!

Osborne's display was so famous that tens of thousands of people
drove along his quiet suburban street each Christmas. This finally pushed
his neighbors over the edge, so they sued. Their lawsuit ended up in the
state Supreme Court. The court concluded that Mr. Osborne had to down-
scale a little.

Although I can understand the neighbors' point of view, I share with Jennings Osborne a fondness for Christmas lights. In fact, putting up the outside lights kicks off Advent for me. This year I spent Saturday afternoon following Thanksgiving untangling strands, replacing bulbs, climbing up on the roof, and trying to remember how my display fits together. Meanwhile, my stereo blasted seasonally appropriate music: Handel's *Messiah* and Bach's *Christmas Oratorio*. Christmas lights and Christmas music — what better way to welcome the Christmas season?

The festive use of lights at Christmas goes back many centuries. Christians often make a connection between lights and the star of Bethlehem. Even more profoundly, our lights can symbolize the light of God coming into the world at Christmas.

In this sermon I'd like to examine the biblical background behind the understanding of Jesus as the light of the world. We will look at the Old Testament for an enriched understanding of Christmas. We will feel again the yearning of God's covenant people for deliverance from bondage. Today we will see that Jesus, as God's promised Servant, comes not just for the people of Israel, but for the whole world. I pray that a deeper knowledge of the prophetic promises will lead you to meet Jesus in a life-changing way this Christmas.

## GOD'S CALL TO THE SERVANT IN ISAIAH 49

Isaiah prophesied in the Southern Kingdom of Judah during the last forty years of the eighth century B.C. He called God's people to repentance even as the Northern Kingdom of Israel fell to the Assyrians in 722 B.C. After Isaiah's death his followers preserved and collected his oracles, which were found to have ongoing relevance to the Jewish people. The earlier prophecies of Isaiah served as a theological basis for additional prophetic activity, especially during the Babylonian Exile in the sixth century B.C. The collection of prophecies in the biblical book of Isaiah speaks of Israel's failure and God's judgment, but also of a future hope for God's salvation.

Isaiah 49:1-6 is one of the so-called "Servant Songs." In these prophecies Isaiah "sings" as if he were another person, the Servant of God. This divine agent is first introduced in chapter 42, where God says: "Here is my servant, whom I uphold, my chosen, in whom my soul delights; I have put my spirit upon him; he will bring forth justice to the nations" (42:1).

In Isaiah 49 the Servant speaks first about his prenatal calling by God (v. 1). Moreover, God has made the Servant's mouth "like a sharp sword" (v. 2). His word, therefore, will cut through to the heart of human need. But God has not yet sent the Servant, preferring to hide him "in the shadow of [God's] hand" until the proper time (v. 2).

In verse 3 God speaks to his chosen one: "You are my servant, Israel, in whom I will be glorified." In the latter chapters of Isaiah the word "servant" refers to different entities, sometimes in a confusing way. At times the nation of Israel is God's Servant (e.g., 44:21). Yet in other passages the Servant, though closely identified with Israel, is a distinct individual. We can see this most clearly in verse 5 of our text. There the Servant says that the Lord "formed me in the womb to be his servant, to bring Jacob back to him and that Israel might be gathered to him." Though he can be called "Israel" (v. 3), the Servant is actually the person who will bring the nation of Israel back into fellowship with God.

But verse 6 adds an unexpected twist to a familiar prophetic promise: "It is too light a thing that you should be my servant to raise up the tribes of Jacob and to restore the survivors of Israel; I will give you as a light to the nations, that my salvation may reach to the end of the earth." The word "light" in the phrase "it is too light a thing" means "small" or "insignificant" or "trifling."[1] In other words, God says to the Servant, "It's too small a thing for you only to restore the nation of Israel. It's worth doing, but it's not enough."

What else will God's Servant do? He will shine "as a light to the nations." We don't hear that sentence the way ancient Hebrew-speakers would have heard it. "Nations" translates the Hebrew word *goyim*, which means "Gentiles," not just "nations." For Jews living in bondage to Gentiles, they would not have heard God's call to the Servant as good news. Not enough to restore Israel? A light to the Gentiles, the bad guys? How striking and even disconcerting that God's salvation through the Servant will include all nations — to the very ends of the earth!

Many Old Testament prophecies speak of national deliverance from the pagan Gentiles who had oppressed God's chosen people. But now a new direction emerges. Yes, the Servant will still restore Israel in her covenant relationship with God, but as "light to the nations" he will include all peoples within God's saving work. It doesn't take much empathy to imagine how shocking this prophecy must have been for the Jews. We can also understand why it might have been conveniently forgotten by many as they yearned for God's restoration of their own nation.

## JESUS AS THE LIGHT FOR THE NATIONS

Now let's jump to a time 700 years after Isaiah and 500 years after the Babylonian Exile. A young Jewish woman gives birth to a child born under questionable circumstances. She and her husband, following their religious tradition, take the infant to the temple in Jerusalem in order to make special offerings. There they meet a man named Simeon. We pick up the story in Luke 2:25:

> Now there was a man in Jerusalem whose name was Simeon; this man was righteous and devout, looking forward to the consolation of Israel, and the Holy Spirit rested on him. It had been revealed to him by the Holy Spirit that he would not see death before he had seen the Lord's Messiah. Guided by the Spirit, Simeon came into the temple; and when the parents brought in the child Jesus, to do for him what was customary under the law, Simeon took him in his arms and praised God, saying,

> "Master, now you are dismissing your servant in peace,
>     according to your word;
> for my eyes have seen your salvation,
>     which you have prepared in the presence of all peoples,
> a light for revelation to the Gentiles
>     and for glory to your people Israel."

Do you hear what Simeon says? This is the one! This is the Servant who spoke in the songs of Isaiah! This is the one who comes as "a light for revelation to the Gentiles." This baby is the light for the nations!

Simeon was the first to identify Jesus as the Servant of God who comes as light for the Gentiles. Many followed him, including Jesus himself. In John 8:12 Jesus says, "I am the light of the world. Whoever follows me will never walk in darkness but will have the light of life." Jesus claims to be the light, not just for Israel, but for the whole world. Through him God's revelation and salvation come to all who believe in him, regardless of their ethnic or national identity (John 1:12–13). What an amazing claim! How utterly preposterous if it is not true! How marvelous if it is!

## JESUS AS LIGHT OF THE WORLD: SO WHAT?

What difference does it make to us if Jesus is the light of the world? First of all, let me state the obvious. You and I can know God's salvation. There may be a few of us here today who are Jewish, but most of us are Gentiles. If God had not sent his Servant as a light for the nations, then we'd be out of luck, or more accurately, out of God's covenant of grace. If Jesus had not come as the light of the world, then we would still be in darkness. But because God has sent Jesus his Servant as light for the nations, we can experience salvation. We can be forgiven! We can know God! We can live forever in fellowship with God through Christ! That's good news. That's the gospel.

The fact that Jesus is the light of the world transforms our lives in another way as well. Speaking to his disciples in the Sermon on the Mount, Jesus says, "You are the light of the world. A city built on a hill cannot be hid. No one after lighting a lamp puts it under the bushel basket, but on the lampstand, and it gives light to all in the house. In the same way, let your light shine before others, so that they may see your good works and give glory to your Father in heaven" (Matt. 5:14–16).

He who is the light of the world passes the torch to his followers—to us! Now the honor and responsibility of the Servant's calling to be the light of the world rests with us.

The Apostle Paul speaks in a similarly striking way in Ephesians 5, "For once you were darkness, but now in the Lord you are light. Live as children of light — for the fruit of the light is found in all that is good and right and true" (Eph. 5:8–9).

Notice that Paul, like Jesus, affirms that we are light. It's not just that we are in the light, or that we should be light. We are already light, as Jesus says, the light of the world. What an incredible affirmation! What an honor! What a responsibility to let our light shine before others so that they might glorify God!

If you're like me, this responsibility seems too heavy to bear. How can I possibly be light in this world, given my dullness and my penchant for darkness? Besides, isn't Jesus the light of the world? How can he say that I am "the light of the world"?

The analogy of a lighthouse helps me to answer these questions. Certain lighthouses can send a beam as far as 28 miles out to sea. That's an amazing distance. A lighthouse is able to shine so far, not just because its light bulb is so bright. But surrounding the bulb in a modern light-house are dozens of small prisms that help to intensify and to focus the light. Though the prisms have no intrinsic light, they are essential to a lighthouse. To be sure, the bulb radiates brightly, but the prisms enable the light to shine far beyond the sphere that would be illuminated by the bulb alone.

And so it is with us. We who know Jesus Christ will not be able to enlighten the world except insofar as we reflect Christ himself, the light of the world. The more we are transformed into the image of Christ, the more we will reflect him in our deeds and in our character. The more we accept our identity as light in the world, the more we will let our light shine before others. Apart from Christ we radiate darkness. When we live in Christ, we are like prisms of a lighthouse, focusing the light of Christ into our world.

## GOD'S CALL TO US

God's vision for his Servant was greater than anything the people of Israel might have expected. The same is true for you and for me. God sees us in ways we cannot see ourselves. God calls us to a mission far beyond what we might imagine for our lives.

If you are not a Christian, if you have not entered into a personal relationship with Jesus Christ, then God invites you into his saving light. Because Jesus came to earth as a baby and died on a cross for you, you can taste the salvation of God, right now, this day, simply by accepting Jesus as your Savior and Lord, by allowing him to be the light of your life. Perhaps you look to Jesus as a good moral example or a wise teacher — or a fine excuse for a holiday. But, as God spoke through Isaiah to the Servant, so he would say to you: "It is not enough that you look to Jesus, my Servant, as a teacher and example; I have sent him as light to bring my salvation to you. Believe in him and you will live!"

If you are a Christian, having entered into the saving light of Christ, then God calls you to live as light in this world. No matter how insignificant you might feel, you are, nevertheless, God's light in the world. Your task, according to Jesus, is to let your light shine, to live so that others might be drawn to the light of Christ in you. As God spoke through Isaiah to the Servant, so he would say to you, "It is not enough that you have received salvation through the light of the world; now share it with others. Live in such a way that your family, your friends, your co-workers, and your neighbors see the light of Christ in you. It's not enough that you get your own spiritual needs met, or even that you grow in your personal faith. You are called to minister, to serve, to share the love of Christ with others, to be a witness to Christ wherever you are."

I believe that God would speak similarly to our church, to this body of believers in Jesus. As the family of God we share life together, loving one another, worshiping, helping each other grow in Christ. These are right and essential to our life as a church. But God has more for us. We are to be a light in this city, a beacon of hope and faith in a world filled with despair and doubt. As God spoke through Isaiah to the Servant, so he would say to us: "It is not enough that you gather to worship me and to love one another, I have placed you in this city to be a light to your community. Reflect my love to your neighbors! Let my truth shine through you!"

Dear friends, I pray for the day when our church will be like the home of Jennings Osborne. I pray for the day when our collection of little lights

— that's you and me — will shine so brightly that people will come just to see what's happening.

Of course, here is where the metaphor breaks down. Because our task is not merely to get people to drive by and look at the light of Christ shining through us. Rather, through our love we invite people into the light, to meet the true light of the world, to experience his salvation, and to join us as prismatic reflectors of his light to others.

Jesus is the Christmas light. This Christmas, come to the light! Allow the light of Christ to enlighten you! Reflect his light in our world of darkness! Amen!

Notes

1. Francis Brown, S. R. Driver, Charles A. Briggs, *A Hebrew and English Lexicon of the Old Testament* (Oxford: Clarendon Press, 1975), p.886.

# COMMENT

Mark Roberts's sermon, "The Christmas Light," takes an obscure Old Testament passage and allows it to speak with power and clarity across time into the lives of modern listeners. The sermon moves very simply from Isaiah's Servant, to Jesus, to us. Isaiah's Servant is to be a light to the nations. Jesus is the light of the world. We are to live as light. Light is the common metaphor uniting those called of God across the centuries.

The power of this sermon lies in the direct continuity it establishes between the Servant and Jesus and us! Here, we as listeners are brought into continuity with centuries of biblical promise and fulfillment. The preacher distills the essence of biblical faith out of the complexity of God's salvation history and proclaims it in simple affirmations. Roberts takes the risk of articulating the gospel in simple terms, in an age when critics might charge that any such effort leads to oversimplified reductionism.

This sermon is simple, but not simplistic. It draws upon the full gospel and presupposes the whole of biblical revelation. But it proclaims the message of the gospel in the Scripture's own simple terms of light and salvation Such a sermon calls us to go back again and again to the essence of the gospel in order to proclaim it and live it with fresh vision and renewed commitment.

## STRUCTURE

In keeping with the simple Servant/Jesus/Us relationship, the main body of this sermon has three sections addressing each of these subjects. These three sections are preceded by an Introduction and followed by a Conclusion. The structure is as follows:

Introduction: Christmas Lights
Body:    1. God's Call to the Servant in Isaiah 49 (Servant)
         2. Jesus as the Light for the Nations (Jesus)

3. Jesus as the Light of the World: So What? (Us)

Conclusion: God's Call to Us

This classic structure lends clarity to the sermon and underscores the continuity between the Servant, Jesus, and the listener. Let's review the sermon step by step and observe what the preacher does in each section.

*Introduction: Christmas Lights.* Here Roberts establishes the metaphor of "light" as the key image for the sermon. He does this by drawing from the news media the story of Jennings Osborne and the Arkansas Supreme Court's ruling about his lavish display of Christmas lights. This story was current in the news at the time the sermon was originally preached. People had heard about it and had seen Mr. Osborne's display on national television news programs. To enter into the ancient biblical story of Christmas light, the preacher begins with a story of dazzling lights on a grand scale right out of the daily newspaper.

Preaching is about making connections between the past, the present, and the future. Watching for those connections in the world around us can be one of the most fun and exciting aspects of sermon preparation. If we are preaching on a regular basis, it is important to train our eyes and ears to watch and listen for the stories, events, and experiences in our lives which God can use in our sermons. The sources of these connections are endless: things that happen in our families and among our church members, stories in the media, books, movies, plays, experiences in our day to day routines. Listen to your life! It is there that God speaks!

After the opening story, notice how Roberts becomes more personal by sharing his own fondness for Christmas lights and the yearly ritual of putting up decorations: "This year I spent Saturday afternoon following Thanksgiving untangling strands, replacing bulbs, climbing up on the roof, and trying to remember how my display fits together." These are not just nice throwaway lines in the sermon. Here the preacher gives us something of himself in a lighthearted way, and the sermon becomes more real and personal. He also taps into our own experiences of untangling lights, replacing bulbs, putting up Christmas trees, and enjoying the special beauty of the sights and sounds of the Christmas season.

In preaching, it's always good to ask ourselves how we can make the sermon more personal by drawing upon our own experiences or tapping into the human experiences that are commonplace among our listeners. When we do this effectively, people more readily identify with the sermon and we gain a better hearing.

At the end of the Introduction, Roberts connects the Jennings Osborne story and his own time on the roof with the biblical story: "Our lights can symbolize the light of God coming into the world at Christmas." Then he tells us what the rest of the sermon is about: "In this sermon I'd like to examine the biblical background behind the understanding of Jesus as the Light of the world.... I pray that a deeper knowledge of the prophetic promises [of the Old Testament] will lead you to meet Jesus in a life-changing way this Christmas." With these words Roberts takes a straight-forward approach in telling the congregation what the sermon is about and what to expect from it. This is a bold and clear way of communicating. After he has his listeners' attention, he tells them up front what he hopes the sermon will accomplish. Sometimes in preaching it's appropriate to lead your listeners along step by step and save the point of the sermon for the end. At other times, however, it's helpful to tell them early on exactly where you're going with the sermon. Mark Roberts's sermon is an example of the latter approach.

*Body 1: God's Call to the Servant in Isaiah 49.* Here Roberts addresses the text for his sermon, the Second Servant Song of Isaiah. He gives a brief sketch of the historical background of the passage in a way that is informative but not overwhelming. If you are familiar with the four Servant Songs of Isaiah (42:1–4; 49:1–6; 50:4–9; 52:13–53:12), you are probably aware of the difficulties of interpreting these passages. Despite the rather clear portrayal of the Servant's mission, the songs do not make the identity of their subject clear. At times Isaiah seems to speak of the Servant as the nation Israel. At other times an individual or ideal figure seems in view. Both may be accurate interpretations of Isaiah's original intent. Roberts acknowledges these issues but is not sidetracked by them. It is important in preaching to acknowledge the difficulties underlying the interpretation of texts without getting bogged down in the scholarly discussion.

Notice in this section how the preacher quickly works down through verses 1–5 of the text encompassing the Servant's calling (vv. 1, 3, 5) and gifts (v. 2). He moves quickly to verse 6, the focus of the sermon. This is a good example of paring the text down to the core idea addressed in the sermon: "a light to the nations." Roberts then notes the "unexpected twist" in the text. The Servant's mission is not simply to the nation of Israel, but to all the nations. "I will give you as a light to the nations, that my salvation may reach to the end of the earth." Roberts points out that Isaiah's emphasis on God's salvation being for "all nations" (Gentiles) is a new direction in Israel's understanding of God.

*Body 2: Jesus as the Light for the Nations.* In this portion of the sermon the preacher turns to the faith of the early church which identified Jesus with the Servant figure spoken of by Isaiah. Quoting Simeon's words in Luke's Gospel, Jesus is the way of salvation prepared by God, "a light for revelation to the Gentiles and for glory to your people Israel" (Luke 2:32). Simeon's words draw upon Isaiah 42:6 and 49:6 (the sermon text) and identify Jesus with Isaiah's promise of the Servant of God who would be a light for the Gentiles. At this point in the sermon Jesus is now linked directly to the Servant figure in Isaiah. Jesus is the "light to the nations." Other New Testament passages proclaim this same truth (John 1:12–13, 8:12).

*Body 3: Jesus as the Light of the World: So What?* Here the preacher proclaims how the Isaiah and New Testament texts apply to us. What difference does it make that Jesus is the light of the world? It means two things. First, we can know God, his forgiveness, and salvation. That's the good news of the gospel! Second, as Jesus is the light of the world, we who know him in faith become light and reflect the light of Christ to the world (Matt. 5:14–16; Eph. 5:8–9).

Note how this third section of the Body of the sermon completes the identification between Isaiah's Servant, Jesus, and us. Those who receive the Servant Jesus in faith share in the light and themselves become light to the world. "Now the honor and responsibility of the Servant's calling to be the light of the world rests with us.... The more we are transformed into the image of Christ, the more we will reflect him in our deeds and in our character." With these words the preacher completes the Servant/Jesus/Us connection and is ready to extend the invitation to us to respond with our lives.

The lighthouse analogy in this portion of the sermon is a good example of a well-placed illustration to help make the distinction between Jesus as the light and our role as "prisms" reflecting the light of Christ himself. Overall, there are few illustrations in this sermon. Roberts has chosen the lighthouse as the only illustration within the body of the sermon. Elsewhere, only the Introduction has illustrative story material. Too many illustrations can become too much of a good thing. Not every point has to be illustrated. In the use of illustrations, less is often more.

Before leaving this section, look back at the sermon and observe the style and the simplicity of the language. Primary words and phrases include: "light," "salvation," "forgiven," "know God," "good news," "we are light," "let our light shine," "live in Christ." The sentences are short. The thoughts are not complex. Simple truth is conveyed in simple words and images.

The preacher uses no technical theological terms or language in this sermon. He quotes no theological textbooks. His exegetical and theological preparation stand behind the sermon but do not get in the way of the simple articulation of the gospel. Some sermons must appropriately wrestle with difficult issues of faith and life. Discussions of theological terms and debates are appropriate if carefully done in the right context. But the sermon before us is an effective example of the principle that less is more. Here "the simple gospel," in the best sense of that phrase, shines with the clarity and simplicity of light, which is the very subject of the sermon.

*Conclusion: God's Call to Us.* In the conclusion there is a threefold invitation: (1) "If you have not entered into a personal relationship with Jesus Christ, then God invites you into his saving light." (2) "If you are a Christian, having entered into the saving light of Christ, then God calls you to live as light in this world." (3) "We [as a church] are to be a light in this city, a beacon of hope and faith in a world filled with despair and doubt."

These are invitations to both faith and action, reaching out to people who are at very different places with regard to Christian commitment. The statements speak to (1) those who may not be committed followers of Jesus Christ as well as to (2) those who have already made that commitment. The call to respond embraces both individual faith (1, 2) and the church (3) as a community of faith. This third invitation is a very important one. It recognizes the communal nature of faith within the life of the church and the responsibility of the church to the outside world. In American Christianity there is often the temptation to focus so much on individualized, privatized faith that we easily neglect the New Testament understanding of the church as a community of faith called to be light to the world around us.

Notice after each call to respond that Roberts paraphrases the first half of his text from Isaiah 49:6. He takes Isaiah's words, "It is too light a thing that you should be my servant [only] to Israel," and puts them in down-to-earth terms relevant to each listener:

1. "It is not enough that you look to Jesus, my Servant, as a teacher and example.... Believe in him and you will live!"

2. "It is not enough that you have received salvation through the light of the world.... Share it with others." "It's not enough that you get your own spiritual needs met.... You are called...to serve."

3. "It is not enough that you gather to worship me and to love one another. I have placed you in this city to be a light to your community.... Let my truth shine through you!"

These are nice examples of paraphrasing the text to make applications to different needs or issues. As you preach, keep this technique in mind and experiment from week to week with amplifying portions of your text by restating it in terms of the needs, issues, and vernacular of your local congregation.

In the closing paragraphs of this sermon Roberts briefly recalls the opening story of Jennings Osborne's light display, acknowledges how the analogy breaks down, and calls us to invite people into the light. He concludes with the focal point of the sermon: "Jesus is the Christmas light." And he reiterates the call to respond: "Come to the light.... Reflect his light in our world of darkness!"

### PROBLEM/TEXT/PROCLAMATION

The problem or need this sermon addresses is that of a greater understanding of Jesus as the light of the world and what it means for us to be light. The preacher allows the biblical texts in Isaiah 49, Luke 2, and elsewhere to answer that question. As a word for the Christmas season, this sermon takes what is for many the unfamiliar Servant Song in Isaiah 49 and proclaims the simple truth of the gospel that we stand in continuity with the Servant and with Jesus.

The word of Yahweh addressed to the Servant of old has now spoken across the centuries and has become the living word of God to us: "I will give you as a light to the nations, that my salvation may reach to the end of the earth." When the ancient Word becomes a living word to us and for us, God has spoken in the power of the preaching event.

### SUGGESTIONS

- Study the four Servant Songs of Isaiah (Isaiah 42:1–4; 49:1–6; 50:4–9; 52:13–53:12) and develop one or more sermons based on them. Read as widely as you can on the historical background, context, and content of these passages. What themes emerge regarding the Servant's character and mission? How is Jesus, as the living, crucified, and risen Christ, the fulfillment of these prophetic passages? How are we as followers of Christ heirs to his servant vocation as a new covenant people of God?
- Isaiah 49:1–6 occurs in some Christian lectionaries as a suggested reading for the season of Epiphany. It is combined with John 1:29–41 and 1 Corinthians 1:1–9. Study these texts together and see what themes emerge from them for a sermon. How could you combine these texts in a sermon?

- If you are not familiar with the meaning of Epiphany as a season of the church year following Christmas, do some reading on the historical and liturgical background of Epiphany. Try preaching on Isaiah 49:1–6 in the period after Christmas, whether or not your particular church tradition observes Epiphany.

- Isaiah 49 proclaims that God's salvation is offered not only to Israel but to the whole world. Do some study on this theme as it appears in the Old Testament in places like Genesis 12:1–3, the Book of Ruth, the Book of Jonah, and Isaiah 40–55. Choose one or more of these and develop a sermon on God's love for the world as found in the Old Testament.

- How does the theme of God's salvation offered to those outside Israel appear in the New Testament, for example, throughout the Gospel of Luke, in Matthew 28:19–20, and Acts 1–2? What problems, needs, or issues do these texts address in your congregation or community?

- If you don't already have an effective system, start a "clip file" or other means of gathering interesting stories, illustrations, and articles for future sermons. The preaching resources listed in the Bibliography at the end of this volume will help you with ideas.

*Gary. W. Klingsporn*

Although there is an immense body of literature on the subject of preaching, the following selected list provides a well-rounded introduction to the most significant works on preaching in recent years. Whether you are an experienced preacher or new to the task, consider making this Bibliography part of your reading list for ministry.

Achtemeier, Elizabeth. *Creative Preaching: Finding the Words.* Nashville: Abingdon Press, 1980.

———. *Preaching from the Old Testament.* Louisville, KY: Westminster/John Knox Press, 1989.

Bartow, Charles L. *The Preaching Moment.* Nashville: Abingdon Press, 1980.

Bodey, Richard Allen, ed. *Inside the Sermon: Thirteen Preachers Discuss Their Methods of Preparing Messages.* Grand Rapids, MI: Baker Book House, 1990.

Briscoe, D. Stuart. *Fresh Air in the Pulpit: Challenges and Encouragement om a Seasoned Preacher.* Grand Rapids, MI: Baker Books, 1994.

Brown, David M. *Dramatic Narrative in Preaching.* Valley Forge: son Press, 1981.

Brueggemann, Walter. *Finally Comes the Poet: Daring Spee or Proclamation.* Minneapolis: Fortress Press, 1989.

Buechner, Frederick. *Telling the Truth: The Gospel as Trag omedy, and Fairy Tale.* San Francisco: Harper & Row, 1977.

Buttrick, David G. *A Captive Voice: The Libera f Preaching.* Louisville, KY: Westminster/John Knox Press, 1994.

———. *Homiletic: Moves and Structures.* P in Homiletic Theology. Philadelphia: phia: Fortress Press, 1987.

———. *Preaching Jesus Christ: An E* Fortress Press, 1988.

Chapell, Bryan. *Christ-Centered F g: Redeeming the Expository Sermon.* Grand Rapids, MI: Baker Books. vent. San Francisco: Harper & Row, 1990.

Claypool, John R. *The Pre he Sacrament of the Word.* New York: Crossroad

Coggan, Donald. *Pre 88.* Publishing Com

Cox, James W., ed. *Biblical Preaching*. Philadelphia: Westminster Press, 1983.

———. *Preaching*. San Francisco: Harper & Row, 1985.

Craddock, Fred B. *As One Without Authority*. 3rd ed. Nashville: Abingdon Press, 1979.

———. *Overhearing the Gospel*. Nashville: Abingdon Press, 1978.

———. *Preaching*. Nashville: Abingdon Press, 1985.

Demaray, Donald E. *An Introduction to Homiletics*. 2d ed. Grand Rapids, MI: Baker Book House, 1990.

Ellingsen, Mark. *The Integrity of Biblical Narrative: Story in Theology and Proclamation*. Minneapolis: Fortress Press, 1990.

Fant, Clyde E. *Preaching for Today*. Rev. ed. San Francisco: Harper & Row, 1987.

Fasol, Al. *Essentials for Biblical Preaching: An Introduction to Basic Sermon Preparation*. Grand Rapids, MI: Baker Book House, 1989.

Freeman, Harold. *Variety in Biblical Preaching: Innovative Techniques and Fresh Forms*. Waco, TX: Word Books, 1987.

Gonzales, Justo L., and Gonzales, Catherine G. *The Liberating Pulpit*. Nashville: Abingdon Press, 1994.

Horne, Chris F. *Preaching the Great Themes of the Bible*. Nashville: Broadman Press, 1986.

Hybels, Bill; Briscoe, Stuart; and Robinson, Haddon. *Mastering Contemporary Preaching*. Portland, OR: Multnomah Press; and Carol Stream, IL: Christianity Today, 1989.

Jensen, Richard A. *Thinking in Story: Preaching in a Post-Literate Age*. Lima, OH: C.S.S. Publishing, 1993.

Killinger, John. *Fundamentals of Preaching*. Philadelphia: Fortress Press, 1985.

Lischer, Richard, ed. *Theories of Preaching: Selected Readings in the Homiletical Tradition*. Durham, NC: Labyrinth, 1987.

Long, Thomas G. *The Witness of Preaching*. Louisville, KY: Westminster/John Knox Press, 1989.

Lowry, Eugene L. *Doing Time in the Pulpit: The Relationship Between Narrative and Preaching*. Nashville: Abingdon Press, 1985.

———. *The Homiletical Plot: The Sermon as Narrative Art Form*. Atlanta: John Knox Press, 1980.

MacArthur, John Jr.; Mayhue, Richard L.; and Thomas, Robert L., eds. *Rediscovering Expository Preaching.* Dallas: Word Publishing, 1992.

MacLeod, Donald. *The Problem of Preaching.* Philadelphia: Fortress Press, 1987.

Miller, Calvin. *The Empowered Communicator: 7 Keys to Unlocking an Audience.* Nashville: Broadman & Holman, 1994.

————. *Marketplace Preaching: How to Return the Sermon to Where It Belongs.* Grand Rapids, MI: Baker Books, 1995.

————. *Spirit, Word, and Story.* Dallas: Word Publishing, 1989.

O'Day, Gail R., and Long, Thomas G., eds. *Listening to the Word: Studies in Honor of Fred B. Craddock.* Nashville: Abingdon Press, 1993.

Pitt-Watson, Ian. *A Primer for Preachers.* Grand Rapids, MI: Baker Book House, 1986.

Robinson, Haddon W. *Biblical Preaching: The Development and Delivery of Expository Messages.* Grand Rapids, MI: Baker Book House, 1980

Stott, John R. W. *Between Two Worlds: The Art of Preaching in the Twentieth Century.* Grand Rapids, MI: W. B. Eerdmans, 1982.

Thompson, William D. *Preaching Biblically: Exegesis and Interpretation.* Nashville: Abingdon Press, 1981.

Westerhoff, John H. *Spiritual Life: The Foundation for Preaching and Teaching.* Louisville, KY: Westminster/John Knox Press, 1994.

Wiersbe, Warren, and Wiersbe, David. *The Elements of Preaching.* Wheaton, IL: Tyndale House Publishers, 1986.

Wiersbe, Warren W. *Preaching and Teaching with Imagination: The Quest for Biblical Ministry.* Wheaton, IL: Victor Books, 1994.

Willimon, William H. *Integrative Preaching: The Pulpit at the Center.* Nashville: Abingdon Press, 1981.

Willimon, William H., and Hauerwas, Stanley. *Preaching to Strangers.* Louisville, KY: Westminster/John Knox Press, 1992.

Wilson, Paul Scott. *Imagination of the Heart: New Understandings in Preaching.* Nashville: Abingdon Press, 1988.

————. *The Practice of Preaching.* Nashville: Abingdon Press, 1995.

# SCRIPTURE INDEX